THE TOURNAMENT IN ENGLAND
1100–1400

THE TOURNAMENT IN ENGLAND
1100–1400

Juliet R. V. Barker

THE BOYDELL PRESS

© Juliet R. V. Barker 1986

First Published 1986 by The Boydell Press
an imprint of Boydell & Brewer Ltd
PO Box 9, Woodbridge, Suffolk IP12 3DF and
Wolfeboro, New Hampshire 03894-2069, USA

ISBN 0 85115 450 6

British Library Cataloguing in Publication Data

Barker, Juliet R. V.
 The tournament in England, 1100–1400.
 1. Tournaments – England – History
 I. Title
 394'.7   DA176
 ISBN 0-85115-450-6

Library of Congress Cataloging in Publication Data

Barker, Juliet R. V.
 The tournament in England, 1100–1400.

 Bibliography: p.
 1. Tournaments — England — History. 2. England —
Social life and customs — Medieval period, 1066–1485.
3. Knights and knighthood — England — History.
4. Chivalry.
 I. Title.
 DA115.B35   1986   394'.7   86-24409
 ISBN 0-85115-450-6

Printed in Great Britain by
St Edmundsbury Press, Bury St Edmunds, Suffolk

Table of Contents

List of Abbreviations

The following is a list of abbreviations used in the notes to refer to titles of works. Full references for all these works are to be found in the bibliography.

APF	Les Anciens Poetès de la France.
Ann.Lond.	*Annales Londonienses de Tempore Henrici Tertii.*
Ann.Mon.	*Annales Monastici.*
Ann.Paul.	*Annales Paulini.*
BL	British Library.
CCR	*Calendar of Close Rolls.*
Cal.Fine Rolls	*Calendar of Fine Rolls.*
CPR	*Calendar of Patent Rolls.*
Chron.Ghisn.	Ardres, Lambert of, *Chronicon Ghisnense et Ardense.*
CRSHR	*Chronicles of the Reigns of Stephen Henry II and Richard I*, ed R. Howlett (R.S., 1885).
CTG	*Collectanea Topographica et Genealogica*, iv (1837).
EETS	Early English Text Society.
Eng.Hist.Rev.	*English Historical Review.*
Froissart	Froissart, *Oeuvres*, ed Kervyn de Lettenhove (Brussels, 1867-77), 25 vols.
HGM	*L'Histoire de Guillaume le Maréchal* ed P. Meyer (Paris, 1901), 3 vols.
Matt.Paris	Matthew Paris, *Chronica Majora*, ed H.R.Luard (R.S., 1872-82), 7 vols.
PRO	Public Record Office.
R.S.	Rolls Series.
Rot.Scot.	*Rotuli Scottiae*, ed Macpherson (London, 1814-9), 2 vols.
SATF	Société des Anciens Textes Francais.
SHF	Société de l'Histoire de la France.

Preface

Throughout the middle ages tourneying was perhaps the most popular of all aristocratic sports. It ranked with hunting and hawking as one of the pastimes in which excellence was sought after and, like them, it acquired a body of customary procedure which was later set out in heraldic treatises and manuals. As a game it epitomized all that chivalry stood for – it celebrated the skills and virtues of the military profession and in particular those of the knightly classes; the handling of weapons and horses and courage and perseverance in the face of personal discomfort and even danger. What made tourneying doubly precious in chivalric eyes was its glorification of knightly ideology. The medieval tourneyer or jouster was not simply putting in a useful bit of martial exercise – he was fighting as the champion of his mistress (real or imaginary) and seeking to win her approbation and that of his companions in arms. To win reputation and renown was his principal object and in the lists it was possible to do this through personal attributes alone. Like the heroes of romance he could sweep all before him, at least temporarily.

The tournament was much more than a game, however. As a gathering in arms of professional soldiers it had great potential for manipulation: in the wrong hands, such as those of political malcontents or feuding barons, it could become an instrument for rebellion, private war and vendetta: in the right hands, as the kings of England were quick to realize, it could become an invaluable propaganda machine. Control over patronage was therefore an issue of great importance and one that raised the tournament beyond the level of mere sport. Just how important tournaments were can be gauged by the fact that they not only survived but flourished, despite two hundred years of consistent ecclesiastical condemnation and prohibition and intermittent prohibitions from secular authorities.

Despite their central role in knightly affairs and their relevance to some of the major political and military issues of the day, hastiludes (to give them the widest generic term) have never been the subject of

1

a major serious study. Two books were written at the beginning of this century, *The History of the Tournament in France and England* by F. H. Cripps-Day (London, 1918, reissued New York, 1985) and *The Tournament: its Periods and Phases* by R. C. Clephan (London, 1919). Both suffered from being too general in outlook and too heavily reliant on romance literature as source material. Since then, however, there has been a dearth of research on the subject. Hastiludes have been accepted as a major chivalric preoccupation, but without any attempt to discover exactly what happened in the various different forms of the game, who attended them and why or what their significance was. Among the exceptions to this general apathy on the subject is the work of Noel Denholm-Young: his most important article, 'The Tournament in the Thirteenth Century', was the first to seriously address the question of how and why medieval governments attempted to control hastiludes. This forms the starting point for any study of the sport, simply because Denholm-Young was the first to fully appreciate the political implications of tourneying. Another important study which has not received the recognition it deserves is the late Ruth Harvey's *Moriz von Craun and the Chivalric World* (Oxford, 1961). This is a masterly review of the social and literary background of tournaments in Germany, France and England which ranges far beyond the narrow confines of the Middle High German poem to which it relates. Two other invaluable short studies were both inspired by the Dunstable tournament of 1309 for which a roll of arms is extant: Tomkinson's article 'Retinues at the tournament at Dunstable in 1309' in *Eng.Hist.Rev.*, 1959 traced the personal ties between the tourneyers listed and their relative positions on the roll; J. R. Maddicott in his *Thomas of Lancaster 1307-22* (Oxford, 1977) gave some consideration to the relationship between the tournament, the April parliament and the presentation of grievances to Edward II. Although important in their own right, all these studies have concentrated on one particular aspect of the tournament and there has been no serious attempt to draw all the different threads together. One of the main drawbacks in doing this is the scattered nature of the sources: references to hastiludes are liberally sprinkled throughout chronicles, financial and administrative records and heraldic manuscripts. For this reason it was necessary to limit the terms of reference of this book, while still attempting a general survey. The year 1400 was deliberately chosen as a *terminus ad quem* because the early fifteenth century saw important changes in the nature of the sport, not the least being the introduction of the barrier which revolutionized the conduct of the joust (tilt between

2

two combatants). The role of heralds, despite its importance for the development of formal tournament organization, has only been touched upon because of the complexity of the subject which makes it deserving of a separate study. The limitation of my terms of reference to England is a somewhat artificial one for, as will emerge all too clearly, English knights tourneyed all over Europe throughout the period and were just as familiar with continental tourneying circuits as with English ones. This makes it admissible to include continental references where these can amplify or elucidate English practices.

Given these limitations, this book sets out to draw as complete a picture of English tourneying up to the turn of the fifteenth century as possible. It examines the intimate and stimulating relationship between war and hastiludes and the political repercussions of tourneying or attempting to suppress it. The implications of pageantry, rather than simply its manifestations, are discussed at length and, similarly, those who actually attended hastiludes are identified and their common characteristics depicted. Finally, the more technical side of the game is considered: what the different forms of encounter were and what developments in armour these called for and encouraged. The end result is, I hope, to place the tournament where it belongs, at the heart of medieval chivalric culture. I would like to thank the following who have assisted me in my research: Dr Juliet Vale, who allowed me to read her thesis ahead of publication; Major Berkeley, the Berkeley trustees and Mr D. H. Smith, B.A., for access to the Berkeley manuscripts; Dr G. Harriss for access to the McFarlane transcripts at Magdalen College, Oxford; Dr C. Allmand, Dr P. Chaplais, Dr J. Maddicott, Dr R. Rogers, Dr C. Tyerman, and Miss H. Waite for assistance on various points. My principal thanks are due to my supervisor Dr Maurice Keen, who has given generously of his valuable time and invaluable talents and without whom this thesis would never have been written. Dr Richard Barber's editorial comments and suggestions have also been much appreciated. I would also like to thank my parents for their continual support and encouragement. Finally, I acknowledge with thanks the support of my husband who has borne with fortitude the side effects of the creative process.

CHAPTER ONE

The Early Beginnings

The historian of the English tournament must necessarily always be looking over his shoulder at developments on the continent, for it was in Europe – most probably in France – that tournaments were first introduced. The highly specialized vocabulary of the sport[1] was dominated by French terminology and French fashions in tourneying, as in other aspects of chivalry, continued to influence English tourneying practices from their earliest beginnings in the twelfth century until the fifteenth century when Burgundian influence became paramount.

The tournament seems to have emerged in the late eleventh or early twelfth century at a period when French knights were introducing a new type of shock combat based on a heavy lance held tightly under the right arm (the 'couched' position) which enabled a rider to put his full weight behind his lance and to unhorse his opponent without losing his own weapon. A closely massed charge by a body of knights with their lances couched in this manner could 'make a hole in the wall of Babylon' according to Anna Comnena,[2] the Byzantine princess who witnessed its devastating effect during the First Crusade. The effectiveness of the manoeuvre very much depended on the ability of the knights to maintain close ranks, and the tournament provided the ideal opportunity for the individual to practise his horsemanship and his management of an unwieldy weapon as part of a team in circumstances which approximated to those of real warfare. It was this action of one team charging another with their lances couched with the object of unhorsing their opponents and seizing their horses and persons as booty which

---

[1] See *infra*: Chapter Seven.
[2] *The Alexiad of Anna Comnena* ed. & trans. E. R. A. Sewter (Penguin, 1979), p. 416.

distinguished the tournament from earlier forms of military sport.[3]

The earliest references to tournaments are ascribed to the eleventh century, but in later chronicles. Geoffrey of Malaterra, for example, who was writing in 1110 records that in 1062, during a siege in the war between Robert Guiscard, duke of Calabria and his brother Roger, count of Sicily, the young men from the two armies jousted against each other and Arnold, the count's brother-in-law, was killed.[4] The early thirteenth century *Chronicon Turoniensis* has an entry under the year 1066: 'Gaufredus de Pruliaco, qui torneamenta invenit, apud Andegavum occiditur.'[5] Though tournaments earlier than the very late eleventh century are likely to be anachronistic, these references do at least show that very early in the twelfth century chroniclers were already anxious to give the sport respectable antecedents in their own local regions. The desire to please patrons who were devoted to chivalric culture by suggesting that their ancestors were also tourneyers was no doubt a powerful one: Lambert of Ardres thus made the eleventh century Counts of Guines attend tournaments and the tyrannical Radulph, count of Guines, meet his end in one in 1034.[6]

Given the vested interests in pushing back the date of the earliest tournaments it is difficult to point to a specific time or place for their introduction. What is certain is that by 1130 they had proliferated to such a degree that the church became concerned at the number of fatalities and the misdirection of knightly energies, and the ninth canon of a decretal issued in that year by the Council of Clermont unequivocally prohibited all military sports of this kind.[7] Ecclesiastical burial was forbidden to those killed in tournaments although the sacraments of confession and the *viaticum* were not to be denied if the victim asked for them in a spirit of penitence. The church thus set her face firmly against the sport at an early period and adopted the attitude which she was to maintain, with varying degrees of firmness, for the next two hundred years. It is perhaps a reflection on how widespread the passion for tourneying had become that it was a council, the highest authority in the

---

[3] See, for example, the cavalry exercises recorded by Nithard in *Carolingian Chronicles*, ed. B. W. Scholz (University of Michigan Press, 1970), p. 164.
[4] Geoffrey of Malaterra, 'De Rebus Gestis Roberti Guiscardi, Ducis Calabriae et Rogerii, Comitis Siciliae' in *Thesaurus Antiquitatum et Historiarum Siciliae*, ed. J. G. Graevius (Lugduni Batavorum, 1723), iv, bk. ii, chap. xxiii, col. 26.
[5] C. Du Cange, 'Dissertations sur la vie de Saint Louis par Joinville', in *Glossarium*, ed. C. Du Cange (Niort, 1887), x, 20.
[6] *Chron.Ghisn.*, pp. 49, 237, 239, 243.
[7] C-J. Hefele & H. Leclercq, *Histoire des Conciles* (Paris, 1912), v, pt. i, 729.

church, which imposed such heavy sanctions. It is also suggestive that the council had to employ a periphrase 'detestabiles ... nundinas vel ferias' to describe tournaments: evidently the sport was new enough for the proper terminology to have not yet reached clerical circles – a fact which tourneyers somewhat ingenuously exploited for their own ends by professing not to understand that the canon applied to their favourite pastime. For this reason, when the Third Lateran Council repeated the prohibition in 1179, their purpose was made clearer by the addition of an explanatory note: 'detestabiles ... nundinas vel ferias, quas vulgo torneamenta vocant'.[8] This same device was used by chroniclers faced with making their meaning clear in the face of a new and technical vocabulary. Otto of Freising, for example, has an incidental reference to a 'tyrocinium, quod vulgo nunc turnoimentum dicitur' which took place in 1127 during an interlude in Frederick, duke of Swabia's wars.[9] Other chroniclers, such as Matthew Paris,[10] simply refer to tournaments as *conflictus gallici*, a generic term which stressed the French origins of the sport without attempting a more precise terminology.

In the second half of the twelfth century the tournament began to feature in chivalric literature, and after Chrétien de Troyes it became a *sine qua non* for all romances and even for the later *chansons de geste*. For the first time, therefore, we begin to get descriptive accounts of tournaments written for chivalric patrons by men who knew and understood the ideology and practicalities of the sport. Chivalric literature no doubt reflected the preoccupations of knightly life in the twelfth century by featuring the tournament so prominently (often to the detriment of the story-line) but on the other hand the glorification of chivalric virtues best displayed in literary tournaments increased the prestige of tourneying in real life and inspired real knights to perform great feats of arms modelled on those of romance heroes. The lives of William Marshal and Arnold of Ardres[11] clearly reveal not only the contemporary obsession with tournaments, which, to judge by the Marshal's history occurred almost fortnightly in northern France and the Low Countries in the 1170s and 1180s, but also the recognition by biographers that skill in

---

[8] *Ibid.*, v, pt. ii, 1102.
[9] Otto of Freising, *Gesta Frederici seu Rectius Cronica*, ed. F-J. Schmale (Berlin, 1965), p. 158.
[10] Matthew Paris, ii, 309.
[11] *L'Histoire de Guillaume le Maréchal*, ed. P. Meyer (Paris, 1901), 3 vols; Lambert of Ardres, *Chronicon Ghisnense et Ardense*, ed. D. Godefroy (Paris, 1855).

the tournament was a prerequisite virtue of the historical as well as the literary hero.

By the end of the twelfth century, therefore, the popularity of the tournament had been established beyond all doubt. Despite clerical disapproval tournaments flourished all over western Europe, in Outremer and even in Byzantium.[12] Knights risked the harshest penalties that church and state could impose to indulge in their favourite sport – a pastime which was stimulated and glorified by chivalric literature. Tourneying was an entrenched habit among the knights of western Europe – a habit that they took with them and established in the lands of the east where crusade or simple aggrandisement led them.

In England in the twelfth century, however, there was rather a different story. William of Newburgh, writing in 1198, declared that tournaments had been prohibited in the reigns of Henry I and Henry II and those wishing to attend them had been obliged to go abroad. He admits that there was a lapse in the effectiveness of this prohibition during the weak government of Stephen's reign, but credits the formal introduction of the sport to England to Richard I's decree of 1194 which recognized five places where tournaments could be held upon purchasing a royal licence.[13]

William of Newburgh's evidence receives confirmation from the very few scattered references that there are to English tourneying in the twelfth century. The earliest known English reference to a tournament occurs in a charter[14] dating from the reign of Henry I in which Osbert of Arden granted a carucate of land to Turchill Fundus in return for the nominal service of carrying Arden's painted lances from London or Northampton to his house at Kinesbury at his legitimate summons and 'cum ultra mare ad turniamenta ire voluero'. This charter, therefore, only contemplates the possibility of tournaments occurring abroad, supporting William of Newburgh's assertion that they were prohibited in England under Henry I.

---

[12] R. P. Honoré de Sainte Marie, *Dissertations Historique et Critique sur la Chevalerie* (Paris, 1718), p. 184.

[13] William of Newburgh, 'Historia Rerum Anglicarum' in *CRSHR*, ii, 422-3.

[14] G. F. Warner & H. J. Ellis, *Facsimiles of Royal and Other Charters in the British Museum* (London, 1903), i, no. 12. I do not believe that the purported reference to jousting in William the Conqueror's *Consuetudines* of 1091 is borne out by the text: see C. H. Haskins, 'The Norman *Consuetudines et Iusticie* of William the Conqueror', *Eng.Hist.Rev.* (1908), pp. 503, 507.

Similarly, his inference that tournaments occurred during Stephen's reign is corroborated by numerous incidental references. Henry of Huntingdon, for example, puts a speech in the mouth of the bishop of Orkney before the battle of the Standard in 1138 contrasting the vast numbers of ill-armed, undisciplined and untrained Scots with the small but well armed English army which was exercised in arms in peacetime so that it was well prepared for times of war.[15] Though the ideas expressed in the speech may be anachronistic for 1138, shortly after the death of Henry I, Henry of Huntingdon's own death in 1155 suggests that the experiences of Stephen's reign may have been in the forefront of his mind when he wrote the passage.

Better evidence for outbreaks of tourneying occurs during the civil wars of Stephen's reign – an association of activities which, as we shall see later,[16] is characteristic of medieval tourneying. In 1140 Ranulph, earl of Chester with only three men-at-arms was able to capture Lincoln castle from the royalist forces under the guise of a courtesy call to the commander's wife, because the military garrison were elsewhere engaged in martial sports.[17] A short while afterwards the royalists displayed their chivalry at the beginning of the battle of Lincoln by trying 'proludium pugne facere, quod iustam vocant, quia tali periti erant arte.' The less chivalrous men of the Earl of Gloucester promptly rode them down on that occasion, but during the siege of Winchester, when less was at stake than on the battlefield, it was the Empress' men who 'por faire chevalerie' daily issued out of the city to tourney with the knights of the besieging army.[18] It seems highly likely that it was also during Stephen's reign that Hugh Mortimer was killed in a tournament at Worcester[19] – he has the dubious distinction of being the earliest known English casualty in the sport.

As the study of later periods of tourneying has shown that chronicle references to tournaments account for only a small proportion of those known to have been held, and there are no royal or seignurial household accounts or heraldic records available for this period to supplement references, it would not be unreason-

[15] Henry of Huntingdon, *Historia Anglorum*, ed. T. Arnold (R.S., 1879), p. 263.
[16] See *infra*: Chapter Two.
[17] J. Beeler, *Warfare in England 1066-1189* (Cornell University Press, 1966), p. 108, quoting Ordericus Vitalis.
[18] William of Malmesbury, *Historia Novella*, ed. K. R. Potter (Oxford, 1955), pp. 48-9; *HGM.*, ll. 175-8.
[19] 'History of the Priory of Wigmore' in *Monasticon Anglicanum*, ed. W. Dugdale (London, 1830), vi, pt. i, 349.

able to infer that the tournament flourished during Stephen's reign. Likewise, a comparison with other times of weak kingship and civil war, such as the reigns of Henry III and Edward II, where evidence is more plentiful, would also point to the conclusion that tourneying was the natural accompaniment of political and military unrest.[20]

With the accession of Henry II it might have been expected that tourneying would have been brought under control and prohibited once again as William of Newburgh suggested. Yet there is evidence to suggest that tournaments were not unknown in England even in his reign. He certainly seems to have patronized them on the continent, for he allowed his knights to tourney during his truce negotiations with Louis VII and he was personally responsible for the publication of a tournament at Beaucaire in 1174 to celebrate his reconciliation with the Duke of Narbonne and the King of Aragon.[21] All Henry II's sons were noted tourneyers, and both Henry, the Young King and Geoffrey of Brittany were permitted to take large companies of young men drawn from England as well as the continental demesnes on foreign tourneying tours of a lavish and spectacular kind.[22] Although this latitude where tournaments were concerned seems to have applied only to his continental lands, it is possible that Henry II allowed a limited number to be held in England in the presence of and under the aegis of his sons. Thus, for instance, according to the life of William Marshal, after his reconciliation with his father in 1174 the Young King and his companions were forced to return to England where they occupied their time in hunting and in tournaments.[23] Likewise, it was in the presence of Prince John that what appears to have been a jousting challenge was fought outside the walls of Chester in 1186.[24]

Whether these tournaments occurred with Henry's approval or without his knowledge, it is interesting to note that the one region where tournaments were unquestionably held during his reign is the area where royal authority was at its weakest – Ireland. Giraldus Cambrensis records at least two occasions on which the Anglo-Norman Geraldine clan held tournaments during the conquest of

---

[20] See *infra*: Chapter Three.
[21] G. Duby, *Le Dimanche de Bouvines* (Gallimard, 1973), p. 113; M. de la Curne de Sainte Palaye, *Mémoires de l'Ancienne Chevalerie* (Paris, 1759), ii, 23 n. 22.
[22] *HGM.*, i, pp. 88ff; Roger of Hoveden, *Chronica*, ed. W. Stubbs (R.S., 1870), iii, 268.
[23] *HGM.*, l. 2394.
[24] Lucian of Chester, *Liber ... de Laude Cestrie*, ed. M. V. Taylor (Record Society of Lancashire and Cheshire, lxiv, 1912), pp. 61-2.

Ireland. While Maurice FitzGerald and O'Roric, the one-eyed King of Meath, held a parley Maurice's nephew and seven of his kinsmen tourneyed 'in the French fashion' within sight of the parley place so that, under guise of this sport, they were ready in arms should the Irish prove treacherous, as indeed they did. On the second occasion, thirty kinsmen of Raymond FitzGerald, the acting lieutenant of Ireland, all bearing the same device on their shields held a tournament ostensibly to welcome to Ireland the newly appointed governor, William FitzAldhelm, but in reality as a show of strength by the displaced lieutenant.[25] It would have been difficult, if not impossible, for Henry II to have stopped his barons tourneying in Ireland so it is interesting to see that even in the twelfth century tourneying was already exhibiting some of the features which were to become prominent in later periods: it was flourishing in areas where royal control was weakest and in a war situation, and it was already showing a tendency to be perverted for political purposes.

The accession of Richard I saw a marked change in royal policy towards hastiludes. Unlike his father, Richard had frequented tournaments on the continent since his youth and was himself an accomplished practitioner of the art. His death was to be lamented by the troubadour, Gaucelm Faidit, because it brought to an end the feats of arms and great daily tournaments which were such a feature of his reign,[26] and the hey-day of the twelfth century English tournament must undoubtedly be placed in his reign. He had himself participated in an unusual informal encounter using sugar canes instead of lances outside the walls of Messina during his journey to the Holy Land in 1191 and he had allegedly conceived a great hatred for William des Barres, a household knight of the French King, who had unhorsed him.[27] When the king himself set such an example of defiance of the church's prohibition while engaged on the church's business, it is not surprising that many of his subjects followed suit. Political uncertainty caused by Richard's long absences abroad, at first on crusade, later in an Austrian prison, provided the opportunity for an outbreak of tourneying in England which provoked the Pope into writing to the English bishops in 1193 strictly forbidding tournaments and ordering all those who wished to exercise themselves in arms to go to the Holy Land.[28]

---

[25] Giraldus Cambrensis, *The Historical Works*, ed. T. Wright (London, 1863), pp. 243, 274.
[26] *Florilegè des Troubadours*, ed. A. Berry (Paris, 1930) pp. 248-50.
[27] Roger of Hoveden, iii, 93-5.
[28] *Ibid.*, iii, 202.

Within a year, however, Richard had returned to England and flagrantly defied the church in this matter by issuing the writ which changed the course of English tourneying history. The writ,[29] addressed to Hubert Walter, his justiciar, announced that tournaments were to be allowed at five named sites in England: between Salisbury and Wilton (Wiltshire), Warwick and Kenilworth (Warwickshire), Stamford and Warinford (?Suffolk, ?Lincolnshire), Brackley and Mixbury (Northamptonshire) and Blyth and Tickhill (Nottinghamshire). A series of graduated fees was set out for each knight wishing to participate: twenty marks for an earl, ten marks for a baron, four marks for a landed knight and two marks for a landless knight. No-one was to be permitted to tourney until he had sworn an oath to pay his fees in full, on pain of personal arrest.

We have already seen how tournaments were taking place in England despite secular and ecclesiastical prohibitions. By licensing them in a limited number of places and under specific conditions Richard I recognized the popularity of the sport and attempted to mitigate its worst effects by exercising some degree of control. The restriction of legitimate tournaments to only five places would, in theory at least, enable the king to keep a watchful eye on them and prevent the indiscriminate destruction of cultivated land and royal forest. The introduction of a licensing system would ensure a healthy income for the king for, as Denholm-Young pointed out, even a fairly small meeting of thirty a side would bring in about two hundred marks;[30] on the other hand, if tournaments were held without the royal licence substantial fines could be extracted from transgressors. As early as January 1195 Robert Mortimer, for example, was obliged to seek recovery of his lands which had been seized into the king's hands because he had tourneyed without licence[31] – an indication that Richard's writ was put into immediate effect. Even if the writ could not be fully enforced due to the impossibility of adequately policing it, it gave the king a means of exerting some influence on tourneying in England and also a means of exploiting the popularity of the sport to the benefit of his treasury. A further advantage, which Richard as an experienced soldier could not be unaware of, was that English knights now had a legitimate opportunity for training themselves in horsemanship and

---

[29] *Foedera*, ed. T. Rymer (Record Commission, 1816), i, pt. i, 65. For a fuller discussion of this decree see *infra*: pp. xx-xx.
[30] N. Denholm-Young, 'The Tournament in the Thirteenth Century' in *Studies Presented to F. M. Powicke* (Oxford, 1948), p. 243.
[31] *Rotuli Curiae Regis*, ed. F. Palgrave (Record Commission, 1835), i, 87.

the management of weapons in a situation which closely approximated that of real battle.

Interestingly, despite the official hardline policy of the church with regard to tournaments, in England churchmen offered little or no opposition to their being licensed by the king; there are very few examples of royally licensed meetings being prohibited by English clerics. The abbot of Bury St Edmunds did formally prohibit a tournament held by eighty young nobles between Bury and Thetford in 1194, presumably because it was too close for monastic comfort. On the other hand, after they had ignored his prohibition without incurring any retribution, he allowed them to receive hospitality in his town and even invited them to dine with him. It was only when the young men got out of hand, celebrating the end of their sport with drinking and singing which kept the whole abbey awake all night and then breaking their oath not to leave the town without the abbot's permission and forcibly battering down the town gates in the process of leaving, that the abbot finally excommunicated them.[32]

By the end of the twelfth century the tournament was flourishing in England as elsewhere in Europe, but with the significant difference that in England it had already become the subject of royal regulation. This gave an added dimension to the English tournament, for unlicensed gatherings swiftly came to be associated with political opposition to the crown. In the reigns of kings who had forfeited the respect and support of their baronage, such as John, Henry III and Edward II, the tournament became a focus for political discontent; on occasion, they even bore a resemblance to private war waged between quarrelling barons and also, which was more sinister, became a pretext for gathering armed men prior to staging a coup. It was no coincidence that the kings who suffered most from political unrest and its concomitant outbreaks of illicit tourneying were not themselves tourneyers.

Both Edward I and Edward III, on the other hand, were warriors of note and had won considerable personal reputations in the lists; they not only patronized the sport but also participated in it with great success. They shared the knightly passion for tourneying and

---

[32] Jocelin of Brakelond, *Cronica*, ed. H. E. Butler (London, 1949), pp. 55-6. It has been suggested, however, that the tournament and the riot were separate and unconnected incidents, so that the excommunication may not have had anything to do with the tournament. See: F. M. Powicke, *Henry III and the Lord Edward* (Oxford, 1947), i, 21.

their subjects were able to identify with their chivalric interests. In their reigns the political overtones of tourneying were diverted into new channels which were extremely valuable to the crown. The Round Table,[33] for instance, was especially popular in the reigns of Edward I and Edward III. This particular form of the tournament was marked by unusual pageantry and feasting; the presence of ladies was an important feature of the Round Table and ensured that singing and dancing were continued long into the night after the sport had ended. This made it very suitable for court celebrations ranging from the purely domestic, such as royal births and marriages, to those of international importance, such as those marking political and military triumphs. In relation to the latter, the Arthurian origins and overtones of the Round Table were frequently exploited to the full, with knights taking on the names and even characters of Arthurian heroes and thus identifying themselves with the ideology and supremacy of Arthur's court. Round Tables therefore became inextricably involved with the Arthurian propaganda which was cultivated by English kings in answer to the French cult of Charlemagne.

If Edward I and Edward III were skilful in harnessing knightly energies and redirecting tourneying activity into useful channels, they were also lucky in that they were aided by changing fashions in the sport which developed independently of their intervention. The most important of these was the decline of the great *mêlée* tournament which had dominated twelfth and most of thirteenth century tourneying. Instead of two teams of knights with up to two hundred men on each side (though smaller numbers were more usual) fighting in their normal armour and with their normal weapons of war over a large area of countryside it became much more common to hold jousts in which each knight would fight for himself in a restricted space marked out by fences. Though the jouster might be part of the home team proclaiming the jousts (a *tenant*), or one of the knights who arrived to take up the challenge (a *venant*), he fought on his own behalf and as an individual against a single opponent. He used only the lance and none of the other weapons, such as the sword and mace, which were available to the tourneyer and since his actions were more open to observation than those of the tourneyer in the confusion of the *mêlée*, they were more closely subjected to a gradual accretion of customary rules of conduct and were liable to be judged not only by the other

---

[33] See *infra*: pp. xx-xxx, xxx-x.

participants and spectators, but also by specially appointed judges and heralds. The development of specialized armour for hastiludes, combined with an increasing emphasis on pageantry, led to a spiralling of costs in the thirteenth century which intensified in the fourteenth century. This too encouraged the popularity of the joust at the expense of tournaments since few knights could afford to equip themselves and a retinue in a manner befitting the occasion. As the sport grew more elitist and its participants fewer, the dangers to the crown decreased. It would be more difficult to gather an army of rebels under the guise of jousting than of tourneying, and there was less disruption of law and order when smaller bands of knights were involved. By the early fourteenth century,[34] the teeth of the sport had been drawn and jousting, rather than tourneying in the strict sense, became the most popular form of encounter.

The rapid advancements which were made in the safety of hastiludes in the fourteenth century caused by improvements in armour, the growth of rules of conduct and the relative tameness of the joust compared to the tournament encouraged some knights to seek their excitement elsewhere. Though hastiludes in border areas between lands of different allegiance were common from the earliest days of tourneying, in the mid fourteenth century the increasingly nationalistic flavour of the wars between England and France gave an added impetus to this type of encounter. Border combats could be fought *à outrance* (with the normal sharp weapons of war) instead of *à plaisance* (with blunted weapons) as had become the usual practice in hastiludes: if the opponent was killed, as was possible in such circumstances, his death was regrettable from the point of view of the loss of a good knight, but of little importance since he was a national enemy. Victory in border combats was not simply regarded as the success of an individual but as the success of the nation which he represented. The bitterness which this ideology instilled into the border combat gave it a greater piquancy in the eyes of the knight anxious to win renown, and greater honour could certainly be won in this more dangerous form of the sport than in hastiludes fought *à plaisance* against fellow countrymen. During Richard II's reign there was a continual stream of applicants seeking licence to go to the marches of Calais or the borders of Scotland to perform feats of arms there.

These border combats were not only more dangerous because of the sharp weapons and animosities involved, but also because the

---

[34] See *infra*: Chapter Three.

fighting usually took several forms. It was common practice for several courses to be run with the lance, followed by courses with the sword, the axe and the dagger: the winner was the combatant who conducted himself best with each type of weapon.[35] The axe and dagger courses were particularly perilous because it was difficult to avoid wounding the opponent. As in other hastiludes, however, the object of the feat of arms was not the death of the opponent (though fatalities were quite common) but to secure his defeat or surrender and thereby prove the general superiority in arms of one of the pair.

By the end of the fourteenth century two distinct types of hastilude had developed out of the unsophisticated *mêlée* tournament of the twelfth century. On the one hand, there was the courtly game fought *à plaisance* for the entertainment of ladies and courtiers: dominated by pageantry, the actual fighting frequently became a subordinate, though still an important, part of the celebrations. On the other hand, to counterbalance this emasculation, there developed the feat of arms: in many ways this was the true heir of the twelfth century *mêlée* tournament involving as it did the use of weapons *à outrance* and the minimum of rules, and being geared to participation rather than spectating. The disparity between the two forms of sport must not be overemphasized, however: the fourteenth century border feat of arms had its audience just like the twelfth century *mêlée*, and the risk of death or serious injury was never altogether removed from hastiludes *à plaisance*. More importantly, the knights who excelled in these courtly games *à plaisance* were usually the same knights who won international renown in border feats of arms – and indeed in war.

Tourneying had become a much more complex sport by the end of our period. There were a great many more variants of the game, each one having its own distinct set of rules and customs. The passing of the centuries had seen the evolution of a tournament ideology which was to have a far reaching effect outside the lists, particularly in the field of war. In many ways, however, tourneying remained much the same. Knights still tourneyed for the same reasons as they had always done, even though it was in a different manner and under different conditions. The holding of tournaments still had political and military overtones which could not be ignored and were still, therefore, liable to be perverted for nefarious ends.

---

[35] See, for example, the terms for the jousting challenges in BL MS. Additional 21357 fos 1-5.

Most important of all, perhaps, tourneying was as central to chivalric life and culture at the end of the fourteenth century as it had been in the twelfth century.

CHAPTER TWO

The Tournament and War

Throughout the period 1100 to 1400 tourneying was closely connected with war. When Richard I introduced licensed tournaments to England his decision was justified on a military basis. According to the chroniclers he had observed that French knights were more skilled and better trained through having frequented the sport than inferior English knights. He therefore permitted them to be held in England so that by participating in this type of *praeludium bellorum* the novice might learn what to expect in real combat – the cracking of his teeth, the sight of his own blood, the blows and the unhorsings.[1] In this manner the tiro was not only given a foretaste of the hardships he might expect to undergo in battle but also learnt how to retaliate and how to handle his horse and weapons to their best advantage.

These experiences are what King Alexander intended his knights to undergo when he was credited with the invention of tournaments in the romance of *Perceforest*:[2]

> affin q[u]e en temps de paix et de repos ilz peussent appre[n]dre les armes sans occire lung lautre et affin que en te[m]ps de guerre ilz fussent mieulx instruictz et propres a grever leurs ennemys et eulx deffendre si on les voiloit assailir ... pour eulx introduyre aux armes et eulx re[n]dre agilles et amollier leurs membres et apprendre a eulx deffe[n]dre au besoing ...

A hundred years after *Perceforest*, despite the changes and developments which had taken place in tourneying practice, the ideology remained the same. Jean de Bueil, in all sincerity, advanced exactly the same ideas in about 1470 in a more succinct manner: knights

---

[1] Roger of Hoveden, ii, 166-7.
[2] *Le Roman de Perceforest* (Paris, 1528), i, 23r.

ought to perform feats of arms 'car ... usage rent maistre et fait l'omme prest et habille.'[3]

By that time there was a school of thought which took these concepts further, believing explicitly that hastiludes should not only be compulsory but also nationally sponsored, so that the knighthood of the realm was kept in good training in the event of war. In 1412, for instance, Christine de Pisan argued that tournaments and jousts ought to be proclaimed in every diocese in France up to three times a year and that their costs ought to be defrayed by means of a levy on royal revenues; French chivalry would then be in trained readiness to withstand an English invasion.[4] This suggestion was still being put forward in England as late as the end of the fifteenth century. Caxton thought it important enough to insert a personal plea to Richard III into his translation of Lull's *Booke of the Ordre of Chyvalrye*: 'that twyse or thryse in a yere or at the lest ones he wold do crye Iustes of pees to thende that every knyght shold have hors and harneys & also the use & craft of a knyght.'[5]

Modern historians[6] have frequently dismissed these appeals as anachronistic hankerings after an earlier, imagined golden age of chivalry and as meaningless chivalric conventions. In the same way, the regular inclusion in late medieval jousting challenges of passages announcing that the challenger wished to learn the *mestier d'armes*, increase his military abilities and experience combat to benefit the order of chivalry, church and state, have been scathingly referred to as 'a courtly formula'. This jaundiced view is shared by other historians who have suggested that the 'Art of War' as taught and practised in hastiludes bore no resemblance to the 'Practice of War'; they have claimed that the lance, the main weapon of knightly sport, became obsolete in warfare and that the infrequency of hastiludes, combined with their perpetuation of anachronistic weaponry and increasingly elaborate settings and ritual, made them simply an exercise in court ceremony.

These assumptions have particular reference to the late fourteenth century and beyond. The connections of the tournament with war are clearer in the earlier period, on which my study concentrates,

---

[3] Jean de Bueil, *Le Jouvencel*, ed. C. Favre & L. Lecestre (Paris, 1887), ii, 71.
[4] Christine de Pisan, *Livre de la Paix*, ed. C. C. Willard (The Hague, 1958), p. 134.
[5] Ramon Lull, *Book of the Ordre of Chyvalry*, trans. W. Caxton, ed. A. T. P. Byles (EETS, 168, 1926), p. 124.
[6] See, for example, A. B. Ferguson, *The Indian Summer of English Chivalry* (Durham, N.Carolina, 1960), pp. 14-7; H. J. Hewitt, 'The Organization of War' in *The Hundred Years War*, ed. K. Fowler (London, 1971), p. 88; Beeler, *Warfare in England*, p. 278.

but some light will, I hope, be cast on the question of their validity. In this chapter I shall begin by considering the relevance of hastiludes to warfare as a training ground and, consequently, their suitability for the recruitment of war retinues, matters clearly germane to that issue. I shall then go on to discuss a second matter that these bring into prominence – the way warfare stimulated tourneying activity; and finally, to examine how advances in the safety of hastiludes were consciously countered by the development of a new outlet for tourneying skills.

The *mêlée* tournament of the twelfth and thirteenth centuries was not only highly relevant to real combat, but was sometimes indistinguishable from it. In early manuscript illuminations it is often impossible to tell whether the fighting is sport or battle, unless there is a *berfrois* of watching ladies or weapons *à plaisance* are being used. As Duby has pointed out, the sole difference between war and the early tournament was one of intention, the death of an opponent being a matter for regret in the latter.[7] Even the fact that the tournament was arranged in advance at a specific time and place and the giving of prizes to the best performers are not without parallels in the conduct of real war.[8]

The most obvious feature of the *mêlée* style engagement was the use of squadron manoeuvres and especially the massed charge with lances couched. The biography of William Marshal always gives particular praise to those companies which were able to maintain serried ranks in the tournament and makes it clear that a charge carried out in this manner was usually irresistible. At one tournament between St Brice and Boeles, for example, the companies were drawn up ready to begin:

> Ja s'aperceivent li conrei:
> Li un correient a desrei
> & li autre sagement vienent,
> Serre en bataille se tienent:
> E il porvit bien son afaire
> Com cil qui bien le saveit faire.[9]

---

[7] Duby, *Dimanche de Bouvines*, pp. 137, 140. It must be noted that the use of mercenaries and the practice of ransoming reduced the number of fatalities in warfare.

[8] *Ibid.*, pp. 121-2; *HGM.*, ii, xxxvii-xxxviii; see also *infra*: p. xx.

[9] *HGM.*, ll. 1417-22. See also *Ibid.*, ll. 2497-500 for another example of a disciplined company faring better than a disorganized one.

The company which was well disciplined enough to keep close ranks in the charge was able to overrun any opposing company by means of the sheer weight and momentum of a closely coordinated charge. The key to success on the tournament field was discipline. If individual knights were carried away by their enthusiasm and left their company to seek prisoners and booty so that the unit became scattered, its capabilities as an offensive and defensive force were drastically reduced. Confusion meant vulnerability.

The same was true of warfare. Where the cavalry was successful on the battlefield it was because they applied the tactics instilled into them on the tournament field. At Lewes in 1264, and again at Evesham in 1265, the decisive blow which changed the course of the battle was struck by a cavalry charge. The author of the *Song of Lewes* claimed that it was despite the military training which the royalists had received in tournaments that they were defeated; God chose to give victory to the smaller, less experienced army of the barons.[10] Though the royalists were indeed tourneyers, Simon de Montfort and his supporters were no less proficient in the sport and had been the chief recipients of royal prohibitions on tourneying in the 1260s.[11] Nearly a hundred years later, at the battle of Poitiers, it was once again a surprise attack on the left flank of the enemy delivered by a small mounted force under the Captal de Buch, (himself a tourneyer), which helped to decide the conflict.[12]

A cavalry charge at the apposite moment could thus turn the scale in a battle, and it was on the tournament field that knights first learnt how to time their charges and concentrate their efforts for maximum effect. This is not to deny that foot soldiers played a vital role in the medieval battle. Indeed, cavalry success was frequently dependent on the defensive capacity of the foot to resist the enemy's horse and the offensive capacity of the archers to create an opening for a cavalry strike by causing heavy casualties and disarray among the enemy ranks. The battle of Falkirk in 1298 is a prime example of the necessity of horse and foot working together. The irregular attacks of the English cavalry were easily repulsed by the Scottish *schiltrons* until the king ordered the English and Welsh archers to come up. Once they had torn gaps in the Scottish ranks with their arrows the knights were able to charge once again and this time deliver the *coup de grâce*. It was the ability of the cavalry to strike

[10] *The Song of Lewes*, ed. C. L. Kingsford (Oxford, 1890), ll. 360-4.
[11] *CCR 1261-64*, p. 133; *CPR 1258-66*, p. 345; *Foedera*, i, 806; *Ann.Mon.*, iii, 238-9; *Ibid.*, iv, 161-2.
[12] R. C. Smail, 'Art of War', in *Medieval England*, ed. A. L. Poole (Oxford, 1958), i, 156.

swiftly and hard which made the knightly charge such an important feature of the medieval battle and one which could decide the fortunes of the day.

On the other hand, whenever the cavalry charge failed to produce the desired effect, it was usually because it had been carried out in a disorderly manner. At the battle of the Standard in 1138 the Scottish cavalry were able to breach the line of the English foot with a successful charge, but were unable to halt and reform. The English, though momentarily scattered, swiftly closed their ranks again and cut off the cavalry from the main body of the Scottish army, rendering both parts impotent.[13]

At both Crécy and Poitiers the English maintained a chosen defensive site with a largely dismounted army, as they had done at Falkirk. On both occasions, the French began the offensive with a mounted charge. At Crécy[14] the French knights were so eager to engage that they attacked before the main body of their army had even drawn up their lines, overriding their own crossbowmen in order to do so. As they charged they were taken in the flank by the English archers who inflicted heavy casualties on both horses and men, so reducing the weight and numbers of the attack as to render it ineffectual. Up to fifteen attacks of this kind were launched at irregular intervals whenever the French had gathered enough knights together. As they received no backing from the rest of their forces, the English were able to destroy the heart of the French army without even a general advance. At Poitiers[15] ten years later, the French knights again opened up the battle with a cavalry charge, although the main body of the army dismounted in imitation of the English. As had happened at Crécy the French charge was completely ineffectual: their numbers were thinned by English arrows and they were unable to maintain close enough ranks due to the marshy terrain which slowed them down.

As contemporary chroniclers were quick to point out the downfall of the French knights was caused by their pride. They had demanded the first place in the army and the right to draw first blood, even though past experience had shown that the charge was most effective when the enemy had been subjected to arrows and crossbow bolts beforehand. They had also been so eager to win personal reputation and glory that they had fought as individuals rather than as a team, which effectively reduced their capacity to

---

[13] Beeler, *Warfare in England*, pp. 88ff.
[14] Smail, 'Art of War', 153-5.

strike an irresistible blow. Though this desire to win personal renown had doubtless been fostered by tournament ideology, the pride which most chroniclers castigated as the cause of defeat in battle was frequently the cause of defeat in hastiludes, and for the same reason. In the poem of William Marshal, for example, at a tournament between Gournai and Ressons the behaviour of the opposing sides was strongly contrasted:

> Li conrei par deca vindrent
> Serre et bataille se tindrent,
> E se de la desreerent
> Par lor orgoil, quer grant gent erent.[16]

This was only a tournament, but the same words could have applied equally well to both Crécy and Poitiers, and even to Agincourt in the following century. Overconfidence in personal abilities and resources was as much a fatal mistake in the tournament as it was in war. The lessons of the lists were highly applicable to the battlefield.

The *mêlée* tournament accustomed the knight to fight as part of a military unit in a disciplined manoeuvre which was always difficult to perform, even on favourable terrain. What was needed on the battlefield was a disciplined, orderly attack in close ranks to maximize the effect of the charge, combined with the ability to check the onslaught and wheel round once enemy ranks had been broken. This was precisely what the tournament could teach. The relevance of the sport as training was further increased by the fact that the companies which took part in tournaments were composed of the same household knights and retainers of the magnates who also gathered under his banner to fight in the same units for warfare.[17] The *mêlée* therefore offered them the opportunity to practise as a team the same tactics which they could employ on the battlefield. If knights frequently forgot, or chose to ignore, the lessons of the tournament when they found themselves in the midst of battle this was not in any way due to the irrelevance of the tactics themselves.

The case for the value of the joust as military training is less strong than that for the *mêlée*, simply because as an individual encounter, rather than a team effort, it had less practical application to battle. On the other hand, since the thirteenth and fourteenth century joust was an informal affair in which it was possible for a

---

15 *Ibid.*, 148.
16 *HGM*, ll. 2497-500.
17 M. G. A. Vale, *War and Chivalry* (London, 1981), pp. 67, 80-85.

challenger to find himself facing more than one opponent at the same time, it gave the knight practise in the art of skirmishing – a form of fighting more common than the set battle. The joust also offered training in the handling of horse and weapons and encouraged accuracy in aiming the lance.

An early example of how experience offered by jousting could serve the knight in good stead when it came to genuine combat occurs in Wolfram von Eschenbach's romance, *Parzival*. The hero encounters one of the Templar guardians of the Grail castle 'and training and impulse both taught him to aim his thrust straight at the knot in the helmet cords – he struck him just where one holds the shield in knightly sport ...' and the Templar was thus successfully unhorsed.[18]

At the end of the fourteenth century, when perhaps it might justifiably be claimed that hastiludes offered little in the way of training for war and pageantry was beginning to swamp the more serious side of the joust, and when the great *mêlée* tournament was dropping out of fashion, a new form of sport emerged which had considerable relevance to warfare. This was the feat of arms already referred to, which was fought with the traditional weapons of joust and tourney, the lance and broadsword, and also with axe and dagger. These were primarily weapons of war and weapons for fighting on foot. This reflected the changing expectations of the knight's role in warfare: he was no longer solely a cavalryman but also a foot soldier who had to be prepared to fight at close quarters. The feat of arms gave him an opportunity to practise his skills on foot with battleaxe and dagger under controlled conditions, as well as to exhibit his superiority in each course.

Throughout the period 1100 to 1400 (and beyond), therefore, there was always at least one form of hastilude available which proffered military training and practice to knights. Though it is true that the courtly joust of the late fourteenth century was more of a pageant than a military exercise, the same was also true of the thirteenth century Round Table. What had happened was that the sport had developed in two directions simultaneously. Certain hastiludes were more suitable as a spectator sport and for this reason developed those ceremonial characteristics which historians have condemned because they detracted from the serious military side of tourneying. On the other hand, side by side with this type of sport, there were more dangerous hastiludes which were primarily oriented

---

[18] Wolfram von Eschenbach, *Parzival*, ed. & trans. H. M. Mustard & C. E. Passage (New York, 1961), p. 239.

towards the participant rather than the spectator, providing the novice with an important form of training for his future military career. To see the late fourteenth and fifteenth century joust as a degenerate descendent of the robust twelfth century *mêlée* tournament is therefore a distortion of vision. The ancestors of the courtly joust are to be found in the tournament *à plaisance* and the Round Table. Similarly, it is the late fourteenth century feat of arms which is the true lineal descendent of the twelfth century *mêlée*, via other hastiludes fought *à outrance*. Although there were dangers in hastiludes *à plaisance* and spectators also attended hastiludes *à outrance*, there still remained a distinct difference of emphasis. The former were primarily entertainment and the latter were first and foremost a serious trial of skill and strength. There can, therefore, be no doubt that hastiludes provided a valuable opportunity for military training throughout the period. The school of thought to which Christine de Pisan and William Caxton belonged was not without justification.

If hastiludes were indeed 'schools of arms' or 'schools of prowess'[19] as contemporaries frequently called them, in which knights practised for war, it is self evident that the same men should be prominent in both. Having learnt the lessons of the tournament they would be ready to follow their leaders on campaign and into battle. This does in fact prove to be the case.

Though tourneying was essentially a sport, for at least the first two hundred years of its history knights were accompanied in the tournament by substantial forces of foot soldiers who often had a share in the actual fighting. In the song of *Gui de Nanteuil*, for example, Charlemagne and Gui's two half brothers brought all their ban host to a tournament at Nanteuil: ten thousand *serjans* armed with bows and arrows were employed there.[20] Although this is an exaggerated picture of reality, there are elements of verisimilitude in it. In 1194, for instance, the Count of Auxerre gave a charter to his burgesses promising not to lead them too far from the county in case of war or *chevauchée*, but reserving the right to lead them to

---

[19] *Perceforest*, i, 23r; S. Anglo, *The Great Tournament Roll of Westminster* (Oxford, 1968), ii, 19; *The Boke of Noblesse*, ed. J. G. Nichols (Roxburghe Club, 77, 1860), p. 76; *The Scrope and Grosvenor Roll*, ed. N. H. Nicolas (Chester, 1879), i, 152, 155. In the *Scrope and Grosvenor Roll*, however, I believe that the deponents meant that tournaments were schools of arms in the sense that blazonry could be learnt there, though this is not the standard interpretation of the text.
[20] 'Gui de Nanteuil' in *APF*, vi, ll. 1781-4, 1841, 2574-9.

tournaments at Chablis, Joigny and Rougemont.[21] The same army of foot soldiers clearly fought for the count in both war and tournament. Baldwin of Hainault continually employed his foot soldiers in tournaments: on one occasion, according to his biographer, he took as many as three thousand to protect him in the *mêlée* because his personal enemy, the Duke of Brabant, was also participating.[22] At about the same time foot soldiers appear in the tournaments attended by William Marshal. A hundred years later they were also present as part of Edward I's returning crusader host at the 'little battle of Chalons'.[23] Up to at least the end of the thirteenth century it was clearly possible to employ foot soldiers in both war and *mêlée* tournament.

More significant for the present purpose than foot soldiers, who were not the principal actors in the sport, was the presence throughout the period of household knights. William FitzStephen described how, in the mid-twelfth century, the young men from the households of the king, bishops, officials and barons who had not yet been knighted, would tourney *à plaisance* in the London suburbs during Lent.[24] At the end of the century, it was the Young King's household knights who accompanied him to tournaments in northern France, and the same men later followed him into rebellion against his father. In 1220 bishop Peter of Winchester replied to charges made by Pandulph, the Papal Legate, that his household had attended tournaments: he denied that they had done so, saying that he would have expelled such sinners from his household, but he admitted that he had had to send away his nephews and certain others of his knights as a preventative measure.[25]

Despite Henry III's personal lack of interest in tourneying, his own household knights were obviously devotees of the sport. They were frequently recipients of royal prohibitions and, on one occasion, a number of them had their arrest ordered for defying one. Even more important, bearing in mind Henry III's normal disapproval of hastiludes and the fact that knights claimed that

---

[21] E. Petit, *Histoire des Ducs de Bourgogne* (Paris, 1888) ii, 187.

[22] Gislebert of Mons, *Chronique*, ed. L. Vanderkindere (Brussels, 1904), p. 101. See also *Ibid.*, pp. 97, 109, 117 for further examples of foot soldiers participating in tournaments.

[23] *HGM*, ll. 2829-30, 2837-9, 3247-50; Henry Knighton, *Chronicon*, ed. J. R. Lumby (R.S., 1895), i, 265-6; *Flores Historiarum*, ed. H. R. Luard (R.S., 1890), iii, 30-1.

[24] William FitzStephen, 'Descriptio Civitatis Londoniae', translated by H. E. Butler in *Norman London: an essay* by F. M. Stenton (London, 1934), pp. 30-31.

[25] *Foedera*, i, 245-6.

tournaments were training for war, was the king's letter of 1228 which ordered all the *familia regis* to attend a tournament at Northampton.[26] More sympathetic kings financed the English tourneying experiences of two Johns of Brittany in 1285-6 and in 1359 each of whom was accompanied by his household knights, and Edward III himself supplied equipment to eleven of his chamber knights tourneying with him at Lichfield in 1348.[27] As late as 1391, royal household knights were prominent among those receiving licences to perform feats of arms against the Scots in the northern marches. One of the few surviving private household accounts suggests that seigneurial household knights were also active tourneyers, for his household knights accompanied Lord Berkeley to jousts at Hertford, Coventry, Exeter and Bristol in 1328 at his expense.[28]

Household knights were, therefore, an important part of the tourneying circuit, consistently providing knights who were keen tourneyers. This links neatly with their military duties, for household knights were the most professional of medieval soldiers and, in the case of the royal household in particular, formed the core of the king's army on campaign.[29] On a lesser scale, the same is true of seigneurial household knights since they too formed the backbone of magnatial retinues on campaign. Moreover, the greater the chivalric reputation of the magnate, the larger his household was likely to be. The *Boke of Noblesse* says of Henry, duke of Lancaster, for instance, that he was 'a chief auctour and foundour in law of armes' and for this reason large numbers of young knights and boys of noble birth from Spain, Aragon, Portugal, Navarre and France were sent to him 'to be doctrined, lerned, and broughte up in his noble court in scole of armes and for to see noblesse, curtesie and

[26] *CPR 1225-32*, p. 202; *CPR 1232-47*, p. 17; *CCR 1227-31*, p. 106; *CCR 1231-34*, pp. 131-2; *Ibid.*, p. 113.

[27] *Records of the Wardrobe and Household 1285-6*, ed. B. F. & C. R. Byerly (London, 1977), pp. 5-7, 20, 22, 26, 34, 47; *Issues of the Exchequer Henry III-Henry VI*, ed. F. Devon (London, 1837), pp. 170, 172; N. H. Nicolas, 'Observations on the Foundation of the Most Noble Order of the Garter', *Archaeologia*, xxxi (1846), p. 26.

[28] *Rot.Scot.*, ii, 111; Berkeley Castle Muniments, Select Roll no. 60, printed in I. H. Jeayes, *Descriptive Catalogue of the Charters and Muniments ... at Berkeley Castle* (Bristol, 1892), pp. 283-5.

[29] See: J. O. Prestwich, 'The Military Household of the Norman Kings', *Eng. Hist.Rev.*, cclxxviii (1981), pp. 1-35; M. Prestwich, *War, Politics and Finance under Edward I* (London, 1972), pp. 41-66; M. Prestwich, *The Three Edwards* (London, 1980), pp. 62-3; R. Nicholson, *Edward III and the Scots 1327-35* (Oxford, 1965), pp. 175-6, 198-9, Appx. 2.

worship.'[30] These apprentices in arms could expect to learn all the *mestiers d'armes* for, like all the great soldiers of his day including du Guesclin, Boucicaut and Thomas, earl of Warwick, Lancaster enjoyed an equally high reputation in war and hastiludes.

In the fourteenth century the same connection between service in war and tournament can be seen in the magnatial retinue which was an extension of the knightly household. Although retaining contracts must have been in use in the thirteenth century, they only begin to survive in any number from the first thirty years of the fourteenth century. Much the same sort of service, though better defined, was obtained by means of the retaining contract as was expected from the old household services. Its conditions might embrace many aspects of life, requiring service in peacetime but also, which is more important for this study, in war and tournament, the latter very often, but by no means always expressly mentioned. The lord would, for this reason, be leading the same men to both hastiludes and campaigns, which again enforces the conclusion that participation in the one prepared the knight for his ultimate function of fighting in the other.

The military aspect of hastiludes is emphasized by the fact that it seems probable that for the *mêlée* tournament at least, the magnate took his usual war retinue. This is suggested by, for instance, the retaining contracts issued by Humphrey de Bohun, earl of Hereford (d.1322), which follow a fairly standard pattern. In 1307 he retained Sir Bartholomew de Enefield for life in peace and war, at home and abroad and in the Holy Land. In peace he was to receive hay and oats for four horses, wages for three *garçons* and his chamberlain dining in hall but 'en temps de guerre et por le turnoi' this was increased to eight horses and seven *garçons*, his chamberlain dining in hall and sufficient horses for himself in war and tournament provided by the earl. In return he was to receive land worth forty marks *per annum* in Annandale, which could be reseized by the earl if he failed to perform the services due.[31] Two years later, the earl retained Sir Thomas de Maundeville in exactly the same terms, with exactly the same number of horses and *garçons*, though Maundeville was only to receive twenty marks because his contract was for a fixed period.[32] The same terms appear again in 1318 in the earl's contract with Sir Peter d'Ouvedale, though if Dugdale's transcript is

---

[30] *Boke of Noblesse*, p.77.
[31] PRO DL25/92 calendared in *Calendar of Documents Relating to Scotland*, ed. J. Bain (Edinburgh, 1881), ii, 505 no. 1899.
[32] PRO DL25/1981.

correct, he was to bring four horses and four *garçons* for peace and eight horses and eight *garçons* for war and tournament, and was to provide his own horse which would only be replaced at the earl's expense if lost in war.[33]

The terms of Bohun's retaining contracts are paralleled in all other extant contracts of this period which mention tournament service.[34] Their survival is of great importance for the military aspect of the tournament since they make it clear that the retaining lords made no distinction between the men they required for war and those they required for tournament. Additional men could be secured to swell the tournament retinue in temporary contracts such as that by which Sir Robert FitzPayn was paid £100 to serve Aymer de Valence in tournaments for one year.[35] Perhaps this was unusual, though there is a parallel here in the use of temporary indentures to swell retinues for war. Normally, however, it seems to have been an accepted part of the retainer's duties in this early fourteenth century period that he would accompany his lord to the tournament. Probably the reason for the comparative rarity of tourneying clauses in extant contracts is simply that few lords felt it necessary to make this commitment explicit.

From a political point of view it is highly significant that those indentures which do include a tourneying clause all date from the early period of retaining contracts. Here we should bear in mind not just the fact that tourneying service was regarded as so important a duty as to merit explicit inclusion in the contract, but also the fact that at this very same period, (the reign of Edward II), tournaments were at the height of their political importance as focal points for discontent.[36] The insistence on tournament service in indentures of his reign therefore assumes a greater and more sinister importance. The lords appear to have been anxious that their retainers would follow them to tournament as well as parliament; this was partly a matter of prestige, for the larger a lord's entourage, the greater his influence was seen to be. It also justified his calling out his normal war retinue for hastiludes, enabling them to practise together as a military unit and, if need be, to exchange the sport for real military

---

[33] Bodleian MS Dugdale 18 fo. 39v, noticed by Denholm-Young, 'Tournament in the Thirteenth Century', p. 240 n. 2.

[34] The terms and implications of this type of contract will be discussed more fully *infra* pp. xxx-xx.

[35] PRO E101/27/11 printed in J. R. S. Phillips, *Aymer de Valence: Earl of Pembroke 1307-24* (Oxford, 1972), p. 306.

[36] See *infra*: Chapter Three for a detailed discussion of the political importance of tournaments.

activity. The complete absence of tourneying clauses in retaining contracts after 1332 reflects the decline of the great *mêlée* tournament, for fewer active knights were required in the jouster's entourage.

The presence of retainers and their forbears, the household knights, at tournaments meant that experienced soldiers were always to be found in the lists, practising (and showing off) their military skills as individuals and as part of a team. For this reason, tournaments were always a fruitful recruiting ground and some men came to hastiludes specifically to enlist tourneyers into their own cause. Gislebert tells us how in 1183 Baldwin of Hainault went unarmed to a tournament between Braine and Soissons purely to recruit knights for his army in view of a war that was threatening him.[37] William Marshal's performances in the lists led the Count of Flanders, the Duke of Burgundy and Jacques d'Avesnes to offer him rents and lordships in an effort to lure him into their households when he was temporarily estranged from the Young King.[38] Similarly, the great chivalric reputation of Edward III inspired several attempts to recruit knights at his tournaments. Gascon ambassadors attended the Windsor Round Table of 1344 to seek help against the French and the Duke of Brabant came to the Windsor jousts four years later to recruit men in his quarrel with the Count of Flanders.[39] In 1362 Spanish, Cypriot and Armenian knights were present at Smithfield in the hope of persuading some of the jousters there to take the Cross and lend their aid to repulse the pagans who had invaded their lands.[40]

Even mercenaries could be found at hastiludes, a factor which further emphasises the feasibility of enlisting tourneyers for real warfare. The men who fought on the English side at the Combat of the Thirty at Ploërmel in Brittany in 1351 were all mercenaries of different nationalities and in 1365 the Pope intervened to prevent a tournament which the Free Companies had proposed to hold against the combined chivalry of Burgundy and Savoy.[41] Professional soldiers as well as well-born knights were to be found at

---

[37] Gislebert of Mons, p. 144.

[38] *HGM*, ll. 6157-70.

[39] Jean le Bel, *Chronique*, ed. J. Viard & E. Déprez (Paris, 1904), ii, 35; Thomas Grey of Heton, *Scalacronica*, ed. J. Stevenson (Edinburgh, 1836), pp. 176-7.

[40] John of Reading, *Chronica*, ed. J. Tait (Manchester, 1914), pp. 152-3.

[41] H. R. Brush, 'La Bataille de Trente Anglois et de Trente Bretons', *Modern Philology*, ix (1912), pp. 523-8; M. H. Keen, 'Chivalry, Nobility and the Man at Arms' in *War, Literature and Politics in the Late Middle Ages*, ed. C. T. Allmand (Liverpool, 1976), p. 40.

hastiludes throughout the middle ages, therefore, and it was logical to seek military aid there.

As the same men were to be found fighting in both hastiludes and warfare from the twelfth to the fifteenth century it is not surprising to find that distinctions between the two were sometimes blurred. Just as the sport sometimes generated real battle so hastiludes were frequently sparked off by military activity. The presence of two hostile armies in close proximity was an ideal opportunity for those knights who were proud of their chivalric reputation and always seeking to better themselves to enjoy a trial of strength. A successful encounter increased morale without materially altering the fortunes of the day, as, for instance, in 1336 and again in 1340 when there was 'jousting of war' between the knights of English and Scottish armies who were in the same vicinity.[42] It was precisely to avoid such combats which could spark off a full scale battle when neither party was fully prepared that the French marshals, having drawn up their lines for the battle of Auray in 1364, gave strict instructions that there should be no jousting or assaults whatsoever.[43] The same impulse to prove their courage and cover themselves with glory led many of the English knights fighting in the Hundred Years War to perform feats of arms which were similarly on the borderline between hastiludes and warfare. In 1360, when Edward III fired the suburbs of Paris, thirty new-made English knights rode up to the gates of the city 'petentes ... opera militaria secundum legem armorum'. They were met by sixty Frenchmen armed with spears whom they quickly put to flight before returning in triumph to their own army.[44] This type of challenge occurs with great frequency in the pages of Froissart, and there seems to have been a general acceptance on both sides in the war that knights would naturally desire to fulfill vows and seek adventures. When an English knight performed his vow to strike the barriers of Paris, for instance, instead of allowing the guard to fire their arrows on him, the French knights shouted to him 'Alés, alés, vous vos estes bien acquittés.'[45]

Chance encounters of skirmishing parties could also lead to jousting challenges in which individuals fought uninterrupted while their companions looked on. Just such a joust was the one between

---

[42] John Barbour, *The Bruce*, ed. W. W. Skeat (EETS, 1870), iii, 483, 493.
[43] Froissart, vii, 36-7.
[44] Henry Knighton, ii, 111.
[45] Froissart, viii, 34-5: see also Cuvelier, *Chronique de Bertrand du Guesclin*, ed. E. Charrière (Paris, 1839), ll. 17, 567-636.

Sir Thomas Colville and a French knight in 1343. The Frenchman had shouted insults against Edward III from the supposed safety of the far side of the river but Colville was so incensed that he forced his horse to swim across, ran three courses *à outrance* against the French knight, killed him and returned to his own party, all without any hindrance from the dead man's compatriots. The fame that Colville won from this encounter was neither transitory nor local, for some years later when he offered to be the Prior of Tynemouth's champion in a judicial duel the opposition withdrew because of Colville's military reputation.[46]

When a knight was killed in this type of encounter it was a matter of regret to both parties, for the appreciation of chivalric excellence transcended purely national hostilities. Thus, for example, when Sir John Coupland killed the French knight, Sir Lancelot Lorris in a joust *à outrance* fought nominally in the name of their ladies, the sorrow of the English observers was expressed by Froissart: 'It was a great pity, for he was an expert knight, young, handsome and much in love.'[47] Similarly, though the Constable of France refused to allow an English esquire, Sir Nicholas Clifford, to proceed on his journey from Vannes to Cherbourg (despite his safe conduct) until he had fought a joust of war against a French esquire, when Clifford killed his opponent and was exceedingly annoyed at having by an unlucky chance slain a valiant and good man at arms the Constable not only took no reprisals but insisted that the accident was just bad luck and that the Englishman should dine with him before departing.[48] Acceptance of a jousting challenge, even in times of open war, could therefore be a form of safe conduct in itself, and one less likely to be breached than the conventional passes issued by captains and commanders.

More elaborate tourneying matches were often arranged on a larger scale during a temporary lull in hostilities or on campaigns when there was little military action. Richard I's army whiled away its stay at Tours during negotiations for peace in the war against France by holding tournaments in defiance of papal prohibition as early as 1197, and in a similar way, Edward III's campaign in the Low Countries nearly a hundred and fifty years later was dismissed contemptuously by Sir Thomas Grey of Heton, for the king did

<hr />

[46] Thomas Walsingham, *Gesta Abbatum Monasterii Sancti Albani*, ed. H. T. Riley (R.S., 1867), ii, 376-7; for a slightly different version of this story see *The Anonimalle Chronicle 1333-81*, ed. V. H. Galbraith (Manchester 1927), p. 18.
[47] Froissart, ix, 135.
[48] *Ibid.*, x, 335-40.

nothing but joust and lead a pleasant life at Antwerp.[49] On both occasions the knights were holding hastiludes among themselves: no outsiders were involved and the sport (at least in the Low Countries) was à plaisance.

Where the participants were the warring parties the hastiludes became much more serious – even if the mood remained fairly light hearted as befitted a sport. This is particularly true of the English and French knights who turned Buckingham's expedition to Brittany in 1380 (and John of Gaunt's expedition to Spain later in the decade) into a series of jousting encounters. On the latter occasion this state of affairs was especially offensive to the Portuguese and Spanish knights, in whose name the war was being waged, for they were excluded from the jousts and from the subsequent banqueting. At one point the jousting had to be stopped abruptly when fighting broke out among the spectators who proved incapable of suspending hostilities to watch chivalric pastimes.[50]

Sieges were very fruitful for inducing hastiludes of this kind since they were often long and boring. The knightly garrison had little to do except guard the walls and make the occasional sortie, and the besiegers were similarly inactive since the mining operations and bombardments were carried out by the foot soldiers of the army. The issuing of jousting challenges broke the monotony, raised spirits and did not alter the physical state of the siege. The Empress' knights garrisoning the city of Winchester against Stephen's queen in 1141 made daily sorties in order to joust against the besiegers; so did the French knights during the year long siege of Calais by the English over two hundred years later.[51] The incentive to tourney had therefore changed very little over the years, despite revolutionary changes in the way sieges were conducted.

The Anglo-Scottish wars also stimulated tourneying, again because sieges were a feature of the border struggle. Alexander Ramsay jousted against an English esquire during the siege of Cupar in Fife although it was the last remaining English outpost in Scotland, and in 1339 David Berkeley and John de Bruce jousted three courses of war during the siege of Perth. A year later, in 1340, when the Scots

---

[49] *Chronica Monasterii de Melsa*, ed. E. A. Bond (R.S., 1868), i, 279; *Scalacronica*, p. 168 is borne out by the royal accounts for the period which reveal a considerable expenditure on jousting equipment: see PRO E101/388/11.
[50] Froissart, ix, 275-7, 323-30; xii, 116-123; P. E. Russell, *English Intervention in Spain and Portugal in the time of Edward III and Richard II* (Oxford, 1955), pp. 467-8, 483.
[51] *HGM*, ll. 175-8; Henry Knighton, ii, 50.

were besieging Percy in Alnwick castle 'grantz ioustes de guere par covenaunt taille' were held.[52]

Further afield, the siege of Rennes in 1357 was the setting for three courses of war between Bertrand du Guesclin, then only a young knight bachelor, and Sir Nicholas Dagworth, which was watched with great pleasure by the opposing armies and all the assembled citizenry. The sieges of Benevento and Salamanca by John of Gaunt's army again produced jousts between the English and French partisans of the Portuguese and Castilians.[53]

Having seen how warfare, whether as campaign or siege, stimulated the holding of hastiludes of varying degrees of formality, it is no surprise to find that tournaments flourished in the border areas of England with France and Scotland, where, even in periods of truce or peace, war was liable to flare up at any time. It became customary for any knight seeking to prove his prowess in particularly hazardous feats of arms to go to the marches of Scotland or Calais where he was rarely disappointed of an equally bellicose opponent. Border areas had always been fertile ground for hastiludes and, as Duby has pointed out, even in the twelfth century when most tourneyers came from the great principalities of northern France, tournaments were held not in the centres of those lands but on their fringes.[54] This was due partly to the fact that these were the least populous and least cultivated areas therefore being more suitable for *mêlées* and partly to the fact that they provided a natural meeting place and natural divisions into teams for men from different provinces.

The efflorescence of border encounters on English territory occurs very late in our period. Although there are some earlier examples, most date from the fourteenth century and especially the last two decades of the century – the very period when hastiludes *à plaisance* were dominated by elaborate pageantry and complex regulations which distanced them from war. It would seem that the more adventurous knights and esquires of this period sought their excitement and the improvement of their chivalric reputation in feats of arms fought *à outrance* against the traditional enemies of

---

[52] Andrew of Wyntoun, *Original Chronicle*, ed. F. J. Amours (Scottish Text Society, 1914), vi, 93, 129; *Scalacronica*, p. 155.
[53] Froissart, vi, 22, 23-4; Russell, *English Intervention in Spain and Portugal*, pp. 466-8, 483; *John of Gaunt's Register 1379-83*, ed. E. C. Hodge & R. Somerville (Camden Soc., 3rd Series, lvii, 1937), p. 406 no. 1233.
[54] Duby, *Dimanche de Bouvines*, pp. 114-5.

England, usually in the borders where neither could claim the advantage of site and they could meet on fairly equal terms. Obviously, the features of this type of hastilude which caused it to be frowned upon by the authorities when held internally, such as the higher risks of fatality and the subsequent risks of feud or even riot, were of less consequence when the opponent was from a hostile nation. An added attraction was the fact that victory over an enemy in such circumstances was doubly precious and more honourable than victory over a fellow countryman. In the reigns of Henry III and Edward II the stimulus to tourney had been provided internally by the political dissensions between the court and baronial parties. Under Edward III, who redirected the nation's energies externally towards wars in France and Scotland, the stimulus came from a different quarter.

To turn first of all to Scotland, it is in the middle of the fourteenth century that there is a dramatic rise in the number of tournaments fought in the Scottish marches; this coincides exactly with the decade in which border warfare flared up due to the return of David II from exile in France until his capture at Neville's Cross in 1347. The jousts of war between Henry Percy and the Earls of Murray and Douglas during the siege of Alnwick in 1340 have already been noted, but it was Percy's fellow organizer of the northern defences against the Scots, Henry, earl of Derby, who was the instigator of two other important feats of arms. In 1341 he and three other knights jousted 'sub foro guerrae' against Douglas and three Scottish knights at Roxburgh and later in the year, when a truce had been declared he and eleven of his household knights, (nineteen according to Wyntoun), tournied against an equal number of chosen Scots. Two of the Scots and John Twyford, a long standing retainer of the Earl, were killed.[55] The latter engagement had arisen after three courses of war jousted by Derby against Douglas were interrupted and terminated incomplete, because Douglas was wounded in the hand by a sliver from his shattered lance. The Scots suggested that the Berwick encounter should be fought with plain shields which the Earl rejected, because it would be counter-productive to prowess if the combatants fought incognito; they also suggested that it should be fought without armour or with bare visages, both of which the Earl rejected out of hand, and it was agreed at his suggestion to fight in war armour and with war weapons. The heralds who supervised the Berwick jousts proposed that each side should choose the prizewinner from the

---

55 Knighton, ii, 23; Andrew of Wyntoun, vi, 104-5.

opposition, and it was a singular example of their courtesy that the Scots chose the knight who had run his lance through William Ramsey's head, and the English chose the Scot who had killed Twyford and would also have killed Richard Talbot if he had not been wearing additional plates contrary to the agreed terms.[56]

The following year, during Edward III's campaign in Scotland, there was a tournament at Melrose held with the king's licence and again there were fatalities on both sides.[57] The last tournament in this series was held in 1348 and was a direct result of the political situation. Edward III had refused to ransom David II thereby provoking the Scots to ravage the northern provinces of England. In revenge, the northerners proclaimed a hastilude at Berwick, but laid in wait to ambush and massacre the Scots coming there, in defiance of tournament conventions but in the tradition of northern self-help against their troublesome neighbours.[58]

This was followed by a quiet period, probably reflecting English preoccupations in France, until there was a sudden resurgence of tourneying activity on the borders in the 1380s. This coincided almost exactly with a combined Franco-Scottish campaign in Northumberland. In 1386-7, for example, Sir Thomas Clifford was given a royal licence

que il puisse faire toutz man[er]s pointz darmes q[ue] luy plerra sibien a pee come a chival en q[u]e conq[ue] lieu en la Marche dEscoce p[ar]entre cy et le fest de Paske prochein a venir.[59]

Similar licences were also issued to many other knights including Richard Tempest and his esquire in 1387, Ralph Neville and six royal household knights in 1391 and John, earl of Huntingdon in 1392. All were to fight in or near Berwick, though safe conducts were also sent to the Scottish knight, Sir William Haliborton and his three companions, coming to Carlisle 'ibidem de guerra hastiludiando' against Richard Redmane and three English knights in 1393.[60] The feat of arms performed in 1390 by lord John de Welles and his challenger, Sir David Lindsay, received a lot of chronicle attention because of its unusual setting on London Bridge, and because Welles

---

[56] Andrew of Wyntoun, vi, 103-115.
[57] Adam Murimuth, *Continuatio Chronicarum*, ed. E. M. Thompson (R.S., 1889), pp. 123, 223-4.
[58] Henry Knighton, ii, 57.
[59] *Rot.Scot.*, ii, 87.
[60] *Ibid.*, ii, 90, 111, 117, 119; *Foedera*, vii, 555, 703, 735, 745.

was defeated at each stage of the combat.[61] Some other feats of arms between noble Scottish and English knights were also performed in London in the king's presence, rather than in the marches in the presence of his lieutenant. Thomas Mowbray, for instance, in his capacity as Earl Marshal of England, fought jousts à outrance in London against the Earl of Murray in 1390 and later in the same year against the Earl of Mar. On the second occasion he was supported by two other knights, including Sir Piers Courtenay who, as Standard Bearer of England, believed himself under an obligation to defend his country's honour in the lists.[62]

One of the advantages of fighting the challenge in London was that the king himself presided, adding lustre to the occasion but also rewarding the combatants with gifts of cash and plate so that even the Scots did not return empty handed in victory or defeat.[63]

If the proximity of a hostile nation to the north of England was an incentive to tourney, the same was true of the south, especially after the capture of Calais in 1347 and the placing of a permanent English garrison in the town. The Calais marches and, to a lesser extent, the borders of English Gascony, played the same role as the Scottish marches and produced a large crop of hastiludes à outrance. Although English knights had frequently gone to France to tourney from at least the reign of Henry I, they had not gone with the express intention of fighting against the French as a body or as individual enemies, even though the division into tourneying teams according to march of origin did tend to pit the English or Angevins or Normans against the French.[64] It is not until the outbreak of the Hundred Years War that English and French knights deliberately sought each other out with the express purpose of tourneying à outrance, and interestingly, this occurs almost exactly contemporaneously with similar developments in the Scottish marches. In the south west of France there were three outstanding encounters: a combat fought between twenty Gascons and twenty Frenchmen in the borders of France and Gascony in 1353 when many of the combatants were killed; the jousts à outrance fought before Chalucet castle by the young Boucicaut, as the Duke of Bourbon's lieutenant, against the Anglo-Gascon knight, Sicart de la Barde; and perhaps

61 Andrew of Wyntoun, vi, 359-62; Ranulph Higden, *Polychronicon*, ed. J. R. Lumby (R.S., 1886), ix, 235.
62 *Rot.Scot.*, ii, 103; *The Brut*, ed. F. W. D. Brie (EETS, 1908), ii, 348.
63 Bain, *Cal. of MSS. Relating to Scotland*, iv, no. 411.
64 *HGM*, ll. 2579-80, 2780-87, 3211-2.

most significant, as being indicative of the shifts in political allegiances in Gascony, the feat of arms performed before the English senechal of Bordeaux by two Gascons, one attached to the French, the other to the English interest, in 1387.[65]

The Calais marches, however, were the most popular venue for this type of combat. In 1380 Boucicaut fought Sir Piers Courtenay and later Sir Thomas Clifford there: the latter combat, which was arranged by Northampton herald, was fought with lances, swords, daggers and axes before Sir William Beauchamp, Captain of Calais and uncle of Clifford.[66] Courtenay was also one of a team of English knights who travelled to Calais to fulfil a jousting challenge delivered by four French knights in the Merciless Parliament of 1388. The following year, when the French king stopped his joust against Guy de la Tremouille after only one course and prohibited the challenge from going on, he fought a secret joust *à outrance* against the Lord de Clary in the Calais marches.[67] The next year, 1390, he was reunited with his old foe, Boucicaut, at the St Ingelvert jousts. Unlike the Clary match, the St Ingelvert jousts had the knowledge and full support of the French king, who was even reputed to have attended in disguise as a spectator.

Originally, there had been doubts about the wisdom of holding such a *feste* at St Ingelvert which lay half way between Boulogne and Calais and therefore in the heart-land of the traditional area for hostile encounters against the English. It was argued that

> les Anglois pourroient tenir ceste chose a atine d'orgueil et de presomption, laquelle chose on devoit bien considerer, car trieves estoient donnees et jurees a tenir le terme de trois ans entre France et Angleterre.[68]

That the English did indeed presume that the challenge was aimed specifically at them, even if they took it in better part than the French had feared, can be deduced from the fact that they formed the vast majority of the visitors. Though the foreign combatants were given the choice of fighting *à plaisance* or *à outrance* it was significant that all the English chose to fight *à outrance*, reflecting

---

[65] Henry Knighton, ii, 76-7; *Livre des Faits du Bon Messire Jean le Maingre, dit Boucicaut* (Collection Universelle des Mémoires Particuliers Relatifs à l'Histoire de France, vi, 1785), pp. 43-5; Froissart, xii, 51-3.
[66] *Livre des Faits du ... Boucicaut*, ii, 47-8, 48-9; *Foedera*, vii, 526.
[67] Henry Knighton, ii, 260; *Foedera*, vii, 580; *Chronique du Religieux de St Denys*, ed. M. Bellaguet (Paris, 1839), i, 392-8; Froissart, xiv, 41-50.
[68] Froissart, xiv, 57.

not only their desire to perform the more honourable feat of arms but also their acceptance of the principle that national enmities were at the basis of the whole event. Indeed, it was the nationalistic feelings engendered by the occasion which caused it to receive so much chronicle attention.[69]

Though St Ingelvert was far and away the largest and most splendid of all the border tournaments, the Calais marches continued to be fertile ground for feats of arms *à outrance*. Jousting challenges passing between English and French knights at the turn of the century and beyond continued to name this area as a suitable compromise for those not wishing to commit themselves to appearing before royal or seigneurial judges in France or England.[70] The national rivalries which prompted such hastiludes and fear of the consequences, including the risk of some important figure being killed and the problem of attitudes hardening, combined to make Richard II issue proclamations in 1396 prohibiting any of his subjects seeking out any subject of France under any pretext whatsoever to perform feats of arms, on pain of forfeiture of all that could be forfeited.[71] The occasion which prompted this withdrawal of royal approval of border feats of arms was Richard's marriage to Isabella of France and his main concern was that the newly made peace between the two countries should not be jeopardized by the foolhardy or reckless courage of a few chivalric entrepeneurs. It is therefore significant that within a few years of this prohibition, when relations between the two countries had once again deteriorated, the challenges to perform hostile and dangerous feats of arms *à outrance* were once more flowing freely across the Channel.

In view of the fact that the English borders with Scotland and France proved to be such fertile ground for those seeking adventures or fighting prearranged challenges in the fourteenth century, it is interesting to contrast this with the total absence of hastiludes of this nature on the other English borderlands with Wales and Ireland. This was not due to an absence of military presence or even of war itself, for warfare in both regions was endemic until the end of the thirteenth century and in Ireland for much longer. The reason seems to be twofold. Firstly, it was not until the fourteenth century that the divergence between hastiludes *à outrance* and *à plaisance* became so great that the former were in effect limited to encounters

---

[69] Froissart, xiv, 55-8, 105-151; *Livre des Faits du ... Boucicaut*, pp. 61-70; Froissart, xiv, 406-20; *Chronique ... de St Denys*, i, 672-82.
[70] BL MS Additional 21357 fo. 2r; BL MS Additional 21370 fos 5r, 11r, 13r.
[71] *Foedera*, vii, 832.

against foreigners, so that there was no real incentive to seek combats in these marches. Secondly, and more importantly, the methods of fighting in Wales and Ireland differed considerably from those in England. Scotland and France shared the same social and military organization as England, so that in each country the man-at-arms was not only a man of rank and high social standing but also a soldier trained in the technique of fighting on horseback with a lance. In Scotland and France, as in England, tourneying and jousting were popular sports which received royal and seigneurial patronage: indeed, Scottish knights were tourneying abroad like their English counterparts.[72] In Wales and Ireland none of these things were true. Even the prince and chieftains, though they rode to battle, almost invariably dismounted to fight and although lances were the main weapons in north Wales, they were not the arms of horsemen but of foot soldiers. There was, therefore, little or no common military background between England and her neighbours, Wales and Ireland, which could have stimulated border tourneying, and it is significant that the only hastiludes in these areas were fought under the aegis of, and by, the Anglo-Norman garrisons and settlers. The conquest of Wales in 1284, which was a victory of chivalry over foot, was marked by a celebration of the skills of knighthood. A Round Table, with its peculiarly Arthurian and Welsh inspirations, was held at Nefyn in 1284, followed by a tournament at Caernarvon to celebrate the birth of Edward, the first English prince of Wales.[73] Both these occasions were presided over by Edward I and although foreign knights attended, no Welshmen are known to have participated. Similarly, the Mortimers' passion for tourneying and their particular devotion to Round Tables, which was probably linked to their political ambitions in Wales, did not mean that they tourneyed against the Welsh. It was the English knights, especially those from the borders, who attended the Mortimer hastiludes, even when they were held in Wales. The great tourneying entourages of the marcher lords were not matched by equivalent entourages of the Welsh princes: in default of other opposition they had to fight among themselves.

The same is true of Ireland, where the Anglo-Normans found themselves fighting a guerilla war similar to that in Wales primarily against foot soldiers armed with battle axes. Again the only tournaments recorded in Ireland occur among the Anglo-Normans

---

[72] A. Behault de Doron, 'La Noblesse Hennuyère au Tournoi de Compiègne de 1238', *Annales du Cercle Archéologique de Mons*, xxii (1890), pp. 89-90 nos 69-72.
[73] *Ann.Mon.*, ii, 402; iv, 491; iii, 313; iv, 489.

settled there, like the Geraldines, who occasionally tourneyed among themselves during the latter years of the twelfth century.[74] The mandate sent to the archbishop and justiciar of Ireland in 1223, ordering the prohibition of all tournaments and the seizure into the king's hands of the lands of those who dared to break the prohibition,[75] could only have been operative against the Anglo-Irish barons and their households, and even that authority was difficult to enforce. Even in the fourteenth century, the only known tourneyers from Ireland belonged to the great Anglo-Irish baronial families, such as James, son and heir of Edward Botiller.[76]

For border tournaments to flourish it was necessary for a common social and military background to exist, so it is not surprising that knights considered tourneying to be one of the bonds of knighthood shared throughout Europe, which transcended national hostilities even if it was stimulated by them. The fourteenth century efflorescence of feats of arms *à outrance* fought on campaign and in the border regions, reflects in many ways both the dissatisfaction with hastiludes *à plaisance* as the only channel for knightly prowess off the battlefield, and the hardening of attitudes linked with the increasing identificatiom of knights with their nationalistic causes, as the Hundred Years War dragged on. As the tournament *à plaisance* became further removed from warfare by a plethora of rules, the tournament *à outrance* became more closely imitative of warfare, in particular by introducing the feat of arms in four stages, which involved fighting on foot as well as on horseback and with sword, dagger and axe as well as lance. War thus provided a stimulus to tourney, while tourneying trained and equipped the knight to fight in war.

This same inter-action between war and tournament is evident in many other ways. In some instances warfare was directly imitative of the tournament and the distinction between sport and genuine military combat became so fine that it was not discernable. This is particularly true of the jousts which, in a manner comparable to the *commençailles* of the tournament, often preceded battle. An early example of this occurred at the battle of Hastings in 1066 when a Norman *mimus* or *histrio* rode out from the ranks of the army brandishing his weapon. An Anglo-Saxon came out to meet him whereupon the Norman speared him through and returned to the

---

[74] Giraldus Cambrensis, pp. 243, 274.
[75] *Rotuli Litterarum Clausarum*, ed. T. D. Hardy (London, 1833), i, 536.
[76] BL MS Stowe 553 fo. 128r.

ranks, having won first blood for the invaders.[77] At the battle of Lincoln in 1141 the royal forces tried to initiate jousting as a 'proludium pugne' but were met at close quarters by the charging knights of the Earl of Gloucester who disdained to observe the niceties and quickly put the royalists to flight.[78] At Bannockburn in 1314 Sir Henry Bohun spurred ahead of his company in an effort to strike down Robert the Bruce with his lance: he missed, and the Bruce split his head open with a battleaxe

> This wes the first strak of the ficht,
> That wes performyst douchtely.[79]

Similarly, at Halidon Hill some nineteen years later, Sir Robert Benhale took up the challenge of a Scottish 'Goliath' to fight a single combat before the assembled troops began battle. Like a second David he overcame his gigantic opponent, even though he attacked on foot armed with only sword and shield.[80] It is notable that both Henry Bohun and Robert Benhale were tourneyers. Bohun had been arrested and his lands had been seized into the king's hands because he had left the king's army in Scotland to tourney in England without licence in 1306: Benhale fought at the Dunstable tournament of 1334, where his arms were among those recorded on the tournament roll.[81]

Knights frequently seem to have carried tournament ideology over into warfare. An early example of this occurred at the battle of Bouvines in 1214 when the French knight, Sir Baldwin Buridan, cheered on his fellows by urging them not, as one might have expected, to think of their reputation or their cause but rather of their lady loves and the tournament.[82] Edward I conducted a showpiece siege of Stirling in 1304 in much the same way as a tournament. He even set up a viewing gallery so that the ladies of the court could watch the trials of a new siege engine called the 'Warwolf'. His grandson, Edward III, was especially susceptible to tournament ideology. In 1347 he and the Black Prince fought as simple knights under the banner of Sir Walter Mauny at Calais just

---

[77] Guy of Amiens, *Carmen de Hastingae Proelio*, ed. C. Morton & H. Muntz (Oxford, 1972), ll. 389-408.

[78] William of Malmesbury, *Hist.Nov.*, pp. 48-9.

[79] J. Barbour, *The Bruce*, ii, 284-5.

[80] Geoffrey le Baker, *Chronicon*, ed. E. M. Thompson (Oxford, 1889), p. 51.

[81] *Cal.Fine Rolls*, i, 553-4; *CCR 1302-7*, pp. 481-2; *CTG*, iv, 393 no. 85.

[82] J. Verbruggen, *The Art of Warfare in Western Europe during the Middle Ages*, trans. S. Willard & S. C. M. Southern (Amsterdam, 1977), p. 232.

as they sometimes did in hastiludes: afterwards, while the Black Prince courteously served his captured French knights himself, his father took off his pearl chaplet and presented it to Sir Eustace de Ribemont saying,

> Messire Ustasse, je vous donne ce chapelet pour le mieulz combatant de toute la journee de chiaus de dedens et de hors, et vous pri que vous le portes ceste anee pour l'amour de mi. Je scai bien que vous estes gais et amoureus, et que voluntiers vous vos trouves entre dames et damoiselles. Si dittes partout la ou vous venes que je le vous ay donnet et parmi tant, vous estes mon prisonnier: je vous quitte vostre prison; et vous poes partir de matin se il vous plest.[83]

Not only the whole idea of giving a prize for distinguished valour but also the terminology was redolent of tournament prizegivings.

It would be wrong to create the impression that hastiludes and warfare were confused in the minds of the knights who fought in both. Though many of the ideas were interchangeable and the same vocabulary was often used to describe both, the sport was quite distinct from real warfare. Indeed, in the fourteenth century it became a chivalric convention to see hastiludes as part of a graduated scale of feats of arms. At the lowest level was the joust. One step higher, because it was more dangerous, was the tourney. At the highest level of all was war. As Geoffroi de Charny, bearer of the Oriflamme, put it, the jouster should be praised for undertaking a feat of arms but more praise was due to the tourneyer and the highest praise of all should be reserved for the warrior:

> Et toutesfois me semble-t-il que en ce fait d'armes de guerres peut-l'en faire en un jour tous les trois mestiers d'armes, comme de jouster, de tournoier et de guerroier; car en guerre convient-il jouster de fer de glaive et ferir d'espee comme a tournoiement, et encontrer d'estoc et d'autres glaives, comme pour la guerre[84]

It was because war was the most important of all *mestiers d'armes* that even chivalrous figures sometimes expressed disapproval of knights jousting and tourneying, particularly when this was at the expense of campaigning. In 1407, for example, Richard Aston,

---

[83] Froissart, xiv, 269-70.
[84] *Ibid.*, i, pt. iii, 466.

captain of Calais, commented on the Senechal of Hainault's jousting challenge to Sir John Cornwall:

> il mest advis que en yceluy temps dessus dit de guerre ouverte peussiez avoir monstre vostre vaillance et plus brief estre pou[r]veu a venir a lonneur du dit fait darmes fust par fortune de guerre ou autrement que entelles manieres user de telles escriptures.[85]

It was reasoning of the same sort that would lead the Jouvencel to refuse two men-at-arms licence to perform a feat of arms, saying that such combats only earned the knight a vainglory which was of little value, did no-one any service, wasted his money and exposed his body to danger in a pointless and needless cause: moreover

> tant qu'il est occupe ad ce faire, il laisse a exploicter la guerre, le service de son Roy et de la chose publique; et nul ne doit exposer son corps, sinon en oeuvres meritoires.[86]

Chivalric opinion, therefore, was quite capable of drawing a strict dividing line between sport and war, particularly when placed in a position of responsibility. Though the more attractive excitement of hastiludes might seduce young knights away from the boring routine of campaign or siege, when it came to actual fighting there was no conflict in duties or in attractions. Even the great *mêlée* tournament was only an imitation of battle.

The connection between hastiludes and warfare was nevertheless an intimate, important and long lasting one. From the twelfth to the fifteenth century, hastiludes provided the opportunity for knights to learn and practice the skills that were required of them in war. As individuals they learnt how to handle their weapons and horses to maximum effect. As members of a team, in all probability the same team of household knights or retainers with whom they fought in war, they learnt how to fight as part of a unit and to obey discipline. The tournament's apologists therefore had some justification in claiming that the sport was a valuable form of military training. This was especially true of hastiludes *à outrance* whose development is closely associated with war. Warfare stimulated tourneying partly because opportunities were rife when knights were gathered in arms on campaign, and partly because the animosities consequent on war

---

[85] BL MS Additional 21370 fo. 7v.
[86] Jean de Bueil, *Le Jouvencel*, ii, 100.

justified alternative forms of combat. Tournament ideology, complementarily, became a powerful factor in the conduct of war among the chivalric classes. At best, as, for instance, in the way ransoms were negotiated and collected, practices evolved through tourneying experiences could exert a civilizing influence on the barbarities of war. At worst, they added gloss and tinsel to the mundane drudgery of campaigning.

CHAPTER THREE

The Tournament and Politics

Because tournaments were so often held in conjunction with military campaigns and because they brought together large numbers of armed men they created a problem of control which was of great importance to royal authority. The dangers arose in three ways. Firstly, hastiludes were dangerous as political gatherings where malcontents could meet to discuss and plan opposition and even sedition: secondly, they could be used as a cover for private feuds and, because of their violence, could sometimes actually generate these: thirdly, if they got out of hand they could cause problems of general disorder which were not confined to the lists. These problems were met in various ways. Some were simply *ad hoc* solutions, such as the generous use of pardons for misdemeanors. Others were more general in their outlook and effect, such as the issuing of royal prohibitions against the sport backed by penalties of varying harshness. More important than prohibitions, because they were more far reaching, were the two tourneying statutes which were unique to England. Richard I's decree of 1194, the first of its kind, established the principle of licensing tournaments which was the foundation for all later attempts to regulate the sport. Edward I's *Statuta Armorum* of 1292 built upon this precedent and attempted to impose restrictions on the conduct of the game which would limit the opportunities for disorder to arise.

In this chapter I shall discuss first of all the problems caused by tourneying which attracted royal attention by posing a threat to its authority. In the second section I shall examine royal reactions to this threat, in particular, the weapons of statutory control and prohibition.

Hastiludes provided an ideal opportunity for knights to meet and discuss political grievances informally. More seriously, they could also serve as a pretext for gathering armed men in readiness for rebellion. The events of Henry III's and Edward II's reigns were foreshadowed as early as 1215 when certain Magna Carta barons planned their rebellion and began assembling armies under the guise of holding tournaments.[1] They continued tourneying among themselves during the civil war which followed: in 1215 Robert FitzWalter postponed a tournament to be held between Staines and Hounslow, on the grounds that if London was left unguarded it might be seized by loyalist forces.[2] In 1228 Gregory IX ordered the papal legate in England to excommunicate all tourneyers and interdict their lands because, he claimed, certain English magnates and barons were meeting together 'sub occasione torniamentorum' to plot and conspire against the young king Henry III.[3] These papal fears were probably justified and were certainly shared by Henry himself, for a large number of royal prohibitions on tournaments preceded Richard Marshal's rebellion, which smouldered for a long time before finally breaking out in 1234.[4] Fears that the tournament might be used for ulterior political purposes similarly inspired other royal prohibitions. In 1260, Henry III prohibited a tournament at Blyth because there were so many quarrels among the magnates that he feared serious consequences if they were allowed to meet in arms. Two years later, a general prohibition on all hastiludes was issued, partly because the king was out of the realm which was therefore vulnerable to sedition, and partly because there were fears of an uprising in the Welsh marches.[5] The ban was given added weight by the issuing of personal prohibitions against tourneying to six marcher lords whose loyalties were suspect.[6]

Edward II also had major problems with tournaments which were used for their own ends by the baronial opposition. There is good evidence[7] to suggest that the eleven grievances presented to the king at the April Parliament of 1309 were discussed and drawn up at the Dunstable tournament held a short while before the official parliament. If this was the case, then Edward II's general prohibition on

[1] Ralph de Coggeshalle, *Chronicon Anglicanum*, ed. J. Stevenson (R.S., 1875), pp. 172-3.
[2] Matt. Paris, ii, 614-5.
[3] *Foedera*, i, 301.
[4] *CPR 1225-32*, pp. 118, 125-6, 142-3, 202, 230, 316, 321, 452, 457, 459, 463, 473, 492, 498, 499; *CPR 1232-47*, pp. 17, 20, 57, 67-8, 70, 84, 86; Denholm-Young, pp. 247-8, 250.
[5] *Flores Historiarum*, ii, 447; *CPR 1258-66*, p. 227; *CCR 1261-4*, p. 133.
[6] *Ibid.*
[7] See J. R. Maddicott, *Thomas of Lancaster 1307-22* (Oxford, 1970), pp. 95-103.

hastiludes combined with the addressing of individual personal prohibitions to the Earls of Hereford, Lancaster, Surrey, Warwick and Arundel,[8] all of which were sent out before the June Parliament of 1309, assumes a greater importance. Edward was presumably trying to prevent a repetition of events earlier in the year and denying the political opposition a chance to hold an unofficial parliament under the guise of a tournament. It was preferable to face an opposition which had not been given the opportunity to concert its views and present a united front.

In 1312, the opposition used tournaments for an even more dangerous end than political manoeuverings. Under the pretence of holding tournaments in different parts of the country, so that suspicions would not be raised by large groups of armed men, the rebel earls gathered an army which they then used to capture and murder Gaveston and ravage the favourite's lands.[9] As in 1309, Edward learnt from his mistakes, although too late, and hearing that tournaments were again planned by the leaders of the baronial opposition in 1313, he repeated the issuing of individual, personally addressed prohibitions to prevent a recurrence of the events of the previous year.[10]

Tournaments were, therefore, a useful weapon against the king in the hands of the disaffected: as gatherings of chivalry, they could be used to sound political opinion and formulate political or even military opposition. Even more dramatically, they could, on occasion, provide opportunities for political assassination, since the presence of armed men would be taken for granted. Plots were apparently uncovered to kill Gaveston at the Stepney tournament to celebrate Edward II's coronation, to kill John of Gaunt at a hastilude in Westminster Hall in 1386 and to kill Henry IV and his sons at hastiludes in Oxford in 1400.[11] A successful assassination was carried out at the Croydon tournament of 1286 when Sir William de Warenne, son and heir of the Earl of Surrey and Sussex, was ambushed and murdered in the lists by his enemies.[12] Presumably nothing was ever proved against his murderers, since there were no reprisals.

Hastiludes provided an ideal opportunity for disposing of a rival

---

[8] *CCR 1307-13*, pp. 158, 159.
[9] *Vita Edwardi Secundi*, ed. N. Denholm-Young (Nelson, 1957), p. 23.
[10] *CPR 1307-13*, pp. 520-1.
[11] *Ann.Paul.*, p. 259; Higden, *Polychronicon*, ix, 55-6; Adam of Usk, *Chronicon*, ed. E. M. Thompson (London, 1904), p. 41; Froissart, xiv, 223-4.
[12] *The Chronicle of Bury St Edmunds*, ed. A. Gransden (Nelson, 1964), p. 87.

because it was so difficult to prove the intention of the killer. When
Roger Leyburn killed Ernald Munteny at the Waltham Round Table
of 1252, an immediate enquiry was held on the spot. Suspicions
were voiced about the 'accident' when the Earl of Gloucester,
himself a noted tourneyer, had the broken shaft pulled out of the
fatal wound: it was found to have the sharp point of a weapon *à
outrance* instead of the blunted end of a lance *à plaisance*. Since the
jousts at the Round Table were supposed to have been conducted *à
plaisance*, and since Leyburn was known to bear a grudge against
Munteny for breaking his leg in a previous encounter, there was
every ground for suspicion. Despite these circumstances, Leyburn
escaped virtually unscathed: in a placatory gesture at the scene of
the accident he voluntarily assumed the Cross, but a month later he
received a royal pardon which acquitted him of any blame in the
matter.[13]

Just as the tournament gave the unscrupulous a chance to revenge
themselves on individuals, it also gave them a chance to wage an
alternative form of private war. In England, royal authority was
powerful enough to abolish the right of a baron to make private war
on his fellows, as the Earls of Gloucester and Hereford found out to
their cost under Edward I; so tourneying was a useful guise under
which to carry on private feuds. In France, tourneying flourished
alongside private war between magnates, but when Philip IV finally
did prohibit all private wars during the king's war in 1296, he also
prohibited all duels, tournaments and jousts at the same time.[14]
Clearly, he regarded them all in the same light. In England too, it
was common practice to issue general prohibitions against hastiludes
during periods of public war: this was intended to prevent knights
being distracted from the serious business of war and to ensure that
the king's peace was preserved in his absence.

In the reigns of Henry III and Edward II private war appears to
have been waged under the nose of the king under the pretext of
military games. The 1240s, for instance, saw a series of tournaments[15] between the rival court and baronial factions which were
distinguished for their violence, their heavy casualties and their
theme of revenge. In 1247, Henry III prohibited the Earl of
Gloucester's tournament against Guy de Lusignan, which was to
have taken place between Dunstable and Luton, for fear of the

---

[13] Matt.Paris, v, 318-9; *CPR 1247-58*, p. 154.
[14] *Ordonnances des Roys de France*, ed. M. de Laurière (Paris, 1723), i, 328-9.
[15] This series is recorded in Matt.Paris, iv, 633 (Dunstable/Luton); v, 17-8
(Newbury); v, 54 (Northampton); v, 83 (Brackley); v, 265 (Rochester).

consequences. The following year, William de Valence, the king's brother and a 'tiro novellus', was deliberately set upon and seriously injured at a tournament at Newbury. This did not dint his ardour, for within a year he defied the king's anger and ordered a tournament at Northampton to go ahead despite a royal prohibition: heavenly intervention, in the form of a snow fall, ensured that his plans were thwarted. In 1249, the warring factions met again at Brackley. William de Valence revenged himself by beating up William de Oddingseles, a knight of the baronial party, and many other bachelors were badly wounded. Finally, as far as the recorded tournaments in this series go, the barons revenged their previous defeat in a large tournament held at Rochester; the vanquished court party found their way to the refuge of the city blocked by a number of English esquires who unceremoniously beat them with clubs and despoiled them. Matthew Paris' comment at the end of his relation of these events sums up the dangers caused by private quarrels pursued under the guise of tournaments: 'crevit igitur ira et odium inter Anglos et alienigenas, et diatim succesive formidabile suscepit incrementum.'[16] It is easy to see how humiliation and defeat in the lists caused an escalation and prolongation of violence and bitterness off the field. Just how seriously these hastiludes were regarded by contemporaries was made explicit at the Brackley tournament of 1249. When Richard, earl of Gloucester, who had always opposed the aliens changed sides and fought with them in the tournament, 'in enormem suae famae lesionem et honoris', it was regarded as a political betrayal.[17] Participation in the tournament could, therefore, be seen as the public declaration of a political allegiance which was much more in keeping with private war than sport.

Later in Henry III's reign, political tensions were again reflected in hastiludes of the period. In 1265, Thomas de Clare, brother of the Earl of Gloucester, planned a tournament at Dunstable against the sons of Simon de Montfort which the king prohibited for fear of the consequences.[18] Another later in the year at Northampton between the main protagonists, Gloucester and de Montfort, did not take place because Gloucester had second thoughts and did not come.[19]

The same sort of political problems appear again in Edward II's reign, and once more we see hastiludes providing a semi-legitimate alternative to private war. Gaveston and his baronial opponents

[16] *Ibid.*, v, 265.
[17] *Ibid.*, v, 265.
[18] *Ann.Lond.*, 65, 67; *Ann.Mon.*, iii, 238.
[19] *Ann.Mon.*, iv, 161-2; ii, 238-9.

clashed several times in the lists: the barons were almost invariably defeated, which further fuelled their hatred of the royal favourite. At the tournament at Wallingford to celebrate his marriage Gaveston had proclaimed that he would hold the field with sixty knights against all comers. On the day, however, he turned up with two hundred knights to ensure that he won the victory. He also won the next tournament at Faversham to celebrate the king's marriage. By this time hatred for him had grown to such a pitch that when a third tournament was proclaimed at Stepney to celebrate the king's coronation, Gaveston feared for his life and persuaded the king to prohibit it.[20]

Hastiludes were, therefore, a convenient cover under which to carry on private feuds. As we have seen, merely by joining one side or another at a hastilude, the tourneyer's action could be construed as a declaration of his political allegiance, so that success or failure in the lists could have a greater significance than a mere sport would otherwise have merited. Indeed, underlying tensions such as these could cause a hastilude to degenerate into a real battle with terrible consequences. In 1237, for example, the political division of the realm was reflected in a tournament at which the knights from northern England took on those from the south: the result was 'non hastiludium sed hostile bellum'.[21] Four years later, the same thing happened at a *fortunium* at Hertford because of the political quarrels among the combatants. Again there was heavy loss of life, including two eminent figures, Gilbert Marshal and Robert de Say.[22]

If quarrels between magnates were sometimes prolonged or exacerbated by the turn of events in the lists, it was not uncommon for hastiludes to actually generate feuds. In 1242 one of the Bisset brothers set fire to the lodgings of Patrick, earl of Atholl, in revenge for his defeat in a tournament at Haddington. The earl and many of his household were burnt to death. Although Bisset offered to prove his innocence in a trial by combat against his accusers, the king forbade it, took the matter into his own hands and banished Bisset from Scotland. The matter did not end there, however, for the feud between the two families was carried over to their adjoining lands in Ireland and was marked by slayings and plunderings.[23] A century later, Sir Walter Mauny travelled to La Réole, which had just fallen

---

[20] *Ann.Paul.*, pp. 258-9; *Vita Edwardi Secundi*, p. 2.
[21] Matt.Paris, ii, 404.
[22] *Ibid.*, iv, 135-6.
[23] Andrew of Wyntoun, v, 99ff; William of Newburgh, pp. 49-50; Bain, *Calendar of MSS Relating to Scotland*, i, xxxvii-xxxviii.

to the English, to see his father's tomb. His father had fought in a tournament at Cambrai where he had accidentally wounded a Gascon knight who later died of his injuries. The family of the Gascon vowed revenge and a bitter feud ensued which was apparently resolved when Mauny's father agreed to undertake a penitential pilgrimage to St James of Compostella. The hollowness of this peace, which had been imposed on the warring parties by the church, became evident when he was ambushed and murdered on his return from pilgrimage by the Gascon's family.[24]

It was presumably with the object of forestalling any private vengeance by the relatives of those killed in hastiludes that royal pardons were issued to the killers. In March 1318, for example, a pardon was issued to William Melksop for killing William de Pouton in a tournament at Luton. Within three months, another was issued to John Maudit for killing Roger de Chedele at a tournament at Cirencester.[25] The pardon was usually granted after an inquest had proved, as far as possible, that the death had been accidental, as in the case of Adam Bernard who had killed Thomas Basset by chance in jousts at Leicester in 1305, his lance having glanced off his opponent's shield and struck him in the belly.[26] The pardon protected the killer not only from the unauthorized summary justice of private revenge but also from pursuit by the king's justices on a charge of homicide. Like most medieval privileges, royal pardons had to be bought, and this could be an expensive business. Robin Hood had to give a helping hand to a knight who had impoverished himself by mortgaging all his lands to a rich abbot in order to buy a pardon for his son who had killed a knight in a joust.[27]

Even if fatalities were avoided, there were still problems of disorder to be encountered. These were almost inevitable when bands of armed men were meeting for combat, however good natured. The *mêlée* style tournament was particularly destructive, not only of lives but also of property, because it ranged over such a wide area of countryside. The tournaments of the late twelfth century frequented by Arnold of Ardres and William Marshal reveal

---

[24] Froissart, iv, 293-4. A literary parallel to Mauny's penitential pilgrimage is found in a late *chanson de geste* in which a Saracen finds it a convenient and unexceptional disguise to wander round Europe as a penitent visiting shrines for killing his brother in a tournament: 'Aye of Avignon' in *APF*, vi, 74-5.

[25] *CPR 1317-21*, pp. 124, 154.

[26] *CPR 1301-7*, p. 313.

[27] 'A Geste of Robyn Hode' in *The English and Scottish Popular Ballads*, ed. F. J. Child (New York, 1956), iii, 57-9.

a scant regard on the part of the tourneyers for the livelihood of farmers in northern France: they took up their positions in vineyards and even trampled over them in the excitement of the chase.[28] In England preachers such as the Dominican John Bromyard championed the cause of the poor who were so often the victims of tourneyers. The poor had their goods seized from them by force or paid for in wooden tallies which were then dishonoured. Their livelihoods were destroyed when their crops were carelessly trampled down by tourneying knights. To add insult to these injuries, the burden of the heavy expenses involved in tourneying was also borne by the poor, who were tallaged to that end by their lords.[29]

Even after changing fashions in hastiludes had reduced the physical destruction to a more confined area, there were still problems of outbreaks of violence. In 1311, for example, a commission of *oyer et terminer* had to be appointed to deal with a complaint from a Cambridgeshire woman who had had her goods seized by a group of armed men contrary to the king's prohibition on tournaments and deeds of arms.[30] Some forty years later, the parson of Grappenhalle in the county palatinate of Chester complained to the Black Prince that he was being persecuted by one of the prince's bachelors, who had seized the parson's torches and his timber from the church to build a *berfrois* for the spectators at a tournament which he had proclaimed at Warrington.[31]

Even monastic houses and towns did not escape without loss. We have already seen how the monks of Bury St Edmunds were plagued by the riotous behaviour of tourneyers in 1194.[32] The problem was still relevant in 1305 when the canons of Salisbury cathedral secured a royal writ to protect themselves from violence by forbidding any tourneyers to lodge within the cathedral close or to take any victuals or other necessities from the canons.[33] The masters and students of the universities of Oxford and Cambridge ensured that their

---

[28] Gislebert of Mons, pp. 116-7; *HGM*, ll. 4834-6. Even in the thirteenth century Nicholas de Yatingden, constable of Windsor, had to account for £4.10.8d worth of corn trampled and lost when a tournament was held in one of the king's cultivated fields at Kenington: PRO E372/115 m1. I owe this reference to Miss H. Waite.

[29] John Bromyard, *Summa Predicantium* (Nuremburg, 1518), fos xcii(r), cxci(r), ccviii(r). See also: Jacques de Vitry, *Exempla*, ed. T. Crane (London, 1890), p. 62; Thomas du Cantupré, *Miraculorum et Exemplorum Memorabilium sui Temporis Libri Duo* (Duaci, 1605), bk. ii, cxlix.

[30] *CPR 1307-13*, p. 369.

[31] *The Black Prince's Register* (London, 1932), iii, 58-9.

[32] See *supra*: p. 10.

[33] *CPR 1301-7*, p. 394.

academic peace and security was not disturbed by obtaining complete prohibitions on all hastiludes within a five mile radius of each city.[34] Townsmen were less privileged, however, one of the worst examples of a hastilude getting out of hand occurring at the Boston Fair of 1288.[35] A *behourd* had been organized to coincide with the fair and when the tourneyers got carried away the fighting spilled out into the market place. The *behourd* became a riot, with tourneyers overturning merchants' booths, setting fire to them, stealing the merchandize and robbing the merchants themselves. Even as late as 1390, and for such a prestigious event as the October jousts patronized by Richard II, special watches had to be laid on in London each night 'so that no danger or disgrace shall befall the city aforesaid'.[36]

The problem of how to contain and control the violence implicit in military sports was a vexed one. In the first instance it was the attendant disorder off the field which attracted royal attention. In this aspect, Richard I's decree was primarily concerned with controlling the number and location of hastiludes and preventing trouble on the way to and from the lists. It made no attempt to interfere in the conduct of the game once it had begun. Tournaments were allowed in five approved places: between Salisbury and Wilton (Wiltshire), Warwick and Kenilworth (Warwickshire), Stanford and Warinford (probably Suffolk), Brackley and Mixbury (Northamptonshire) and Blyth and Tickhill (Nottinghamshire). The choice of sites appears rather arbitrary for they were certainly not 'conveniently placed to cover the needs of the whole of England' as Denholm-Young suggested.[37] Only one site, between Blyth and Tickhill, lay north of the Trent which was the usual administrative dividing line of the realm. The western counties of England were completely uncatered for, even though the Welsh marches were a fertile breeding ground for hastiludes with their heavy concentration of seigneurial armies and castle garrisons.

The fact that the north and west of England were left without a site is significant, for these were the most politically and militarily unstable areas of the realm. The dangers implicit in allowing bands of armed men to gather in counties where royal authority was at its

---

[34] *CPR 1266-72*, pp. 446, 447; *CPR 1301-7*, p. 395.
[35] Walter of Guisborough, *Cronica*, ed. H. Rothwell (Camden Soc., lxxxix, 1957), pp. 224-5. A *behourd* was an informal joust, see *infra* pp. 000-00.
[36] *Memorials of London and London Life*, ed. H. T. Riley (London, 1868), p. 522.
[37] Denholm-Young, pp. 243-4.

weakest may have been so weighty a consideration that Richard deliberately chose his sites elsewhere. Bearing this in mind, it is equally significant that all the sites which were licensed straddled major routes to London which made them more accessible not only to knights travelling from other counties but also to government control. Another factor relevant to the enforcing of the decree was that the chosen sites also lay within the spheres of territorial influence of the three earls who were appointed as sureties of the charter. It therefore seems that the five licensed tourneying grounds were chosen not because they were evenly spread out over the kingdom but because they were capable of being kept under surveillance.

The three men chosen to act as guarantors of the charter were equally carefully selected. Two of them, William FitzPatrick, earl of Salisbury, and Gilbert de Clare, earl of Gloucester, were senior earls and the third, Hamelin de Warenne, was an illigitimate son of Geoffrey Plantagenet, Richard I's uncle. The rank of the guarantors presupposed that they would have the influence necessary to ensure that English tourneyers abode by the terms of the charter. Likewise, their involvement in military affairs ensured that they had the tourneyers' respect and the king's confidence. According to Roger of Hoveden, the charter itself was placed in the custody of William FitzPatrick, even though he was in Normandy on the king's service in 1194 and remained there until his death two years later.[38]

The actual administration of the charter was not put into the hands of the guarantors or their nominees, but was left with royal servants. The collection of fees payable for tourneying was entrusted to Theobald Walter, brother of the justiciar.[39] The licence itself cost 10 marks; additionally there were individual fees, graduated according to the rank of the tourneyer, which were explicitly set out in the charter: twenty marks for an earl, ten marks for a baron, four marks for a landed knight and two marks for a landless knight. In this context it is significant that the charter did not cater for any tourneyer being of lower rank than that of a landless knight, and that it specifically prohibited foreigners from tourneying in England. The exclusion of foreigners seems contrary to the spirit of tourneying, since the widely differing origins of tourneyers was a feature of tournaments in northern France and the *chevaliers d'estranges terres* was a stock figure in romance hastiludes. The reason for their exclusion would seem to be pragmatic. It would be difficult to

[38] Roger of Hoveden, iii, 268.
[39] *Ibid.*

enforce the collection of fees from foreign tourneyers and impossible to seize their lands into the king's hands if they presumed to tourney without licence. In addition, the consequences of a fatal accident might be far more complex, and perhaps more far reaching, if the victim was of foreign extraction.

The fees for licences were to be collected by two clerics and two knights of the justiciar. These men were to be present on the day of the tournament and receive the oaths of the earls and barons that they would pay their fees in full before permitting anyone to tourney, on pain of personal arrest. These careful arrangements to ensure that tourneyers paid for their licences suggest that Richard expected to make a considerable profit in allowing tournaments. A small indication of the scale of those profits is given in the Pipe Rolls of his reign and just after. In Lincolnshire in 1198 Geoffrey FitzPeter accounted for 100 marks 'de torneamentis' and in Northamptonshire in 1201 David, earl of Huntingdon accounted for 25 marks 'pro torneamentis'.[40] The potential income from fines for tourneying without the king's licence was even greater, for the transgressor was at the king's mercy. Ralph FitzStephen, for example, was fined twenty pounds (a much greater sum than he would have paid to obtain the royal licence) 'de periurio tornamento' in 1200.[41] His perjury must have arisen from his breaking his oath not to tourney before paying his fees or giving his oath to keep the peace. Given the popularity of the sport, Richard was assured of a healthy income from tournaments, whether they were legitimate or not.

A special form of oath was drawn up for the archbishop's men to administer to would-be tourneyers to ensure that the movement of armed men about the country did not endanger the peace. It was specifically laid down that from the moment of their setting out from home, all tourneyers and their men were to pay reasonable market prices for their food and other necessities. Nothing was to be taken by force or unfairly, on pain of having to make amends. The royal rights of vert and venison were given special protection in another clause of the oath which prohibited tourneyers from breaching the king's forests. Indeed, the prevention of loss or damage to the royal forests was one of the principal objects for licensing English tournaments, according to the preamble of the

---

[40] Pipe Roll Soc., new series, vol. ix, 64; *Ibid.*, vol. xiv, 178. I am grateful to Dr Pierre Chaplais for these references.
[41] *The Rolls of the Justices in Eyre for Lincolnshire and Worcestershire, 1221*, ed. D. M. Stenton (London, 1934), p. 81.

writ. Finally, any tourneyer who was in feud against another had to swear not to harm that man in the tournament itself, nor in the journeys to and from the tournament. If he refused to give this form of truce he could be distrained to do so or, failing that, he was not to be allowed to tourney at all.

The writ and the oath between them catered for the eventualities about which Richard was most concerned. They restricted tourneying to areas where supervision was possible and they protected the king's subjects and his forests from violence. Where offences were committed, remedies were also provided and it was heavily stressed that the tourneyers were subject to the justiciar as well as the king in all matters of enforcement, ensuring that Richard's long absences abroad would not provoke defiance of the writ.

This first royal attempt to control tourneying was not unsuccessful: all future royal policy towards English tourneying was based on the enforcement of the licensing system set up in 1194, though the limitation to five official tourneying sites fell into abeyance fairly rapidly because it was impractical. Unlike France, where the crown obdurately opposed the sport, in England royal interest in and influence on tournaments was felt very early. Through Richard's writ the mechanism for royal exploitation of hastiludes, particularly for propaganda purposes, was set in motion.

The writ of 1194 set a precedent for external regulation of tourneying in England. In 1245 another committee of three earls was at work administering a royal prohibition on hastiludes and fining transgressors.[42] The composition of the committee was significant. Richard, earl of Cornwall was Henry III's brother, Simon de Montfort was steward of England and the Earl of Norfolk was Marshal of England. The royal representative was thus aided in his work by the two premier hereditary officers of the realm. In 1267 the end of the civil wars was marked by a public edict allowing tournaments once more, which caused a flood of foreign tourneyers into England and the holding of an unprecedented number of tournaments. Three members of the royal family, the lord Edward, his brother Edmund and their cousin Henry of Almain (son of Richard of Cornwall), were responsible for securing the edict and may also have been involved in its administration.[43]

By 1292 there was a familiar format for tourneying legislation.

---

[42] *CCR 1242-7*, p. 363.
[43] *Ann.Mon.*, iv, 212.

Edward I's *Statuta Armorum* were built upon these foundations but went further in attempting to control the actual conduct of the sport. The initiative for the legislation came from the tourneyers themselves, for the statutes were based upon a provision[44] made by the earls, barons and certain magnates of the realm which the king ratified at their request.

There are many misconceptions about the statutes. They were not, as has often been suggested,[45] intended to limit the weapons and armour of the tourneyers themselves. In fact, the statutes make a vital distinction between principal tourneyers and their servants. The former are referred to as *grans seigneurs*, the latter are *escuiers*, *garçons*, *hommes a pee*, or simply 'those who serve at the tourney'. The statutes were only concerned with the problem of armed servants and attendants who were frequently the troublemakers at tournaments. Prior to the statutes their numbers had been un-limited, as far as we know, which could cause unwelcome disruption of the sport if they got out of hand and rioted. At Rochester in 1251, for example, it was the esquires who blocked the route of the defeated party and beat them with staves and clubs. As the tournaments between the court and baronial parties of the period reveal so clearly, victory and defeat alternated rapidly so that every tourneyer, whichever side he belonged to, risked this type of humiliation at the hands of non-knightly combatants.[46] No doubt this explains the fact that it was the chivalry of England which appealed to Edward I to rectify the matter, since their own sport was interrupted by outbursts of rioting among attendants.

The statutes began by prohibiting any tourneyer of whatever rank from taking more than three armed esquires to serve him in the tournament. These three were each to wear a cap of their lord's arms to make them immediately and clearly identifiable. According to the Harleian text,[47] only these three esquires were permitted to pull a tourneyer from his horse legitimately. If anyone else did so, the tourneyer had his horse restored and the wrongdoer forfeited his own horse and harness and was sent to prison for three years. The implication of this clause, incidentally, was that the horse was the legitimate booty of the three esquires if captured in the proper way.

No knight or esquire serving at the tournament (as distinct from the principal tourneyers themselves) was to be armed with a sharp

---

[44] The provision is printed in *Statutes of the Realm* (London, 1810), i, 230-1. The *Statuta* are printed in *Rotuli Parliamentorum* (London, 1832), i, 85.
[45] See Appendix I.
[46] Matt.Paris, v, 265; iv, 633, 649; v, 17-8, 83.
[47] See Appendix I.

sword, knife, cudgel or mace. They were restricted solely to the broadsword ('espee large pur tournoir') which again suggests that these esquires were expected to have a limited fighting role in the sport. The numbers of more menial servants, including *garçons* and *hommes a pied*, were not restricted, nor were they to be specially identified like the three esquires, but they were absolutely forbidden to carry any offensive weapons on pain of imprisonment for one year (Harleian version) or seven years (printed version). Because some of these servants would be required on the field to help their lord remount, to bring fresh weapons, to tend his horses and to carry his banner they were permitted to wear a certain amount of defensive armour for their own protection. All those on the field, with the exception of the principal tourneyers themselves (*grans seigneurs*),[48] were only allowed to wear knee pieces (*mustilers*), thigh pieces (*quisers*), shoulder pieces (*espaulers*) and a bascinet. This armour would give them a certain amount of protection from accidental knocks, but would not make them secure enough to encourage them to get properly involved in the fighting. The audience was not forgotten: all those coming to watch the sport were to be completely without weapons and without defensive armour, on pain of imprisonment. Even the heralds were included in this restriction. The kings of heralds and minstrels (or possibly marshals)[49] were forbidden to carry any concealed arms and permitted only to carry their blunted swords of office. Like the esquires serving the tourneyers, they were to be clearly identifiable by means of their armorial tabards. Problems after the tournament ended were anticipated with the provision that only those esquires performing the duty of carving their lord's meat were to accompany tourneyers to the festivities. This possibly explains the many references to the chamberlain dining in hall which occur in tournament retainers.[50]

The *Statuta Armorum* were an extremely far-reaching attempt to impose some sort of disciplined structure on the tournament, thereby reducing the risks and consequent casualties. Their primary purpose was to ensure that each group coming to the tournament was quickly and easily identifiable, and that the carrying of weapons was strictly limited to the tourneyers and their three attendant esquires. In this way it became easier to regulate which people were

---

[48] See Appendix I.
[49] Lib.Horn and Cay versions of the *Statuta Armorum* quoted in the printed edition. See also Denholm-Young, p. 261.
[50] See *supra*: p. 12.

on the field and what functions they were legitimately allowed to perform. The tourneyers themselves were personally unaffected by these new rules, for their arms and armour were unrestricted, but their retinues were severely curtailed. The numbers and equipment of the tourneyer's following were also cut down to a minimum which allowed them to remain useful to their lord but less dangerous to others.

These statutes of Edward I shed an interesting light on the role of esquires in tournaments. The three armed esquires were obviously intended to have a restricted but active fighting role on horseback, since they were provided with broadswords which were a cavalry-man's weapon.[51] On the other hand, the limitations of their defensive armour must have effectively excluded them from the preliminary lance combats. Their being allowed to acquire legitimate booty in their own right if they managed to pull a knight from his horse in the combat put them on a par with the tourneyers themselves, and it must have been in this way that young men gained their first experiences of the sport before they were knighted and were promoted to tourneyer's rank.

The effectiveness of the *Statuta* is difficult to assess. In the short term, their effect was noted immediately by the Dunstable annalist who recorded a particularly fierce tournament at Dunstable in the same month as the statutes were enacted, in which no groom (*ribaldus*) or foot soldier was allowed to carry any weapons except a small shield with which to repel the horses' hooves.[52] Even this annalist did not make explicit the connection beween the innova-tions of this tournament and the *Statuta Armorum*, and no other chronicle sources mention the introduction of the statutes. It seems likely, therefore, that the limitations of the statutes were not completely innovatory but rather that statutory force was given to customary regulations which had been voluntarily imposed and were difficult to enforce. This would explain the absence of comment in chronicles. In the longer term, the statutes still received little or no chronicle notice, though it is possible that their effects were felt. For instance, nothing more is heard of rioting foot soldiers and esquires at tournaments and though there were occasional outbursts of violent tourneying, there was never again anything approaching the violence of the tournaments of the 1240s and 1250s.

---

[51] It is interesting to speculate whether these three esquires were the forerunners of the 'lance' unit in warfare.
[52] *Ann.Mon.*, iii, 373.

The *Statuta Armorum* were unique in tourneying history because of their legislative status. Together with Richard I's decree of 1194 they set out the general precepts upon which the more particular day to day policy of the government was based. This more detailed aspect of the official approach towards control of tourneying has to be studied through the royal writs of prohibition. From these it is clear that royal attitudes towards the sport varied considerably, and it is no coincidence that the largest number of secular prohibitions were issued in the reigns of Henry III and Edward II. Neither king had any aptitude for military leadership or military games, and so could not successfully participate in hastiludes and win their knightly subjects' respect, as Edward I and Edward III were able to do. Henry III seems never to have fought in hastiludes or even attended one. This may be due to his remarkable piety which might have encouraged him to obey church precepts against tourneying. He may also have been influenced by the theory current in France which prevented French kings from entering the lists once they had been anointed with the chrism at their coronation because it would derogate from royal dignity for God's anointed king to be assaulted, even in sport.[53] Though piety might explain Henry's personal abstinence from tourneying, it cannot have been so driving a force as to prevent him allowing others to tourney, for he not only licensed tournaments from time to time, but he also on one occasion ordered all his household knights to attend one. Edward II's attitude to tournaments was rather more ambivalent: he personally attended several hastiludes during his reign, but his one attempt to proclaim and patronize a tournament was apparently a dismal failure.[54]

The explanation for the hostility of both kings towards the sport, as expressed in the sheer volume of their prohibitions, lies in the political instability of their reigns. The meeting in arms of disaffected and discontented barons with their large armed retinues in tow was obviously undesirable in the context of reigns afflicted by political divisions and even outright rebellion. General bans were backed up by specific prohibitions of individually named tournaments and prohibitions addressed individually to the leading trouble makers. If this only succeeded in multiplying the number of illegal and unlicensed tournaments, at least there was a legal mechanism which could be set in motion against offenders.

In fact, however, a repressive attitude towards tournaments was not confined solely to Henry III and Edward II: when hastiludes

---

[53] Duby, *Dimanche de Bouvines*, p. 118.
[54] *Ann.Paul.*, p. 264.

conflicted with their own political interests, both Edward I and Edward III could be equally ruthless in issuing prohibitions, despite their own love of the sport.

One of the commonest reasons for prohibiting tournaments, irrespective of the attitude of the monarch, was because war was being waged. This necessitated the presence of as many active knights as possible in the king's army and it is clear from the number of knights who deserted the royal army in Scotland so that they could tourney in England in 1302 and again in 1306[55] that tourneying was not only a distraction from the serious business of war, but on occasions could prove more attractive to knights stuck on a boring campaign with little military action. Similarly, it was sometimes necessary to issue a general prohibition to cover the meeting of a parliament or the holding of councils of the realm to prevent the chivalric classes, who were the administrators and councillors, abandoning their political duties in favour of more attractive pastimes. During the parliament of Northampton in 1328, for example, Edward III had to issue a general prohibition because a series of hastiludes had been proclaimed in the county, 'by reason whereof certain magnates in the parliament of Northampton propose going to the said tournaments, leaving the king's affairs.'[56] It was also deemed prudent to prohibit all tournaments during the absence of the king from the realm, for fear of disturbances or even rebellion when the kingdom was particularly vulnerable.[57]

The reason for issuing the prohibition was usually clearly set out in the king's writ: this emphasized the necessity of the ban by making it clear that it was justified. It was comparatively rare for a general prohibition to be issued for arbitrary personal reasons. One such instance was the sending out of a prohibition in 1323 on any other tournament at Northampton or elsewhere in the realm, at the request of Thomas, earl of Norfolk, and Edmund, earl of Kent, the king's brothers. They were thus protecting the great tournament held at Northampton with the king's licence at which they were presumably the leaders of the two parties. The tournament was not only held in Edward II's presence, but was also the setting for him

---

[55] *CCR 1302-7*, p. 66; *Cal.Fine Rolls*, i, 543-4. For further examples of prohibitions issued because of war see: *CCR 1296-1302*, p. 373; *CCR 1302-7*, pp. 433, 459, 535-6; *CCR 1307-13*, p. 269. See also PRO SC1/49 no. 45 for a personal prohibition addressed to Aymer de Valence in 1319 because of the Scots war.
[56] *CCR 1327-30*, p. 382. For similar examples see: *CCR 1307-13*, p. 257; *CPR 1301-7*, p. 40.
[57] See, for example: *CCR 1261-4*, p. 133; *CCR 1318-23*, p. 243; *Foedera*, iv, 386; *Ibid.*, i, pt. i, 685, 709.

to confer knighthood on Geoffrey Scrope and three other young aspirants.[58]

It has been suggested by Denholm-Young[59] that the fact that most prohibitions were issued only a few days before the hastilude was due to be held made the prohibitions themselves ineffectual: the meeting could not be cancelled and the knights prevented from coming to the prearranged site in so short a space of time. The *caveat* that he attached to this, that some of these writs are 'genuine' and others are 'purely formal', is not particularly helpful, however, unless there is an observable distinction between them. The distinction, as I see it, appears to be one of intention: the 'genuine' ones were intended absolutely to prevent hastiludes taking place under any pretext whatsoever. 'Purely formal' ones, on the other hand, merely indicated the king's opposition to a hastilude which had been planned without his licence, and probably against his wishes. An examination of the writs suggests that 'genuine' prohibitions, such as those intended to cover war, the king's absence abroad or large scale administrative meetings, were not often issued at the last minute.[60] Usually they were sent out in plenty of time for the proclamation to be made. They were also distinguished by having a clause explaining the justification for the ban and extremely heavy penalties were attached, including loss of life and lands.

It is the 'purely formal' ones which were generally issued in the same week as the tournament and the penalty for disregarding them could be arrest, imprisonment and, more importantly, forfeiture of goods and lands. The key to the 'purely formal' ones is that they were not a general blanket ban on all hastiludes, as is sometimes believed,[61] but simply meant that no hastiludes were to be held without the king's prior knowledge and approval, that is, without his special licence. There is a radical difference between not allowing any tournaments at all, as in 'genuine' prohibitions, and allowing them only once a specific royal licence had been obtained, and penalizing breaches of this rule which had been set out so firmly in

---

[58] *CPR 1321-4*, p. 339; *CCR 1323-7*, p. 136. Scrope received £26.13.4d from the king compared to only 100s. given to James Botiller for his expenses in attending the tournament presumably because Edward II had already decided to knight Scrope at the meeting: See BL MS Stowe 553, fo. 128r.

[59] Denholm-Young, pp. 245-6.

[60] An example of a last minute 'genuine prohibition' occurred on 30 January 1284 when a prohibition issued on a tournament due to take place the next day was to be delivered 'post haste' (*Cal. Chancery Warrants*, p. 18).

[61] See, for example, C. Bullock-Davies, *Menestrellorum Multitudo: minstrels at a royal feast* (Cardiff, 1978), p. 41.

Richard I's decree.

Whenever the king heard of a hastilude planned without his authority, which might well be only a few days before the event was due to take place, he would issue a 'formal' prohibition. This would be sent to the place where the hastilude was planned, perhaps only the day before or the day of the tournament. It would have been totally impractical to try to prevent hastiludes taking place by sending prohibitions up and down the country, because the king had no way of knowing who would attend. On the other hand, by sending royal messengers to the lists where they could proclaim the ban to all the tourneyers together, the plea of ignorance could not be made. Once the prohibition had been read out, the knights could either pay for a licence which would enable them to tourney legitimately, or they could refuse to buy a licence and either disband the tournament or proceed and incur the penalties. In either case the king was sure of raising revenue – his main object when issuing purely 'formal' prohibitions.

The significance of sending either clerics, usually the abbots or priors of nearby religious houses, or soldiers, usually the king's own sergeants at arms, therefore becomes clear. These were the same men who were employed as messengers delivering renunciation of homage and challenges in the days before heralds. Clerics[62] had the advantage of being literate and could therefore record the names of those who either bought a licence or tourneyed against the prohibition: additionally, they could invoke the threat of ex-communication against the intransigent. Occasionally the cleric was a member of one of the military orders, as when the Master of the Templars was sent to prohibit a tournament at York in 1243,[63] thus combining the advantages of being both cleric and soldier. Addition-ally, of course, monks and members of the military orders were sacrosanct in their persons (as heralds were later to be) so that the king's messages would be treated with respect. Usually, however, the messengers were the king's own sergeants at arms. Nominally, at least, they were sent to arrest the tourneyers and commit them to the sheriff's prison,[64] but actually, as members of the royal household, they were more reliable as enforcers of prohibitions than sheriffs, who were frequently accused of condoning the unlicensed tournaments of their fellow knights and neighbours.

---

[62] See, for example, *CPR 1232-47*, pp. 57, 70, 86, 119, 131, 133, 136, 148, 156, 173, 222, 266, 269, 452, 477.
[63] *CPR 1266-72*, p. 722.
[64] See, for example, *Foedera*, iii, 438, 438-9, 597, 982-3.

Arrest, imprisonment and seizure of lands were the usual punishments for tourneying without a licence, as we have seen, and these penalties (especially the forfeiture of land, which was a more complicated process than personal arrest and therefore required more documentation) can be seen being put into effect from the earliest days of licensed tourneying in England. In 1196 Robert Mortimer sought the king's peace and found pledges for having tourneyed without a licence.[65] In 1235 three knights temporarily lost their lands for tourneying without a licence at Cambridge, an offence that was repeated by twelve other knights ten years later, with the same result.[66] In 1302 Giles de Argentine, a habitual offender, and six fellow knights were arrested for leaving the king's army in Scotland to attend jousts at Byfleet in Surrey, as were a further sixteen knights who committed the same offence in 1306.[67] In 1305, ten knights were arrested for the slightly different misdemeanor of tourneying against the charter of Cambridge University which prohibited all hastiludes within five miles of the city.[68] This type of evidence suggests that when breaches of prohibitions were blatant or serious enough the king was prepared to take action against the offenders; he also had the added inducement of an income from fines.

One of the greatest practical difficulties in seeking to control illicit tourneying was to find out which knights had actually tourneyed. For this reason, sheriffs were sometimes ordered to certify the names of offenders to the king: even the names of those who had set up their inns as lodgings for tourneyers were demanded on occasion.[69] Many other ingenious attempts were made to forestall illicit tourneying. On several occasions it was made an offence to sell or supply tourneyers with arms, victuals or other goods, or even to give them shelter or lodging. In 1233 the mayor and bailiffs of Northampton were ordered to close the town gates to shut out some illegal tourneyers and to prevent them entering the town for supplies.[70] The penalties threatened for those who aided or abetted tourneyers in any of these ways were comparable to those imposed on the tourneyers themselves.

Just how ineffectual such prohibitions proved to be, despite the severity of the penalties, is clearly shown by the monotonous

---

[65] *Rotuli Curiae Regis*, p. 87.
[66] *CCR 1234-7*, pp. 210 (*bis*), 212; *CCR 1242-7*, pp. 361, 363.
[67] *CCR 1302-7*, pp. 66, 481-2; *Cal.Fine Rolls*, i, 543-4.
[68] *CCR 1302-7*, p. 299.
[69] *Foedera*, iii, 835, 836; *CPR 1232-47*, p. 266.
[70] *Ibid.*, p. 20.

regularity of the issuing of bans. The only time when prohibitions do seem to have been generally observed was in periods of extreme danger to the kingdom. At such times, the ban was usually issued at a council of the realm. One of the Provisions of Oxford, for example, agreed a prohibition on all hastiludes until one month after Michaelmas in order to preserve the peace, 'by the common consent of the earls, barons and certain bishops.'[71] Similarly, Edward III issued a general ban on hastiludes in 1331 with the consent of 'all his council in the Parliament of Westminster'.[72] Chivalric approval of prohibitions of this kind appears to have been one of the most effective ways of curtailing tourneying activity. Interestingly, when the barons came to power in 1258 they proposed a totally new method of enforcing prohibitions. Instead of having their lands seized, offenders were to serve the king in his army at their own cost for one year – a penalty for which the financial equivalent was a fine of fifty pounds.[73] As tourneyers themselves, the barons no doubt appreciated that the onerous duties of a year's free service in the army was a more compelling reason for abstaining from hastiludes than the usual penalties imposed by the king.

The attitude of secular authorities to hastiludes in the thirteenth and early fourteenth centuries was therefore an ambivalent one. The reason for this was that no consistent line of policy was ever evolved and upheld, and royal reactions to tourneying were based on a pragmatic assessment of the prevalent political situation of the day. When it was necessary to concentrate knightly resources in a particular war effort or when there were obvious dangers of hastiludes being used for political ends by the disaffected, then a repressive policy had to come into operation. When there was internal and external peace it was possible to relax the more stringent prohibitions and allow hastiludes to take place, but always with the proviso that this should be with the knowledge and approval of the king, as expressed by his royal licence.

Edward I and Edward III went one step further than this: though they could be as repressive as Henry III or Edward II whenever hastiludes conflicted with their own interests, it was their personal patronage of the sport at other times that took much of the political danger out of tourneying. Their presence at, and participation in, hastiludes made it difficult for political opponents to gather there or use them for their own ends. More important than this, however,

---

[71] *Ibid.*
[72] *CCR 1330-33*, p. 397.
[73] *CPR 1258-66*, p. 5; Denholm-Young, p. 251.

was the way both Edward I and Edward III turned the tournament to political advantage. In their hands, hastiludes became vehicles of royal propaganda, and it is in this context that the devotion of both kings to the legendary king Arthur becomes important.

Round Tables were the ultimate celebration of Arthurian values. They were remarkable for their sumptuous settings, the extravagance of their *largesse* and their involvement of women in the pageantry which was carried over from the hastiludes into the peripheral celebrations. Frequently the participants appear to have assumed the arms, names and even characters of the Arthurian knights of romance, and when the king himself assumed the role of Arthur, there could be no mistaking this deliberate association of Edwardian and Arthurian ideology. Moreover, the timing of English Round Tables was often politically significant. Edward I held one at Nefyn on the north west coast of Wales in 1284 to celebrate his conquest of the principality. This Round Table marked the culmination of an English campaign which had been continually and closely associated with the cult of Arthur: the tombs of Arthur and Guinevere at Glastonbury had been visited and reopened in 1278 and four years later Arthur's crown was found in Wales and sent back to Westminster Abbey to be displayed as a trophy of war. By continually associating Arthurian matter with his conduct of the campaigns in Wales Edward I closely identified himself with the once and future king. This had two benefits as a form of propaganda: firstly, it proved to the Welsh that the semi-legendary king, who was popularly believed to be sleeping at Avalon with his knights ready to rise again in their hour of need, was dead and could not resurrect, even against the English conquerors; secondly, it associated Edward and his knights with all the virtues of the romance heroes, including their invincibility. The choice of a Round Table, rather than any other type of hastilude, to celebrate the conquest of Wales was therefore an important and significant one.

Equally significant, bearing in mind their own political pretensions in Wales, was the Mortimer connection with Round Tables. It was Roger Mortimer who, in 1279, held the great Round Table of a hundred knights and a hundred ladies at Kenilworth, the home of his close associate, Edmund, duke of Lancaster, the younger brother of Edward I. The whole affair was marked by prodigious expense since all present were housed, fed and entertained at Mortimer's own cost. On the fourth day the whole gathering transferred to Warwick where the celebrations continued and a golden lion was awarded as the prize for the hastiludes. According to the Wigmore chonicle, Blanche, queen of Navarre and wife of Edmund, presented Mortimer with several wine barrels filled with gold as her contribution to the expenses and thereafter, in token of his gratitude, he bore a carbuncle on his armour.[74] Similarly extravagant Round Tables were held by other members of the Mortimer family. Geoffrey Mortimer, Roger's grandson, held one in Wales for all who would come to it because he was 'so ful of pride and wrecchednesse'.[75] Geoffrey's father, Roger Mortimer IV, celebrated his elevation to the earldom of March in 1328 by holding a series of Round Tables in the presence of his lover, Queen Isabella, at which there was profuse expenditure.[76] Since the Mortimers were conspicuous for their political aspirations in both Wales and England, their patronage of Round Tables is of great importance, particularly as they were very conscious of their alleged Arthurian descent. A genealogy of the Mortimer family drawn up for them in the last quarter of the fourteenth century emphasized their descent from Arthur and the other semi-legendary kings of Wales, Cadwallader and Brutus. Arthurian ancestry was also stressed in other ways, such as naming one member of the family Iseult, after the lover of Tristan.[77] It is therefore no coincidence that those men who most identified themselves with the once and future king, including the Mortimers, Edward I and Edward III, should have been the most conspicuous patrons of the Round Table.

Pretensions to political power in Wales were not the only stimuli to holding Round Tables. Edward I held one in 1302 at Falkirk on the Firth of Forth,[78] the site of his victory over the Scots in 1298. He also held another at an uncertain date which was interrupted at intervals by messengers bearing news of political and military disasters; his knights, under their various *personae* as Arthurian characters, swore to undertake the adventures and when the play acting was over, Edward held the actors to their promises.[79]

Edward III's most important Round Table was held at Windsor castle in 1344. After the normal celebrations were over, an attempt was made by Edward III to found a new order of chivalry which, in

---

[74] *Monasticon Anglicanum*, vi, pt. i, 350.

[75] *The Brut*, i, 262.

[76] Robert of Avesbury, *De Gestis Edwardi Tertii*, ed. E. M. Thompson (R.S., 1889), p. 284; *Monasticon Anglicanum*, vi, pt. i, 352.

[77] M. E. Giffin, 'Cadwalader, Arthur and Brutus in the Wigmore Manuscript', *Speculum*, xvi (1941), pp. 109-20, esp. pp. 111-3, 115-6, 117.

[78] *Ann.Lond.*, p. 104.

[79] R. S. Loomis, 'Edward I: Arthurian Enthusiast', *Speculum*, xxviii (1953), pp. 118-9. See *infra*: pp. xxx-xxx.

direct imitation of romance, he called a Round Table. In fact, the new order was more like a society of knights than a chivalric order, for the inspiration was purely secular and Arthurian. From a political point of view, Edward III's order of the Round Table, though transient, was a chivalric coup. His plans were too ambitious and were never fully carried out, but despite their ultimate practical failure, they had immense prestige in chivalric circles at home and abroad. According to at least one English chronicler, Philip of France found it necessary to found a similar order so that he could lure the knights of Italy and Germany to France and thereby prevent their being enticed to England.[80] The fact that Edward's Round Table was open to foreign knights as well as Englishmen made it a useful political tool in his war against France: it was an attractive bait with which he could woo foreign knights to his cause. Similarly, the more successful and long-lived Order of the Garter, which fourteenth century knights considered to be a direct descendant of the Arthurian Round Table,[81] was also open to foreign knights. The restriction of membership to twenty-four knights at any one time made the order more prestigious and highly sought after than the less elite order of the Round Table, and the Garter knights were frequently challenged as representatives of English chivalry by foreign knights anxious to test their prowess.[82]

Though the Round Table was the ultimate propaganda weapon of royal patrons of hastiludes, other forms of the sport were used to the same end. In 1333-4, and again in 1342, Edward III organized a series of hastiludes to celebrate the end of campaigns in Scotland; on the later occasion more than two hundred and fifty knights took part including six earls and the king himself, who fought as a simple knight-bachelor. Another series of hastiludes in 1348 celebrated the English victory at Crécy.[83] The importance of these celebrations was not confined simply to England. They increased Edward III's prestige abroad, especially when men such as the Comte d'Eu praised his generosity in allowing his French prisoners to tourney and in awarding them the prizes in preference to himself.[84] At such times, hastiludes were as much a show of strength – a demonstration of military superiority – as an occasion for chivalric sport. Even political victories could be celebrated with tournaments. In 1330, for example, the crushing of the Earl of Kent's rebellion was marked by

[80] *Chronicon a Monacho Sancti Albani*, ed. E. M. Thompson (R.S., 1874), p. 17.
[81] The foundation of the two orders is often confused, e.g. Froissart, iv, 203-6.
[82] BL MS Additional 21370 fo. 1r.
[83] N. H. Nicolas, 'Observations', pp. 26-30, 36-42.
[84] Geoffrey le Baker, *Chronicon*, ed. E. M. Thompson (Oxford 1889), p. 101.

jousts and tournaments, and later in the same year, Edward III celebrated the fall of Mortimer in a series of hastiludes in London while at the same time stirring up popular support by a generous display of pageantry and *largesse*.[85]

It was, therefore, possible for hastiludes to be used as instruments of royal propaganda by those kings who were personally adept at, and patrons of, the sport. A well timed tournament was a public declaration of military superiority celebrating victories of all kinds. If it was carried out in a suitably spectacular and profusely expensive manner it increased royal prestige and attracted knights from home and abroad so that the king's praises would be carried far afield. The chivalric reputation which Edward I and, more particularly, Edward III won throughout Europe was based, to a large extent, on a highly successful manipulation of hastiludes to their own ends. This contrasts sharply with the reigns of Henry III and Edward II, when the patronage of tourneying was allowed to slip out of the king's hands into those of the barons. Instead of being a powerful propaganda machine on behalf of the king and royal policy, hastiludes became centres of disaffection and opposition. The weapon, in the wrong hands, was therefore turned against the king. The importance of patronizing tournaments cannot be overestimated because of the political consequences. This is evident in the reign of Richard II when, despite political troubles strongly reminiscent of the reigns of Henry III and Edward II, hastiludes did not become a danger to the crown. This was partly because the changing fashions of tourneying had made much smaller jousts more common than in the thirteenth and early fourteenth centuries, but also because Richard II was a lavish patron of the sport, thus forestalling any attempts to win the patronage from him. Had he not financed and attended hastiludes as he did, it is possible that tourneying might have become the preserve of his enemies, particularly as Henry, earl of Derby, was a devotee of the sport.

The control of hastiludes was, therefore, a matter of vital importance to the crown. Since it had proved impossible to suppress tourneying by royal prohibition it was better to patronize hastiludes judiciously than to allow this patronage to pass into the hands of others. It was preferable to exert some influence over the sport than to allow it by neglect or repression to become the weapon of the disaffected.

[85] *Ann.Paul.*, pp. 352-3, 353-4, 354-5.

CHAPTER FOUR

The Tournament and the Church

As we have seen, two methods of exerting influence and controlling hastiludes were open to secular authorities, particularly in England. Firstly, there was the weapon of prohibition and statutory limitation: secondly, there was the more subtle weapon of patronage which could be used effectively to coax knightly enthusiasm into acceptable channels. For ecclesiastical authorities the problem was made more difficult by the fact that patronage was impossible given the church's moral stance in relation to tournaments. Their only means of controlling the sport lay in the negative attitude of prohibition, backed by ecclesiastical penalties.

In this chapter I shall look first of all at the Council of Clermont canon of 1130 which set out what was to remain official church policy with regard to tourneying for the next two hundred years. I shall then turn to examine the arguments against the sport which were promulgated in clerical writings and from the pulpit. Finally, I shall look at the most interesting aspect of clerical criticism, the argument that tourneying detracted from crusading. Inevitably, perhaps, due to the universal application of the church's teaching and attitude, I shall rely heavily on continental sources which are nonetheless highly relevant to the position of the church in England.

The position of the church with regard to tourneying was set out very early in an uncompromising statement at the Council of Clermont:

> Detestabiles autem illas nundinas, vel ferias, in quibus milites ex condicto convenire solent, et ad ostentationem virium suarum et audacie temerarie congrediuntur, unde mortes hominum ut animarum pericula saepe proveniunt, omnino fieri interdicimus.

Tournaments were thus completely prohibited, on the grounds that they caused unwarranted loss of life and the committing of mortal sins. The canon went on to declare that anyone mortally wounded in the lists was allowed to receive penance and the *viaticum*, if repentant, but was to be refused ecclesiastical burial.[1] The church's opposition was clearly stated in this way at the very period when the passion for tourneying was sweeping Europe, and officially it remained inflexible until John XXII's bull, *Quia in futurorum*, in 1316.

Though the reasons for the church's hostility were clearly set out in the canon, there was some confusion caused by the way in which it was worded. The periphrase 'Detestabiles ... illas nundinas, vel ferias' was hardly a precise description of tournaments: contemporaries were able to exploit the imprecision by professing to believe that the canon did not refer to hastiludes, just as they were later to be casuistical about the terminology of secular prohibitions. Later commentators, endeavouring to explain the phrase, suggested that tournaments were called fairs because knights attended them for gain.[2] In fact, the explanation is more obvious than this, for markets and fairs were frequently held in association with tournaments. The organizer of a tournament in the romance of Parthonopeus de Blois suggested that to ensure its success all the merchants of the realm should be summoned to hold a fifteen day fair at the tournament where they could sell horses, armour, shields, covertures and everything else a tourneyer could desire. The merchants could hire out their tents as lodgings to the tourneyers, some of whom could lodge in the real town, the rest in this new 'town'. While knights won glory in the lists the merchants could win profits on the sidelines.[3] How great these profits could be is suggested by Sarrazin who complained at the beginning of his *Roman du Hem* that King Louis' ban on hastiludes had impoverished not only *jongleurs*, heralds and merchants but also armourers, saddlers and sellers of food and wine: all had lost their main source of income.[4] In England we find the same connection. Though not all hastiludes were as clearly associated with fairs as the Boston fair *behourd* of 1288, the presence of merchants is taken for granted in the prohibitions which

[1] Hefele & Leclercq, *Histoire des Conciles*, v, pt. i, 729.
[2] Raymond de Penafort, *Summa Sancti ... de Poenitentia et Matrimonia* (Farnborough, 1967), p. 161.
[3] *Partonopeus de Blois*, ed. G-A. Crapelet (Paris, 1834), ii, ll. 6547-620.
[4] Sarrazin, 'Le Roman de Ham', ed. F. Michel in *Histoire des Ducs de Normandie et d'Angleterre* (SHF, 251, 1840), pp. 216-8.

forbade the selling of goods to unlicensed tourneyers.[5]

Clerical criticism of hastiludes and the opportunities for sin that they presented flowed unabated from the pulpits and pens of preachers, though criticism was at its most vociferous in the late thirteenth century. One of the commonest accusations was that tourneyers committed all the seven deadly sins. The seeking after *los et pris*, which was such a powerful motivating force with most tourneyers and which was central to the tournament ideology of romances, was characterized as mere pride and vainglory. Envy arose from the success of one party at the expense of another, as was inevitable at such sport, and ire flourished in the heat of combat. Idleness in religious observance was caused by the dedication of knights to attending tournaments instead of hearing mass, while covetousness for acquiring horses, harnesses and ransoms was the sole motivation of some tourneyers. After the sport was over, gluttony and lechery reigned in the feasting and dancing consequent upon the festivities. The courtly love ethic which inspired tournaments in the first place was simply the chivalric euphemism for lust, and it was lust that drove tourneyers to accept 'sum pryvy present' from their mistresses, in the hopes of receiving the ultimate feminine reward for success at the sport. Nor could these sins be avoided in any other form of hastilude: jousting and attending *behourds* were just as sinful as tourneying.[6]

Clerical fulminations of this kind were common and they did not lack foundation. Henry, duke of Lancaster, for instance, in his *Livre de Seyntz Medecines* confessed that lechery had led him to fight in jousts, 'por grant desir d'estree preisez, puis amez et puis perduz'. He confessed to pride in his physical strength and beauty as a young man and to boasting of his deeds, and even lying about them, so that he might be more honoured.[7] As Lancaster was aware, however, it was not the actual sports he engaged in that were bad in themselves, but that his own intentions in tourneying had been tainted with sin. This argument had already been put forward by Humbert of Romans, who condemned the extravagant expenses, vain intentions and malice consequent upon tourneying, but suggested that the sport itself was tolerable if it was fought with the right intention.

5 *Foedera*, iii, 820; *CPR 1232-47*, p. 20, 266; For comparable prohibitions in France see *Ordonnances des Roys de France*, i, 421-2.

6 Robert of Brunne, *Handlynge Synne*, ed. F. J. Furnivall (London, 1862), pp. 144-6; see also Jacques de Vitry, *Exempla*, pp. 62-4; A. Lecoy de la Marche, *La Chaire Française au Moyen Age* (Paris, 1886), pp. 392-5.

7 Henry of Grosmont, *Le Livre de Seyntz Medecines*, ed. E. J. Arnould (Anglo-Norman Text Soc., ii, 1940), pp. 77-8, 15-6.

This he defined as a desire to train oneself to be a good knight, so that one could be a more effective soldier for Christ in the Holy Land.[8]

Indeed a considerable range of opinion on the subject was to be found within the Church. On the one hand there was the reluctant and qualified approval expressed by preachers such as Humbert of Romans; on the other hand, there was the obdurately hostile attitude which found its expression in papal bans and in popular horror stories calculated to frighten knights into obedience to them. The most common of these were reported visions of tourneyers suffering for their sins in hell where their earthly tourneying activities were parodied in a grotesque manner, such as being compelled to dress in burning armour, bathe in sulpherous baths and receive the unwelcome sexual attentions of demons in the shape of toads.[9] It was presumably such visions which caused Roger Tony to revive on his deathbed and cry 'Vae, vae, mihi, quare unquam torneamenta exercui, et ea tanto studio dilexi', so that he could warn his brother against sharing his own fate.[10] Another popular horror story was the return to earth of ghostly tourneyers who came to punish their killers or to relive their fatal combats.[11] The origins of the belief in the return to earth of ghostly tourneyers is easily traced, for knights killed in tournaments were refused ecclesiastical burial, according to orthodox church policy, hence their souls could not achieve eternal rest. In one of the popular *fabliau*, for example, when a knight was killed in a tournament, the action was halted and the corpse hastily buried beneath an elm tree.[12]

In reality, the church could sometimes be obdurate on this point of ecclesiastical burial. In 1163, for instance, the Pope refused a request, backed by the archbishops of Rheims and Canterbury, that a knight killed tourneying should receive ecclesiastical burial, because he had received numerous requests from kings, princes and barons for the same thing and had no wish to set a precedent which would render the ecclesiastical prohibition ineffectual.[13] More often than not, however, the church appears to have given way, though

---

[8] Humbert of Romans, 'De Eruditione Religiosorum Praedicatorum' in *Maxima Bibliotheca Veterum Patrum* (Lyons, 1677), xxv, 559.

[9] Thomas du Cantupré, bk. ii, cap. xlix; John Bromyard, fo. cxciv.

[10] Matt.Paris, iii, 143-5.

[11] *Ibid.*, iii, 367-8; Thomas du Cantupré, bk. ii, cap. xlix; Ruth Harvey, *Moriz von Craûn* (Oxford, 1961), pp. 248-50.

[12] M-L. Chênerie, ' "Ces Curieux Chevaliers Tournoyeurs" des Fabliaux aux Romans', *Romania*, 97 (1976), p. 346.

[13] *Materials for a History of Thomas Becket*, ed. J. C. Robertson (R.S., 1881), v, 36.

somewhat reluctantly. Only twelve years after this incident, for instance, Conrad, son of the Marquis of Lusatia, was killed in a tournament and was refused church burial. His relatives therefore came to archbishop Wichmann of Magdeburg's council to ask for a proper interment because the dead man had made confession and expressed penitence, been absolved from excommunication and consequently received the sacraments and taken the Cross before he died. He had obviously done everything possible to save his soul in the face of compulsory excommunication and exclusion from church burial (and he had been lucky in having a priest prepared to perform the holy offices for him in such circumstances); it was only when his relatives all swore solemnly on holy relics to abstain from tournaments for ever that the archbishop relented and secured papal approval for the burial. Even so, the corpse remained unburied for two months – long enough to ensure the relatives would at least begin to comply with their oath.[14]

In England, where papal authority was not so strong and relations between church and state were less strained, there are no records of major disputes over the ecclesiastical burial of tournament casualties. The chronicles of Wigmore Abbey record that both Hugh and John Mortimer, killed in tournaments in 1227 and 1318, were buried in the abbey among their ancestors. Similarly, Gilbert Marshal was buried with his father and brothers in the New Temple in London after receiving a fatal wound at the Hertford *fortunium* of 1241.[15] In about 1267 the lord Edward sent the body of Sir John de Vaus, killed in a tournament at Thirsk, to Durham priory where the monks not only received it with honour but also inscribed his name in their book of martyrs so that masses could be sung for his soul annually on the anniversary of his death.[16] Nor was this treatment accorded only to those of prominent social status, whose family patronage was important to the local church. The annalist of Dunstable priory records that the body of an unknown knight killed in the Dunstable tournament of 1292 was received into the priory and buried there.[17]

Indeed, normal ecclesiastical practice, in England at least, seems to have diverged quite considerably from ecclesiastical theory, as promulgated by the Pope and hard line preachers. The theological

[14] *Monumenta Germaniae Historica, Scriptores*, xxiii, 155-6; Harvey, *Moriz von Craûn.*, pp. 116-7.
[15] *Monasticon Anglicanum*, vi, pt. i, pp. 350, 351; Matt.Paris, iv, 135-6.
[16] *Durham Annals and Documents of the Thirteenth Century* ed. F. Barlow (Surtees Soc., clv, 1945), pp. 96, 97.
[17] *Ann.Mon.*, iii, 376.

casuistry of someone like Gregory IX, for example, who argued that a man who died while present at a tournament but without actually having participated or having any intention of participating, should not be refused church burial,[18] was irrelevant to the situation in England where, even at the height of official church opposition to hastiludes, English clerics cooperated with tourneyers. The man on whom rested the responsibility for administering Richard I's decree allowing tournaments in England was none other than the archbishop of Canterbury, albeit in his role as the king's justiciar.[19] Even so pious a king as Henry III did not regard the papal prohibition as absolute and final, for in 1228 he personally offered to seek a papal licence allowing tournaments in England, and in 1252 the monks of Waltham Abbey not only allowed a Round Table to take place on their lands but also buried the corpse of Ernald Munteny within the abbey.[20]

There were practical benefits to be obtained by turning a blind eye to local tournaments. The relations of a tourneying victim were usually more anxious to endow masses and offer oblations than if he had died of natural causes, so the church benefitted financially from receiving the corpse that should have been excluded. Moreover, the church and, in particular, the mendicant orders, were frequently the objects of tourneyers' *largesse* as the latter paraded through the streets to the lists. They also received substantial oblations whenever they held masses for knights going to tournaments[21] – and that friars were prepared to perform this office for those about to defy the church's prohibition again reflects the equivocal attitude of those clerics who were in daily contact with chivalric circles. Most knights appear to have attended mass before submitting to the dangers of the tournament or joust: a popular early medieval miracle story described how one pious knight, who always attended mass before tourneying, stopped off on his journey to a tournament to pray to his patron, the Virgin Mary. He arrived late at the lists to find that the Virgin had assumed his own shape, tourneyed in his place and won the honours of the field for him.[22] This type of alternative

---

[18] *Decretales D. Gregorii Papae IX* (Turin, 1621), cols 1717-8.
[19] *Foedera*, i, 65.
[20] *CCR 1227-31*, p. 113; Matt.Paris, v, 318-9.
[21] See, for example, *Register of the Black Prince*, iv, 428, 475; A. Taylor, 'Royal Arms and Oblations in the Later Thirteenth Century', *Tribute to an Antiquary: essays presented to Marc Fitch*, ed. F. Emmison & R. Stephens (London, 1976), p. 111 n. 29.
[22] Caesarius of Heisterbach, *Dialogus Miraculorum*, ed. J. Strange (Cologne, 1851), ii, 49ff.

literature, which enjoyed a wide vogue, must have substantially weakened the church's hard line attitude towards tourneying, as indeed must the practical need not to offend that class of society on whose charity the church primarily depended.

The reason most often given by the church for reissuing prohibitions on tourneying was that a crusade was imminent. Just as secular authorities prohibited hastiludes before and during wars to prevent the dissipation of their forces so the church prohibited them during the preparations for a crusade to prevent knights being lured from the service of the Cross by more pleasurable and less arduous military sports. The earliest instance of the crusade being put forward as a justification for prohibiting hastiludes occurs in a papal letter to the bishops of England, written in 1193. The pope firmly forbade all tournaments and suggested that any knight who wished to exercise himself in arms should dedicate himself to the more virtuous and more salutiferous cause of the Holy Land.[23] This letter anticipated by half a century the first formal conciliar ban on tournaments because of an approaching crusade.[24] Ninety years later, John Peckham, archbishop of Canterbury, ordered the bishop of Bangor to prohibit all those magnates and knights who had taken the Cross from participating in the Round Table at Nefyn in 1284, on pain of excommunication. If after three warnings, they persisted in tourneying, 'per quod non minus consumptione bonorum quam mutilatione corporum timetur', they were to be denied ecclesiastical burial if they met with a fatal accident there, despite their privileged crusader status.[25] Having enlisted a number of knights for the Cross, Peckham had no intention of losing them through financial embarrassment or personal injury. Interestingly, Peckham made no attempt to prohibit the knights who had not taken the Cross from tourneying, perhaps because he feared to anger the king who had organized the Round Table. Only two years before the papal ban on hastiludes was lifted in 1316, Clement V issued a prohibition on all tournaments, jousts and Round Tables because of his crusading plans. The reasons he cited were the same as those which had impelled Peckham: he justified his position by declaring that it was not simply the moral dangers to the soul and the deaths of men that concerned him, but the consumption of money and the loss of

---

[23] Roger of Hoveden, iii, 202.
[24] This was issued at the Council of Lyons: see Matt.Paris, iv, 460; *Ann.Mon.*, i, 271.
[25] *Registrum Epistolarum Fratris Johannis Peckham*, ed. C.T.Martin (R.S., 1885), iii, 775-6.

horses, both being resources vital to the success of the crusade.[26]

The problem with maintaining a rational opposition on the grounds that hastiludes depleted the resources of men and money available for the *negotium crucis* was that there was no way of proving that the sport did hinder the crusade. There was no hard evidence that knights attended tournaments instead of crusading, or that the two activities were in any way incompatible. In fact, as knights often claimed, tourneying could actually promote the crusades. Richard I's great tournament in England in 1189 which attracted a large number of foreign knights and at the end of which the king and his fellow tourneyers took the Cross,[27] may have been a literary fiction, but it had many parallels in reality. Ten years after this fictional tournament, the counts of Champagne and Blois, followed by many of the high barons and knights of France, took the Cross at a tournament at Écry before setting out on the Fourth Crusade.[28] Similarly, the Hesdin Round Table of 1235 and the Trazegnies tournament of 1251[29] were the settings for mass assumptions of the Cross by the very men – trained and experienced knights – whom the Church was most anxious to recruit. Even as late as 1390, when church opposition to tourneying had been officially withdrawn, the St Ingelvert jousts proved a fertile recruiting ground for the French crusading expedition to Tunisia.[30] Far from being an alternative to crusading, tourneying could be conducive to it: a gathering of chivalry such as the tournament, where the emphasis was on knightly ideology and the winning of *los et pris*, was an ideal place for preaching the crusade. At the very least, some of the tourneyers might be shamed into taking the Cross by the example of their fellows and betters.

Hastiludes could also provide recruits and finances for the cause of the Holy Land in a more roundabout way. When Roger Leyburn killed Ernald Munteny at the Waltham Round Table of 1252, for example, he vowed to go on crusade as a self-imposed penance,[31]

[26] *Conciliae Magnae Britanniae et Hiberniae*, ed. D. Wilkins (London, 1737), ii, 437-8.

[27] Jakemes, *Le Roman du Castelain de Couci*, ed. M. Delbouille (SATF, 1936), ll. 6838ff.

[28] Geoffroi de Villehardouin, *La Conquête de Constantinople*, ed. M. Natalis de Wailly (Paris, 1882), pp. 4-6.

[29] *Monumenta Germaniae Historica, Scriptores*, xxiii, 937; *Ibid.*, xxv, 543.

[30] F. R. H. Du Boulay, 'Henry of Derby's Expeditions to Prussia 1390-1 and 1392', *The Reign of Richard II*, ed. F. R. H. Du Boulay & C. M. Barron (London, 1971), p. 162; A. Goodman, *The Loyal Conspiracy* (London, 1971), p. 57; J. J. N. Palmer, *England, France and Christendom 1377-99* (London, 1972), p. 185.

[31] Matt. Paris, v, 318-9.

and this was, no doubt, a fairly common practice. The bishop of Soissons in 1207 lifted an excommunication imposed on certain nobles who had tourneyed against the ecclesiastical prohibition, on condition that the offenders paid large fines 'in Terrae Sanctae subsidium'. Similarly, Philip IV intended to improve his own crusading finances by confiscating one year's revenues from the lands of those who tourneyed against his prohibition in 1314, and turning them over to his crusading coffers.[32]

If fines for tourneying against prohibitions might go to help the *negotium crucis*, there was also a not inconsiderable amount to be gained from the voluntary bounty of individual tourneyers. William Marshal, for instance, gave away all his winnings at the Joigny tournament, dividing them between captured tourneyers to help them pay their ransoms, and those knights who had taken the Cross.[33] On a larger scale, and presumably with the agreement of both parties, an early fourteenth century indenture records that if Nicholas Cryel should fail to perform his obligations to Stephen de Segrave and the penalty clause of his retaining contract be consequently implemented, the thousand mark fine should go, not to Segrave, but 'a la croyserye vers la tere seinte'.[34]

The conflict between tourneying and crusading alleged by the church found no place in knightly ideology. Though the sport was an essential and honourable feat of arms which ought to be practised by all men-at-arms, the ultimate goal of the knight who sought honour in this world and the next was to go on crusade. As Baudouin de Condé put it,[35]

> Ains qu'il soit chevaliers parfais,
> Li couvient qu'il voist outre mer
> Por sa prouece confremer.

Geoffroi de Charny echoed this idea, and reflected on the practical problems of the would-be crusader faced with leaving his friends, his weeping mistress, his hounds and falcons and the pleasures of jousting and tourneying for the ordeal of a long sea voyage and the

---

[32] *Regesta Pontificum Romanorum*, ed. A. Potthast (Berlin, 1874), i, 266 no. 3127; *Ordonnances des Roys de France*, i, 540.
[33] *HGM*, ll. 3558-62.
[34] Berkeley Castle Muniments, Select Charter no. 490. For a more detailed discussion of this charter see *infra*: pp. 000-00.
[35] Baudouin de Condé, *Dits et Contes*, ed. A. Scheler (Brussels, 1866), i, ll. 408-10.

martyrdom of fighting God's enemies in a strange land.[36] Though there were undoubtedly great attractions to make a knight stay at home, not the least being the fame and reputation which it was possible to acquire in hastiludes alone, these were not as highly regarded as the fame of a knight who had both performed well in the sport and also fought in the Holy Land. When Sir Giles de Argentine was killed at Bannockburn, it was not his undoubtedly great tourneying reputation but his crusading enthusiasm that earned him unsolicited praise from the Scottish chronicler, John Barbour;[37]

> He was the thrid best knycht, perfay,
> That men wist liffand in his day;
> He did mony a fair Iourne.
> On Sarisenis thre derenzeis did he;
> And in-till ilk derenze of thai
> He vencust Sarisenis twa;

Many of the romance heroes chose to end their days in perfecting their secular knighthood by going to the Holy Land to fight in God's cause.[38] They were not short of imitators in reality, even though real knights tended to see the crusade as only an episode (albeit an important one) in their careers rather than the culmination.

As in so many other cases, reality fell short of the ideal and it seems that the motivation of some crusaders was not as pure and single minded as it ought to have been. Ulrich von Liechtenstein was reproved by his esquire for declaring that he would go on crusade to win his lady's favour, but vindicated his motives by declaring that God wanted men to love and serve womankind and therefore He would not be angry with him[39] – a view that was hardly in line with orthodox crusading theory. Similarly, the

---

[36] A. Piaget, 'Le Livre de Messire Geoffroi de Charny', *Romania*, xxvi (1897), pp. 402ff.

[37] J. Barbour, *The Bruce*, ii, bk. xiii, ll. 321-6.

[38] Baudouin de Condé, ii, 202ff; *Le Roman du Castelain de Couci*, pp. 222ff; *The Thornton Romances*, ed. J. O. Halliwell (Camden Soc., 30, 1844), pp. 87, 256.

[39] Ulrich von Liechtenstein, *Service of Ladies*, ed. & trans. J. W. Thomas, (University of North Carolina Studies in the Germanic Languages and Literatures, 63, 1969), p. 207.

recruiting songs written for the crusade urged all knights to go to the Holy Land

> Qu'on i conquiert paradis et honor
> Et pris et los et l'amour de s'amie.[40]

Tournament ideology was here being applied to holy war just as it was applied to secular war, despite the incongruous, and in some cases blasphemous, effect. The crusade itself was sometimes referred to as a tournament between heaven and hell ordained by God; in the early thirteenth century *Ancrene Wisse* Christ appears as a tourneyer fighting on behalf of his beloved, 'love', and in *Piers Plowman* he appears as a jouster going to defeat the Devil in the jousts at Jerusalem.[41] There was clearly some difficulty in trying to clothe ecclesiastical teaching in the language and ideology of chivalric preoccupations when the two were so disparate. On the other hand, this dichotomy was only obvious to the church. To the knights who went on crusade there was no inconsistency apparent. According to Robert the Monk, the knights on the First Crusade ran at the quintain during their leisure moments, and Richard I and his household tourneyed against the French king's household at Messina on the Third Crusade.[42] Both Joinville in 1250 and Henry, earl of Derby in 1390-1 clearly expected to participate in hastiludes while they were on crusade, for both took tourneying equipment with them.[43]

By the early fourteenth century, however, the church began to come under pressure to allow tournaments. Knights might go on crusade for the wrong reasons, or even tourney while involved in the *negotium crucis* itself, but they still became crusaders and this was better, it was argued, than the otherwise serious risk of antagonizing the chivalry of Europe by punishing those who indulged in chivalry's favourite pastime. One of the most powerful

---

[40] *Les Chansons de Croisade*, ed. J. Bédier (Paris, 1909), p. 33; see also *Ibid.*, pp. 32-3, 104, 139.

[41] *Ancrene Wisse: parts six and seven*, ed. G. Shepherd (Thomas Nelson, 1959), p. 22; *The Vision of Piers Plowman*, ed. W. W. Skeat (EETS, 1950), p. 323. See also: *Les Chansons de Croisade*, ed. Bédier, p. 10; Huon de Mery, *Le Tornoiement de l'Antéchrist* (Rheims, 1851) and A. Langfors, 'Le Tournoiement d'Enfer', *Romania*, xliv (1915-7), pp. 511-58.

[42] Robert the Monk, *Historia Hierosolymitana*, quoted by Du Cange *Dissertations sur la Vie de saint Louys*, p. 25; Roger of Hoveden, iii, 93-5.

[43] *Mémoires de Jean, Sire de Joinville*, ed. F. Michel (Paris, 1859), p. 96; *Expeditions to Prussia and the Holy Land Made by Henry, Earl of Derby 1390-1 & 1392-3*, ed. L. Toulmin-Smith (Camden Soc., new series, lii, 1894), p. 113.

advocates for allowing tournaments was Pierre du Bois. Although he was writing at the instigation and under the patronage of Philippe le Bel, his views were of great importance because they set out the pragmatic reasons in favour of removing the prohibition on hastiludes. He argued[44] that any papal prohibitions would be ignored as they had been in the past, thereby teaching the knights of France to despise ecclesiastical sentences and causing them to incur excommunication. Once excommunicated, they were useless as tools of the church for this status debarred them from taking the Cross. Even if they did go on crusade, success would be withheld from the Christian armies because of the moral state of the excommunicated tourneyers within their ranks. In that case, it was better to overlook the minor sin of tourneying so as to avoid the greater evil of risking another failure against the pagans. In a revolutionary reversal of orthodox church policy, du Bois even suggested that instead of penalizing knights for tourneying the church should make participation in the sport a privilege granted only to those who took the Cross. In this way a powerful incentive would be given to the enlisting of future crusaders.

Eventually, in 1316, the Pope conceded defeat and issued the bull *Quia in futurorum*.[45] When he did this, John XXII naturally had to seek to justify his decision to reverse the policy of the church for the last two hundred years. He therefore claimed that, contrary to past belief, tournaments did not impede the crusade but their prohibition had actually caused some knights to refuse to take the Cross. Others had gone even further and had refused altogether to take the belt of knighthood so that the crusade was in danger of failing through a deficiency in trained soldiers.

The circumstances in which the bull was issued were intriguing. It must be significant that papal opposition to tourneying was officially withdrawn by John XXII, who was not only a Frenchman but also the first of the popes during the Babylonish Captivity to reside at Avignon. Even more significant, is the fact that the bull was one of the first issued by John XXII, dating from Lyons on September 16th, 1316 – only eleven days after his coronation. Furthermore, he declared in it that his opposition was withdrawn expressly at the request of the French princes and magnates. It

---

[44] C. V. Langlois, 'Un Mémoire Inedit de Pierre du Bois', *Revue Historique*, (1889), pp. 88-90.

[45] 'Extravagantes tum Viginti Joannis Vicesimisecundi', *Sextus Decretalium Liber a Bonifacio Octavo in Concilio Lugdenensis editus* (Venice, 1566), pp. 55-8. Also printed in *Corpus Juris Canonici*, ed. A. Friedberg (Leipzig, 1881), ii, col. 1215.

would seem ,therefore, that this new Pope was under exceptional secular French pressure, particularly as a crusade organized by France was in the offing. No doubt he found it politic to give way on hastiludes in order to win support for his own position and crusading policies.

Although official church opposition to tournaments was in this way removed, making it more acceptable for monarchs and those in secular authority to tourney themselves, it was still possible for it to be provoked again. In 1368, for example, a papal chaplain was sent to Lionel, duke of Clarence

> to warn him, under pain of excommunication, not to hold the tournament (in itself reprobated by the sacred canons) which he and many other nobles are said to have agreed and sworn to carry on as a hostile and deadly combat. Faculty is granted for relaxation of any oaths and obligations that have been made and taken.[46]

It would be fascinating to know what had caused the prince and his companions to vow to hold a hastilude *à outrance*. It is possible that it was the imminent renewal of war against France, since papal intervention and the nature of the combat suggest that it was something on an international scale. What is also interesting about the prohibition is that the pope was aware of the necessity of absolving the knights from their chivalric vows to undertake the combat if the encounter was to be effectively prevented.

By the fourteenth century, the church had come to terms with the fact that she could not eradicate a sport which was so deeply embedded in knightly ideology. Despite a consistent hard line policy of repression and prohibition from the early days of tournaments, the sport had grown more, not less, popular. In England, ecclesiastical authorities had to oppose not only the chivalry and nobility of the realm but also the king himself since Richard I had deliberately flouted church teachings by licensing the sport, thus setting the seal of royal approval on them. Edward I, like Richard, personally fought in hastiludes despite the fact that the papacy condemned this as *indecens*: Gregory X used all the arguments calculated to appeal to a monarch of the standing of the king of England: it was

---

[46] *Calendar of Entries in the Papal Registers Relating to Great Britain and Ireland*, ed. W. H. Bliss & J. A. Twemlow (London, 1902), iv, 287-8.

contra gravitatem, quam ut Rex et Princeps inclitus te convenit
exhibere, personam tuam periculose ac indecenter exponas; attende
quod alii Reges se ludis huismodi non immiscent

but to no avail.[47] When kings set their subjects such a bad example
by ignoring ecclesiastical prohibitions there was little that the
papacy could do except accept the situation with as good grace as
possible. By 1316 John XXII was merely bowing to the inevitable
by withdrawing his sanctions against the sport. The withdrawal was
not without effect, however; despite the fact that it simply accepted
the *status quo*, John XXII's bull removed the last impediments that
existed to unrestrained indulgence in the sport. Providing that his
sovereign had licensed the game, an Englishman could now tourney
freely without moral scruple. The removal of these restrictions
seems to have had an effect on the conduct of the sport, for there
was an appreciable increase in the pageantry attendant on hastiludes
at this period. Chronicle notices similarly proliferate both in
number and in the detail with which they record encounters. It
would therefore seem that perhaps there had been a lingering sense
of reticence about the morality of tourneying which the church's
withdrawal finally relieved, allowing a new effloresence of tourneying pageantry.

---

[47] *Foedera*, ii, 29. See also *Ibid.*, p. 30.

CHAPTER FIVE

The Tournament as Spectacle

Historians of the so called 'decline of chivalry' point to the fifteenth century as the period when hastiludes reveal an 'unmistakeable taint of decadence' having degenerated from a robust unselfconsciousness into the 'mere externals of lavish spectacle and empty ritual.'[1] In fact, allegory and a sense of theatre had had an important part in hastiludes *à plaisance* since at least the thirteenth century. Pageant and banquet, for example, featured as prominently in this early period as they did in the fifteenth century courtly joust.

In this chapter I shall examine first of all the manifestations of pageantry from the twelfth century to the end of the fourteenth and, more importantly, the inspirations which lay behind this development of the ceremonial aspect of the sport. Then I shall turn to a second characteristic of hastiludes *à plaisance* which increasingly elaborate pageantry brought into prominence: the progression of women from a purely passive inspirational role to a much more active participation in attendant ritual.

One of the most fruitful sources of inspiration for hastiludes was chivalric romance literature, though it was their stories, settings and ideology rather than the bloodiness of their combats that was imitated. All the great heroes of romance were tourneyers from Lancelot, the best knight of the secular world, to Galahad, the perfect knight of God. After the seminal work of Chrétien de Troyes even the *chansons de geste*, which had hitherto ignored the sport, began to include tourneying skills among their heroes' accomplishments. Gui de Nanteuil, for example, was described as a good knight who willingly attended tournaments, even though he

---

[1] Ferguson, *The Indian Summer of English Chivalry*, p. 14; J. Barnie, *War in Medieval Society* (London, 1970), p. 57; Similar views are expressed throughout R. Kilgour, *The Decline of Chivalry* (Cambridge, Mass., 1937).

possessed many rich lands and so was not obliged to frequent them to earn a living as many poor bachelors had to do.[2] His prowess was more commendable than theirs because it was disinterested. The medieval passion for tourneying was also anachronistically attributed to classical heroes such as the emperor Aurelius and Alexander the Great who were credited with being the most renowned jousters of their day.[3] Likewise, the protagonists of the semi-historical romances, which were based on the lives of real knights such as Fulk FitzWarin and the Chatelain de Couci, were skillful tourneyers.[4] The cult for laudatory biographies of contemporaries knights such as William Marshal, and later, Marshal Boucicaut and Richard Beauchamp, naturally led the biographers to stress the pre-eminence of their heroes in the lists.[5]

If tourneying occupied such an important place in chivalric literature it is not surprising that knights sought to imitate their literary heroes and thereby associate themselves with some of the glamour and prestige attached to knights of romance. Many knights who were tourneyers owned copies of the romances and were, therefore, familiar with their contents. Thomas, duke of Gloucester owned eighty-three books on his death in 1397, including romances of Hector of Troy, Bevis of Hampton, Lancelot, Tancred, Alexander, Fulk FitzWarin and Godfrey de Bouillon, as well as the life of William Marshal and innumerable histories, chronicles and books of pseudo-Arthurian prophecy.[6] Similarly, Simon Burley, who was executed in 1387, left twenty-one books, over half of which were romances and chivalric histories.[7] Even a little known knight of relatively small income like Sir Fulk Penbridge (d.1325) left two books of romances to his eldest son along with other items of value in his will.[8] While the possession of expensive books was not within every man's means, many must have heard the *chansons de geste* and the romances recited or sung by minstrels in royal and seigneurial households. In the last decades of the twelfth century, for example,

---

[2] 'Gui de Nanteuil', *APF*, vi, ll. 162-3.
[3] Robert of Gloucester, *Metrical Chronicle*, ed. W. A. Wright (R.S., 1887), i, ll. 2893-901; *Perceforest*, passim.
[4] *The Legend of Fulk FitzWarin*, ed. J. Stevenson in Ralph de Coggeshalle *Chronicon Anglicanum* (R.S., 1875); *Le Roman du Castelain de Couci*.
[5] *HGM*; *Livre de Faits … du Boucicaut*; *Pageant of the Birth, Life and Death of Richard Beauchamp*, ed. Viscount Dillon & W. H. St John Hope (London, 1914).
[6] Viscount Dillon & W. H. St John Hope, 'Inventory of the Goods and Chattels belonging to Thomas, duke of Gloucester', *Archaeological Journal*, liv (1897), pp. 300ff.
[7] PRO E154/1 no. 19 m2.
[8] BL MS Stowe Charter 622.

Arnold of Ardres employed several *jongleurs* and ancient knights, each of whom specialized in a particular field of story telling, including tales of the Holy Land, Arthurian romances and Carolingian *chansons de geste*.[9] The stories and ideology of the romances would have been familiar to all knights, whatever their economic standing, from royal princes down to the humblest household knights, and their influence is perhaps the most striking aspect of tournament pageantry.

This influence can be seen in many ways. One of the most popular literary devices, for instance, was the wearing of the arms of another knight or fighting completely incognito. This was probably the inspiration for the occasions on which real knights also put aside their own personal arms for the day. The advantage in doing this was that if the disguised knight won the prize it had to be by virtue of his prowess rather than his rank or reputation. This probably explains why Theobald de Verdun, Thomas de Vere and John Mowbray, who were all high born and wealthy men, chose to fight as simple knights at the Dunstable tournament of 1309, and why Edward III also fought as a simple knight bachelor at the Dunstable tournament of 1342.[10] Edward III seems to have particularly enjoyed this method of proving himself since on several occasions he attended hastiludes wearing the arms of other knights. In 1348 he appeared at the Lichfield jousts in the arms of Sir Thomas de Bradstone and at the Canterbury hastilude in the arms of Sir Stephen Cosington;[11] some years earlier he had fought in the arms of 'Lionel', presumably his son, at the Dunstable tournament.[12] On both of the latter occasions the same suits decorated with the arms of the chosen knight were worn by several other knights as well as the king himself, suggesting that the arms were adopted by a team of jousters or tourneyers as their common device. This seems to be the explanation for the production of thirteen shields of the arms of Sir Robert Ufford and Sir William Montague for the hastiludes at Langley in celebration of the relevation of the Queen in 1341, the chosen knights probably leading the team of *tenants*.[13]

By wearing the arms of chosen knights the king and his fellow tourneyers not only satisfied their desire to win admiration when they revealed their true identity but also honoured the individual

[9] *Chron.Ghisn.*, p. 127.
[10] A. Tomkinson, 'Retinues at the Tournament at Dunstable 1309', *Eng.Hist.Rev.*, lxxiv (1959), p. 80; Adam Murimuth, pp. 123-4.
[11] N. H. Nicolas, 'Observations', pp. 40, 42; PRO E372/207 m50.
[12] PRO E101/389/14 m3; PRO E361/2 m12.
[13] PRO E101/390/2 m5.

whose arms they borrowed. It was therefore highly significant that when, in the poem *The Vision of Piers Plowman*, Jesus jousted against the devil in Jerusalem he did so not in his own arms but in those of Piers, thus symbolizing the Son of God's assumption of human form and his identification with human needs.[14] On a more pragmatic level, some tourneyers on the Dunstable Tournament Roll of 1309 seem to have temporarily (possibly only for the purposes of the actual tournament) adopted a difference based on the arms of their company leaders; thus, Sir Thomas Ferrers quartered the Bohun arms on his own and Sir Thomas le Blund bore a version of the Beauchamp arms, thereby publicly declaring their allegiance.[15]

Just as tourneyers imitated the romances in adopting the arms of another knight for a tournament so they imitated the popular literary device of appearing each day at a three day tournament in different coloured armour. Gawain, Arthur, Lancelot, Cliges and Ipomedon all changed the colour of their armour each day of the sport[16] to prove that it was their personal strength of arms and not their reputation that won them the prize. In the same way as they rejected wearing their personal arms because identification might lead some to suppose that they had an unfair advantage of rank or reputation, they rejected wearing the same arms throughout a tournament so that they could wipe the slate clean and win glory anew under a different identity. The ultimate revelation that the victors of each day were one and the same man increased his prestige more than simply appearing in his true identity throughout would have done. The most outstanding example of an English knight making play with this literary format for a tournament is the series of jousts organized by Richard Beauchamp, earl of Warwick at Guines in the Calais marches in 1414. Although everyone concerned was well aware of his true identity, he issued letters of challenge to the French under three separate *personae*, the Green Knight with the black quarter, the 'Chevaler Vert' and the 'Chivaler attendant'. The first two challenges were taken up in the same spirit by Frenchmen calling themselves the 'Chevaler Rouge' and 'Chivaler Blanke', and the third by Sir Colard Fynes. On each day of the jousts Beauchamp wore the arms of one branch of his ancestors. The first day he wore the Tony arms, on the second the Maudit arms

[14] *The Vision of Piers Plowman*, ll. 22-8.
[15] Tomkinson, *Op. Cit.*, pp. 73-4; *CTG*, iv, 65 nos 27, 45.
[16] For a full discussion of the literary three day tournament see J. Weston, *The Three Days Tournament* (London, 1902).

and on the third the arms of his semi-legendary ancestor, Guy of Warwick, quartered with those of Beauchamp; the arms of Tony and Maudit were displayed on his horse's trappers so that there was no mistaking that Beauchamp himself had fought each of the challenges. Although the incognito applied only to the letters of challenge, the changing of arms was reminiscent of romance stories and had the added advantage in this case of glorifying Beauchamp's noble ancestry.[17]

The scenarios and stories of chivalric literature were also imitated by real knights in their efforts to bring some of the excitement and panoply of ideal chivalry into reality. The continent furnishes numerous examples of this. In 1278, for example, the lords Bazentin and Longueval held an Arthurian inspired festival at Le Hem. Anticipating the elaborate *pas d'armes* of the fifteenth century, the jousting played only a part, though a very important part, of the proceedings. A sister of Longueval presided over the whole affair as Queen Guinevere, and the *tenants* were all members of her court. Robert, count of Artois played the part of the *Chevalier au Lyon*, complete with lion, and had his own adventures rescuing some of the queen's damsels and sending their captors to submit to the queen. Comic relief was provided by a knight taking the part of Sir Kay who lived up to his romance reputation for rudeness and unchivalrous behaviour and, to emphasise the literary influences which had guided the celebrations, the festival was written up by a herald or minstrel called Sarrazin as a poem entitled *Le Roman du Hem*.[18]

Arthurian romances were an especially fruitful source of inspiration for tournament scenarios, but role playing of the type which was practised at Le Hem was most commonly associated with one particular chivalric gathering, the Round Table. The Table itself was a direct borrowing from Arthurian romance and it was natural that hastiludes fought under its auspices should have a peculiarly Arthurian flavour. There was certainly a strong element of role playing with the names, arms and even characters of the Round Table knights being adopted by their medieval copyists. The knights at the earliest Round Table on record, which was held in Cyprus in 1223, 'contrefirent les aventures de Bretaigne et de la Table Ronde, et moult manieres de jeus'.[19] Similarly, at the coronation of Henry of

---

[17] *The Pageant of . . . Richard Beauchamp*, pp. 52-61.
[18] Sarrazin, 'Roman du Hem'; For further continental examples of Arthurian inspired festivals see Harvey, *Moriz von Craûn*, p. 206; P. S. Booth, *Tannhauser and the Mountain of Venus* (New York, 1916), pp. 9-10.
[19] Philippe de Novare, *Mémoires 1218-43*, ed. C. Kohler (Paris, 1903), p. 7.

Cyprus as king of Jerusalem in Acre in 1286, the celebrating knights

> contrefirent la table reonde et la raine de Femenie c'est asaver
> chevaliers vestus come dames et josteent ensemble; puis firent
> nounains quy estoient ave moines et bendoient les uns as autres; et
> contrefirent Lanselot et Tristan et Pilamedes et mout d'autres jeus
> biaus et delitables et plaissans[20]

The knights here were playing the parts of the most celebrated
Arthurian heroes and enacting their adventures; the Queen of
Femenie was queen of the Amazons, hence the knights jousting
together dressed as women.

Another early example of Arthurian role playing is the tourneying
tour undertaken by Ulrich von Liechtenstein in 1240. He presented
himself as king Arthur returned from Paradise to reestablish the
Round Table and any knights who broke three lances against him in
the jousts could be admitted to a Round Table society, providing
that they too assumed Arthurian names. By the time he had
gathered enough knights to actually hold a Round Table at
Katzelsdorf, near Neustadt, he was accompanied by a Lancelot,
Gawain, Yvain, Erec, Tristan, Parsival, Ither and Segremors, who
held the field with him against all comers.[21] Similar Round Table
societies formed for the purposes of jousting festivals were popular
in the Low Countries in the thirteenth and fourteenth centuries.[22]

In England, role playing of Arthurian characters is only specifically recorded on two occasions, although almost every chronicle
reference to Round Tables suggests that they were affairs of
exceptional expense and pageantry. In 1328 Sir Geoffrey Mortimer,
the third son of Roger, earl of March, held a Round Table in Wales
which was open to all comers: the young Mortimer personated the
'Kynge of Folye' and 'countrefede ye maner & doyng of Kyng
Arthurez table; but openly he failede ...'[23] It is probably to this
same year that an undated set of royal accounts belongs, recording
the expenses of carrying a castle made of canvas from Wigmore to
Woodstock, and of purchasing and carrying four dozen lances from

---

[20] *Les Gestes des Chiprois*, ed. G. Raynaud (Société de l'Orient Latin, v, 1887),
p. 220.
[21] Ulrich von Liechtenstein, *Service of Ladies*, p. 20.
[22] M. Lucien de Rosny, *L'Épervier d'Or* (Valenciennes, 1839), pp. 6-8; R. Withington,
English Pageantry (Cambridge Mass., 1918), i, 88; J. Vale, *Edward III and
Chivalry* (Woodbridge, 1983), pp. 25-41.
[23] *The Brut*, i, 262.

Hereford to London and Bedford.[24] Since the Mortimers not only had family connections with Wigmore, Woodstock and Hereford but also held Round Tables in 1328 at Wigmore and Bedford in celebration of Roger Mortimer's elevation to the earldom of March,[25] it seems most likely that the account refers to tournament scenery and equipment which was being carried from one Round Table to another. Castles were a popular piece of scenery since they could be attacked and defended, they could house captured damsels who had to be rescued by jousting in the lists, as at Le Hem, or they could serve as the station at the end of the lists from which the jouster would emerge. It is even possible that the canvas castle was the sort of Round Table house or tent often referred to in romances, in which the feasting after the hastiludes and other games took place. Although this canvas castle, complete with poles and pegs ready for assembly, is the only reference to tournament scenery of any kind in England, a passage in the royal household accounts of 1344 alluding to heather and sand being strewn on the bridges of Windsor Castle 'ne frangerentur cum magno cariagio tabule rotunde'[26] could be construed as meaning a great cart bearing a Round Table rather than the heavy traffic consequent upon holding the festival.

There are no such financial accounts to confirm a Round Table of uncertain date held by Edward I. According to the Dutch historian and writer of romances, Lodewijk van Velthem, this Round Table was held in 1284 on the occasion of Edward's marriage to the daughter of the king of Spain.[27] In fact, Edward married Eleanor of Castile in Spain in 1254, and his second marriage, to Margaret of France, took place in 1299. No other source suggests that a Round Table was held in connection with either marriage, though one was held at Nefyn to celebrate the conquest of Wales in 1284, Velthem's putative date. This may be significant in view of the fact that Velthem's account of Edward I's Welsh campaigns contains a core of truth around which fantastic adventures, culled from romances, have been embroidered.[28] Velthem's veracity must be regarded as suspect but cannot be totally dismissed because Edward was a great

---

[24] PRO E101/382/17.
[25] Robert of Avesbury, p. 284; Henry Knighton, i, 449.
[26] W. H. St John Hope, *Windsor Castle: an architectural history* (London, 1913), pt. i, 123 n. 30.
[27] R. S. Loomis, 'Edward I: Arthurian Enthusiast', pp. 118-119.
[28] G. Huet, 'Les Traditions Arturiennes chez le Chroniquer Louis de Velthem', *Moyen Age*, xxxvi (1913), pp. 173-97; T. M. Chotzen, 'Welsh History in the Continuation of the Spiegal Historiael', *Bulletin of the Board of Celtic Studies*, vii (1933), pp. 42-54.

patron of chivalry, and of Arthuriana in particular. Round Tables were held many times in his reign: at Kenilworth and Warwick in 1279, Warwick in 1281, Nefyn in 1284 and Falkirk in 1302.[29] At least two of these, Nefyn and Falkirk, were personally arranged by Edward himself.

The interest in Velthem's account lies in the fact that, as at Le Hem, the pageantry and role playing were carried beyond the tournament field. The whole affair is referred to as a play:

> According to custom a play (*spel*) of king Arthur was enacted ... the best were chosen and named after the knights of old who were called those of the Round Table.[30]

The knights playing Arthurian roles acted as the team of *tenants* and defeated the *venants* in a great tournament. Just as at Le Hem, the knight playing Sir Kay afforded comic relief, being set upon by twenty young men who cut his saddle girths in the tournament so that he fell off his horse.

The parallels with the Le Hem tournament are obvious although, according to Velthem, a political message lay behind the masquerade. After the tournament Edward I held a banquet, making the Round Table knights sit with him: between each course an esquire rode into the hall in haste demanding aid against various troubled parts of the realm and taunting the courtiers for cowardice. Those playing Arthurian roles each swore to undertake a campaign against one of the rebellious lands: the king then revealed that these challenges were also part of the play, but he insisted on holding them to the promises which they had made in their fictitious characters, and the festival ended with preparations for a real campaign. The two Round Tables which Edward is known to have sponsored, Nefyn and Falkirk, were both similarly associated with military campaigns, but unlike Velthem's Round Table, they were held not at the beginning but at the conclusion of successful wars.

Another interesting feature of the Velthem account is that the third esquire who rode into the hall to challenge the knights to undertake the king's wars was masked and dressed to appear as the Loathly Damsel, a figure who first appears in Chrétien de Troyes *Perceval*. 'She' had long coarse braids of hair, buck teeth, a nose a

---

[29] *Ann.Mon.*, iii, 281; iv, 281, 445; Walter of Hemingburgh, *Chronicon*, ed. H. C. Hamilton (London, 1849), ii, 8; *Ann.Lond.*, p. 104; *Vita Edwardi Secundi*, ed. N. Denholm-Young (Nelson, 1957), p. 6.
[30] Loomis, 'Edward I: Arthurian enthusiast', p. 118.

foot long and rode on an ass, so that she was a distinctive and easily recognizable figure from romance. Damsels delivering challenges from knights were a common motif in romance literature, but it was very rare that they were in fact men mascarading as damsels; it was not unknown, however, for it was two knights dressed as damsels that Sir Degrevant sent to deliver his challenge in one of the Thornton romances.[31] Similarly, but firmly in the realms of reality, it was a knight who was issued with red robes in 1378-9 so that, dressed as a damsel, he could ride before the young Richard II and deliver to him a letter containing a jousting challenge. Just as in Velthem's account, and in the romances, the challenge was delivered during the course of a banquet in the great hall of Windsor Castle. On this particular occasion the king himself and the three knights who were to perform the challenge were all clad in red harness and garments decorated with golden suns, which suggests that further pageantry was in store.[32]

Windsor Castle, which had strong Arthurian associations, was also the scene of a great Round Table in 1344. The importance of this particular event was not so much the pageantry surrounding the proceedings, but rather the novel attempt to create something permanent out of the transitory celebrations. At the conclusion of the hastiludes and banquets, the knights who had participated gathered together in the royal chapel at Windsor. There they witnessed Edward III swearing a corporal oath upon holy relics that

> ipse ad certum tempus ad hoc limitatum, dummodo sibi facultas arrideat, mensam rotundam inciperet, eodem modo et statu quo eam dimisit dominus Arthurus quondam rex Angliae, scilicet ad numerum trecentarum militem, et eam foveret et manuteneret proviribus numerum semper inaugendo.[33]

Afterwards, the knights, including six earls, all swore the same oath before the gathering dispersed. This oath was the only religious colouring given to any of the proceedings, for this nascent order of the Round Table was a purely secular organization. Indeed, one chronicle account omits even this short religious ceremony, and places Edward's oath at the banquet celebrating the end of the hastiludes: it was here too that he received the oaths of three

---

[31] *The Thornton Romances*, p. 226, ll. 1171-84.
[32] PRO E101/400/4 m3. Though he wore the same costume as the *tenants* this does not mean that the twelve year old king jousted; he was simply the patron of the event.
[33] Adam Murimuth, p. 231.

hundred knights chosen to receive membership of the order 'sub certa forma ad dictam rotundam tabulam pertinente'.[34] The usual oath of Round Table knights in the romance was to protect damsels, widows, orphans and all those lacking aid in just quarrels, and this was probably what Edward III's knights swore what to do.

Edward also announced his intention to hold a Round Table at Pentecost, the traditional season in Arthurian romances for holding festivals and beginning adventures, and to build a most noble house in which the Round Table could be held. His plans were put into effect immediately, and work began at Windsor castle building a Round Table which was circular in shape, with a two hundred foot diameter, and had forty thousand tiles covering its walls.[35] A total of nearly £510 was spent on the materials and wages of the masons, carpenters and other workmen employed on the building works before they were abandoned. A further £26 13s 4d was finally paid to the Prior of Merton in 1356, in full satisfaction for fifty-two oaks taken from the prior's wood near Reading for the Round Table.[36] Whether the wood was used up in the building works, or whether it was intended for an actual round table at which the feasting could be held, is not clear, though the number of oaks taken suggests the former explanation.

While an Arthurian inspiration obviously lay behind the attempt to found a permanent Round Table, the building of the Round Table house was in direct imitation of the *franc palais* from the romance of *Perceforest*. This magical palace was found to have letters inscribed over the doorway which encapsulated the spirit not only of the *franc palais* but also of the Edwardian Round Table.

> Or sachez tous que desormais
> Est cy lentree au franc palais
> Ou les preux acquerront honneu[r]
> Et tous les faillans deshonneur.[37]

It should be noted in this context that Edward's intentions in founding the Round Table were, according to Jean le Bel, 'pour plus essauchier l'onnour de ses chevaliers qui si bien l'avoient servi qu'il les tenoit pour proeux.'[38]

---

[34] *Ibid.*, pp. 155-6.
[35] *Chronicon a Monacho Sancti Albani*, p. 17; Walsingham, i, 263; St John Hope, *Windsor Castle*, pt. i, 123 n. 31, 124, 113-8.
[36] *Ibid.*, p. 118; *Issues of the Exchequer*, p. 164.
[37] *Perceforest*, ii, 122r.
[38] Jean le Bel, *Chronique*, ed. Viard & Déprez, ii, 26.

The construction of the Round Table house at Windsor was almost exactly the same as that of the *franc palais*. The Windsor house was circular and two hundred feet in diameter: similarly, it was said of the *franc palais* that

> au premier estage il estoit dune tour ro[n]de gra[n]de a merveilles car le palais avoit plus de deux cens pied de long p[ar]my le travers.[39]

Within the palace there was a vast table which could seat three hundred knights – the same number as were included in Edward's version – and above each place, on the wall, there was a nail. Another magic verse, this time written on the table, declared that noone could sit at the table unless his shield hung on the nail, and these chosen ones were to be called the 'chevaliers du franc palais'. A great tournament was held to discover which knights were worthy to sit at the table; likewise, hastiludes preceded the foundation of Edward III's Round Table at Windsor.[40]

How far Edward got in organizing his nascent order and the refinements of the Round Table house is not known for, after the first enthusiasm, building work gradually ceased and the house was never completed because the money was urgently needed elsewhere.[41] It was evident that Edward's plans had been too ambitious, but despite their ultimate practical failure, they carried immense prestige, particularly in chivalric circles.

Edward III's order of the Round Table represented one of the first attempts to found a military order of secular knights. Although it inspired a great many other orders, none of them were so firmly based on literary precedent nor so secular in tone. Although the knights retained their identity and did not attempt to play the part of Arthurian heroes as they did in hastiludes, the romance overtones of the whole affair were obvious to all. Even the choice of Windsor castle, Edward III's birthplace and favourite place of residence, was a significant one since it had reputedly been built by king Arthur and been the site for the foundation of the original Round Table.[42]

Edward III's plans for founding the order of the Round Table have sometimes been confused with the foundation of the order of the Garter.[43] In fact, the Garter seems to have been founded in

---

[39] *Perceforest*, ii, 120r.
[40] *Ibid.*, 120v, 121r, 121v; Adam Murimuth, pp. 155-6.
[41] *Chronicon a Monacho Sancti Albani*, p. 17.
[42] *Ibid.*
[43] Jean le Bel, ii, 26.

connection with the Crécy campaign and the division of its members into two groups according to their seating position in St George's chapel, one headed by Edward III, the other by the Black Prince, suggests that two potential tourneying teams were in the sovereign's mind when he founded his order.[44] It is even possible that the division originated in a hastilude since there seems to be no guiding principle in the choice of membership in each group. What is certain is that foreign knights regarded Garter knights as prime targets for jousting challenges. Membership of the order was seen as proof of military skill and, as it suggested that they were the elite of English chivalry, they had to bear the burden of representing England in hastiludes abroad.[45]

The 'matter of Britain' continued to be a fertile source of inspiration for the setting and conduct of hastiludes of all kinds from the thirteenth century onwards, but other influences were also at work. The chivalric response to ecclesiastical condemnation and prohibition of tournaments, for instance, was to use hastiludes as a form of anti-clerical satire. As early as 1227 Ulrich von Liechtenstein had refused to joust against a knight dressed as a monk, wearing a cassock over his armour and a tonsured wig on his helm, on the grounds that chivalric sport was not a suitable employment for a man of the cloth. When he finally acceded to the request of the other knights present and did perform a joust against the 'monk' Ulrich took especial care to unhorse him for his disrespect for the clergy – a curiously ambivalent attitude for a knight who was himself dressed as the Lady Venus.[46] In England, where anti-clerical feeling was traditionally strong, there were several occasions on which the tourneyers assumed clerical roles. In 1288 the esquires who held a *behourd* at Boston Fair divided themselves into two teams, one wearing monastic and the other canonical habits. In 1362 jousts planned for Cheapside at which the *tenants* were to take the roles of the seven deadly sins, which the church had taught were all committed by tourneying, were hindered by the divine intervention of several days of pouring rain.[47]

More immediate causes probably underlay two other hastiludes in which knights took the roles of churchmen. In 1343 Robert Morley held a famous tournament against all comers, which was still

---

[44] See Juliet Vale, *Edward III and Chivalry*, pp. 76-91.
[45] BL MS Additional 21370 fos 1r, 1v, 2v.
[46] Ulrich von Liechtenstein, pp. 124, 128.
[47] Walter of Guisborough, pp. 224-5; John of Reading, p. 151.

remembered over forty years later by a deponent in the Lovell v. Morley case in the Court of Chivalry, in which he played the pope and the other *tenants* played twelve cardinals.[48] Similarly, in 1394 twelve English nobles dressed in the robes of an abbot and his convent to hold the field against all comers.[49] Both these jousts were held just after the English had quarrelled with the pope over papal provisions to English benefices. Parliament in 1343 had petitioned against this practice and in 1393 had enacted a stiffer statute of Praemunire; the adoption of clerical roles was therefore an indication of lay feeling on the subject.

Irreverence, rather than anti-clericalism, may have prompted Enguerrand de Balliol, a knight from northern England who participated in the jousts at Le Hem, to appear as a demon ('an guise d'un malfe'), even though the general theme of the festival was Arthurian.[50] Similarly, Geoffrey Mortimer's Round Table at which he assumed the role of the 'Kynge of Folye' may have been intended as a joke, if he intended to be taken as jester. More seriously, he could have been personating the stock romance figure of the knight driven mad by his mistress' indifference or cruelty.[51]

Often, however, the adoption of roles could be intended as a compliment to the person imitated. This was the interpretation put upon Edward III's wearing the arms of Stephen de Cosington and Thomas de Bradstone in hastiludes in 1348.[52] In the same way, when Edward III, four of his sons and nineteen noblemen dressed up as the Lord Mayor and aldermen of London in the hastiludes to celebrate the marriage of John of Gaunt and Blanche of Lancaster in 1359, the gesture was taken as a compliment to the city of London which had hosted some of the festivities.[53]

Most of the disguises discussed so far have been practical imitations of real or literary persons, but in the later history of the tournament allegorical masquerades were much more popular. Ferguson hails the festivities of 1581 in which four courtiers calling themselves 'the four foster children of desire' challenged the defenders of 'the fortress of perfect beauty' to jousting combats as 'a new era, the age of a truly romantic chivalry' but, as Sidney Anglo comments, there

[48] PRO C47/6/1 m2; Adam Murimuth, pp. 124, 230.
[49] 'Annales Ricardi Secundi et Henrici Quarti' in Johannis de Trokelowe et Henrici de Blaneford, *Chronica et Annales*, ed. H. T. Riley (R.S., 1866), ii, 165.
[50] Sarrazin, p. 311.
[51] *The Brut*, i, 262; see also *Perceforest*, ii, 16v.
[52] N. H. Nicolas, 'Observations', pp. 40, 42; PRO E372/207 m50.
[53] John of Reading, pp. 131-3.

is evidence for a 'fourteenth century allegorical tradition of which practically all traces have disappeared'.[54] This evidence includes the seven deadly sins tournament but a more interesting and more complex festival took place in 1401 at Westminster Hall in honour of the Princess Blanche whose marriage had just been arranged. Thirteen jousting challenge letters in connection with this festival are extant.[55] Some of these take the form of letters of introduction by patrons such as Phoebus' letter on behalf of 'n[ost]re tresame enfaunt de n[ost]re Chambr[e] Ferombras de la Fontain' and Nature's letter on behalf of her nursling Ferant de Ferers. Others take the form of direct challenges by champions such as *Ardant desireux*, Lancelot de Libie and *Voulente dapprendre*. Historical figures including Cleopatra, Penelope and the Sultan of Babylon rub shoulders with such figments of the imagination as the knight *Nonsaichant* who was on a quest seeking a lady called Grace, and *Le Povoir Perdu*, a knight from the realm of Love, who was being detained a prisoner by a lady called *Plaisance* in the court of the Princess Blanche. Each challenger named a certain type of knight, in keeping with his assumed character, whom he wished to joust against. The Sultan of Babylon, for example, wanted to fight against the knight who most wished to reconquer Jerusalem, and Ferant de Ferers against the knight who had spoken of love to the largest number of ladies. Not only were most of the characters assumed by the jousters or their patrons firmly in the allegorical convention, but also the letters themselves were written in a style of courtly chivalry more familiar in a later age. This is best illustrated by a quotation from the beginning of the letter by 'Nature':

> Nature Nourice de vie executeur du tout puissant Roi des Roys a t[re]sexcellent Princesse Dame et Fille au t[re]spuissant Prince Roi Dalbion salut et tresparfite dileccion. Nous qui ordonnons a hom[m]e et best leurs vivres selon' le hault com[m]aundement du creato[u]r de tous creatures savons de certain que ainsi com[m]e n[ost]re subgiet Priapus qui est dieu de Jardins derbes et de Fleurs renouvelle et refressh' la face de la terre en la noble season' Davrill' qui estoit povre et sans vestur' par limportable yver qui est Roi de Froidur' Region' et trace par entre la terre si reprent sa co[n]jointur' et subtill' mantell' plain de dulceur et de Fleurs Droit ainsi toutz

---

[54] Ferguson, *Indian Summer of English Chivalry*, p. 16; S. Anglo, 'Financial and Heraldic Records of the English Tournament', *Journal of the Society of Archivists*, ii (1960-64), pp. 188-9.
[55] BL MS Cotton Nero Dii fos 260v-262r. Another text is in Bodleian MS Douce 271 fos 40v-47v.

estaz au monde vivans attendans honneur sont vestuz et nourriez de v[er]tueuse science par g[ra]cious gouv[er]naunce et contenement de v[ost]re excellent noble cuer Roial com[m]e de vray mireur et exemplair de tout honneur bontie et gentillesce a cest v[ost]re noble feste pour veoir la gouv[er]naunce de v[ost]re excellent estat et pour apprendre le fait desbatement darmes.[56]

The existence of these elaborate courtly letters suggests that similar letters probably lay behind earlier tournaments in which the participants assumed real or imaginary roles and that this type of hastilude was already deeply imbued in courtly allegory and masquerade. The fact that the letters were mainly written by patrons of the would-be jousters also suggests that they might have participated in the pageantry before the actual combats, leading their *alumni* to the lists. Such opportunities for dressing up in elaborate costumes as were offered by the letters were unlikely to have been missed.

In many cases this type of masquerading seems to have been confined simply to the procession of tourneyers to the field. This is particularly true of the wearing of masks which were, of course, impractical when actually fighting. One of the most notable examples of masking occurred in William Montague's Cheapside tournament of 1331, when the sixteen *tenants* paraded through the streets of London all splendidly clothed and masked in the likeness of Tartars.[57] This novel idea may have owed something to Rusticiano da Pisa's version of Marco Polo's *Travels* which appeared at the beginning of the fourteenth century, since Rusticiano was himself the author of romances and the *Travels* told tales of adventures which were calculated to appeal to a chivalric audience.

Masks were also worn by the knights and esquires processing through the London streets to Robert Morley's Stepney jousts in 1330; similarly, Edward III provided masks and costumes for the knights and ladies entering the cities where jousts were to be held in 1348 – two hundred and eighty-eight for Lichfield, forty-four for Canterbury and twelve for Bury, with an unspecified number for Reading.[58] It was also Edward III who bought nineteen masks made from the expensive material samite, together with seventy cheaper ones made from sheepskin, for hastiludes at Northampton in 1342, while in 1329 his purchases for jousts and tournaments had included

---

[56] BL MS Cotton Nero Dii, fo. 261r.
[57] *Ann.Paul.*, pp. 354-55.
[58] *Ibid.*, pp. 354-5; Nicolas, 'Observations', pp. 29, 30, 39; PRO E372/207 m50.

'false visages'.[59] Whether these masks simply hid the identity of the wearer or whether, like the false visages, they were intended to give him a new identity is not clear.

The popularity of masking owed much to the gradual relocation of the sport from large areas of open countryside to the narrower confines of town and city, since the necessity of travelling from lodgings to the tournament field encouraged the processional aspect of fourteenth century hastiludes. For some contemporary chroniclers, such as the author of the *Annales Paulini*, the procession was far more important than the actual tournament, since the former were discussed in great detail and the latter were dismissed in a few trite and conventional phrases. No patron could be unaware of the effect produced by companies of knights, esquires and ladies, often clad in the same livery for visual impressiveness, riding through the crowded streets. It was a supreme opportunity for the nobility to display their wealth so as to impress their social inferiors and even their peers. So common did the tourneyers' parade through the streets become that, according to Stow, the route from the Tower to one of the most popular tournament sites at Smithfield, acquired the name of Knightriders Street.[60]

The procession was usually held on the first day of the jousts and marked the opening of the festivities. Frequently, the patron of the hastilude would issue suits of the same colour or cloth to all who participated in this parade. It would be tedious to recall every occasion on which the royal household accounts record the issuing of robes for hastiludes, but even at relatively minor ones, which pass unnoticed by the chroniclers, colour themes in clothing appear. At the Northampton hastiludes of 1342, for example, nine tunics were pleated and buttoned and given green hoods for the king and his eight knights who were fighting there. A further twenty-five of the same design were made for twenty-two esquires of the king and queen and three minstrels who formed the king's company.[61] At Lichfield six years later, blue tunics with white hoods were issued to the king, eleven of his chamber knights and twenty other knights: twenty-eight ladies who were to accompany the procession were also given blue gowns with white hoods.[62]

Some of the more dramatic costumes did catch the eye of the chroniclers. Robert Morley and his twenty-five knights who held

[59] PRO E101/389/14 m2; PRO E361/3 m13r.
[60] Stow, *Survey of London*, ed. C. L. Kingsford (Oxford, 1908), i, 245.
[61] PRO E101/389/14 m1.
[62] Nicolas, 'Observations', pp. 26-9.

the field at Stepney in 1331 all rode through the city streets wearing tunics and mantles of green cloth lined with red sendal, the mantles being embroidered with golden arrows. They were accompanied by more than fifty esquires all clad in white tunics with a green right sleeve: gold arrows were also embroidered on their sleeves.[63] Similarly, in 1390, Richard II led twenty knights (or, according to the *Brut*, the twenty-four knights of the Garter) all bearing the same device of the white hart chained and gorged with a golden crown displayed on their clothes, armour, shields and horses' trappings from the Tower to Smithfield through the streets of 'la neufe troy' in the company of twenty ladies who also displayed the same device.[64]

The wearing of such liveries clearly improved the tourneyers' parade turning it into an eyecatching and colourful display with which to impress the assembled citizenry. The colours could be carried on to the lists as well so that the *tenants* were easily distinguishable and so as to emphasize the fact that they were brothers in arms for the occasion.[65] It is possible, moreover, that the wearing of suits of the same colours and design by the knights, squires, ladies and their servants in the tournament parade was a contributary factor in the growth of liveried retainers in the fourteenth century, since they had clearly shown the prestige attached to such displays of wealth and influence.

In this discussion of the processional aspect of hastiludes *à plaisance* in the fourteenth century, it has become increasingly evident that women were playing a much more active and important role in the associated pageantry. Like so much else connected with this type of ceremonial, the growing involvement can be largely attributed to the influence of romance literature. Since the mistress, the hostess and the damsel in distress were the motivating forces behind most romance adventures and sometimes even enjoyed a considerable active role in the story, it is not surprising that women should have become involved in the tournament pageantry of reality. The actual fighting still remained a man's preserve, but as settings grew more elaborate and pageantry more prominent, so the opportunity for women's involvement grew.

---

[63] *Ann.Paul.*, pp. 353-4.

[64] BL MS Lansdowne 285 fos 46v-47r; *The Brut*, ii, 343.

[65] See M. G. A. Vale, *War and Chivalry*, p. 84 for two knights who agree to wear the same livery and device in peace and war including tournaments as public proof of their brotherhood.

It is therefore no coincidence that women are first mentioned in connection with tournaments contemporaneously with the production of Chrétien de Troyes' seminal works. Until the late twelfth century there is no indication that women even watched hastiludes or attended the evening celebrations after the sport had ended. Indeed, spectators of either sex are rarely mentioned, but the festivities seem to have been strictly men-only affairs at which there was feasting, drinking and exchanging of chivalric news.[66]

The first mention of ladies being present at a real tournament occurs in the poem of William Marshal. Most of the tournaments he attended were in the traditional male dominated vein, but in about 1180, when he arrived for one outside the castle of Joigny, he found the Countess and her ladies already at the lists. At their request, he obliged them by entertaining them with a song until the action began.[67] Their presence, and the uncharacteristic courtly act of the Marshal, suggest that romance influence was already beginning to filter through, and that the courtly anecdote was not unexpected nor out of place in a chivalric biography. By the first half of the thirteenth century, the presence of women seems to have been taken for granted on the continent. In England, however, there was a considerable lapse of time before their presence at hastiludes was noted. The first instance does not occur until 1279 when Roger Mortimer held a Round Table at Kenilworth for a hundred knights and ladies.[68] The absence of evidence for England probably reflects the lack of chronicle interest in tournaments at the time, rather than any exclusion of a feminine audience. Even Matthew Paris, whose connections with the tourneyer Richard, earl of Gloucester had led him to take an almost unique interest in chivalric affairs, failed to record their presence. This may be due to the fact that he mainly concentrated on recording hastiludes *à outrance* at which a female audience would have been inappropriate. It seems highly unlikely that the chronicle silence for Edward I's reign reflects reality. Not only did Edward encourage pageantry and patronize Round Tables at which the presence of ladies was common, but also, as a king who had ladies present in viewing balconies at the siege of Stirling, in all probability he would have invited them to his hastiludes.

It is not until Edward III's reign that ladies are regularly mentioned as spectators. Since this was also the period when

---

[66] See Jocelin of Brakelond, pp. 55-6; *HGM*, ll. 3013ff, 4329ff.
[67] *Ibid.*, ll. 3452ff.
[68] *Scalacronica*, p. 109. I do not believe that the reference in *Ancrene Wisse*, pp. 22, 56-7 is historical; it is simply a literary device.

chroniclers began to take an interest in tournaments, this may be a vicious circle, their presence being noted more often simply because more hastiludes were recorded, but this cannot completely account for the change. The patronage of Queens Isabella and Philippa may have done something towards making their presence more respectable and more fashionable: it seems more likely that the growth of pageantry coupled with the increasing popularity of smaller hastiludes made spectating more interesting and more feasible. Ladies attended in large numbers, for so many of them were crushed into Queen Philippa's *berfrois*, the stand built for viewing jousts, at the Cheapside hastiludes of 1331 that the whole structure collapsed, severely injuring many of the occupants.[69] On three occasions Edward specifically ordered the presence of ladies in large numbers: in 1342 five hundred ladies of high lineage were summoned to attend the London *feste des joustes* held in honour of the Countess of Salisbury upon whom, according to Jean le Bel, he had amorous designs: two years later, for his Round Table he summoned

> par tous pays dames et damoiselles, chevaliers et esquiers, et que chascun, sans point d'excusation, y venist pour faire celle grand feste a Windesore.[70]

On this occasion, the ladies of noble birth from southern England and the wives of the London burghers were banqueted by the queen in the great hall of Windsor castle while the king feasted his knights, this separation of the sexes at the banquet being in full accord with the practices of the *franc palais* of *Perceforest*.[71] On the third occasion, Edward III held a great festival at Windsor in 1358 to celebrate the conclusion of peace with France and 'pour mielx festier et honnourer le roy Jehan', who was still his prisoner, Edward commanded the presence 'des plus belles et mielx habillees' ladies of England.[72]

The attendance of ladies was therefore considered to add lustre to hastiludes and enabled the prolongation of the festivities. For the combatants their lady spectators were an inspiration to perform greater feats of arms since, according to chivalric lore, a wise woman would bestow her love on the most 'preux'. The herald Maigniens summed up these ideas when he preached to the ladies at Chauvency:

[69] Geoffrey le Baker, p. 48; *Ann.Paul.*, pp. 354-5.
[70] Jean le Bel, ii, 2-4, 27.
[71] Adam Murimuth, p. 155; *Perceforest*, ii, 129r.
[72] Jean le Bel, ii, 240.

> Car d'amor ont le movement
> De hardement et proesce,
> De courtoisie et de largesce,
> Que hardemens et cortoisie
> Et bonne amors et nete vie
> Doivent avoir tuit chevalier
> Qui lor cors welent essaucier.[73]

Whilst it became a chivalric duty for knights in romances to have a mistress in whose name they undertook all manner of adventures, this attitude undoubtedly left its mark on real knights. Even that supreme pragmatist, the Chevalier de la Tour Landry, despite the fact that his offspring were all daughters, could demand of his wife

> Lady, why shall not the ladies and damsels love paramours? For in certain, me seemeth that in good love and true, may be but wealth and honour, and also the lover is better therefore, and more gay and Jolly; and also the more encouraged to exercise himself more oft in arms.[74]

Eglantine, in the *chanson de geste* of Gui de Nanteuil successfully put this theory into practice, surrounding herself with beautiful ladies to inspire her lover and his men to fight harder and rescue her from her captors, while according to his biographer, even William Marshal and his fellow tourneyers at Joigni were inspired to win the tournament by the bright eyes of the Countess and her ladies.[75]

The idea of love for a mistress motivating knights to commit great deeds of arms was paid at least lip-service in the descriptions and conduct of real tournaments. It also received a more formalized expression through the mouths of heralds. One of their roles at hastiludes, which was an extension of their duty of praising the skill and bravery of the jousters, was to urge the ladies to bestow their love on the knights who suffered the martyrdom of combat for their sakes and to reprove them for their harshness in compelling knights to risk life and limb in the sport. When two momentarily stunned knights were believed to have been killed in the jousts at Chauvency, a herald responded by crying to the ladies:

---

[73] *Le Tournoi de Chauvency*, ll. 954-9.
[74] *The Book of the Knight of La Tour Landry*, ed. G. S. Taylor (London, 1930), p. 139.
[75] 'Gui de Nanteuil', *APF*, vi, 62 esp. ll. 1965-8; *HGM*, ll. 3464-70, 3524-6, 3538-41.

> Or, esgardez a quel escil
> Dames, cis chevalier se metent,
> Terres et cors pour vos endetent,
> Et or sont en peril de mort!
> Si m'ait Diex, vos avez tort!
> Tout est par vos amors conquerre![76]

Similarly, the entry of the hero during a joust in the *Dis dou Chevalier a la Mance* was greeted by the heralds crying

> Ensi com lor mestiers apporte;
> 'Amours au cevalier qui porte
> La mance, bien le doit porter,
> Car il se seit biel deporter
> De lances froissier et brisier!
> Bien se doit la dame prisier
> U la pucielle u iestre quinte
> De qui tels bacelers s'acquinte!'[77]

Heralds were also responsible for producing the elaborate formal jousting challenges of the late fourteenth century which encapsulated the same ideas. Their letters declared that the challenges were made to win the love of the knights' mistresses, and often ended with a courteous prayer that the God of Love would grant the correspondent the grace of his lady.[78] There was, therefore, an acknowledgement of the inspirational role of women in tournament procedure, even if it was only a courtly formula without any solid foundation in reality.

Motivation by a mistress could be a two edged sword, however. Instead of making the knight more eager for combat in war and tournament it could make him abandon them altogether: Erec, in Chrétien de Troyes' romance of that name, was so absorbed in his new wife that he deserted the tournament field earning himself dishonour, and Aucassin was so overwhelmed by his love for Nicolette that he had no desire to become a knight or frequent tournaments.[79] Geoffroi de Charny commended temperate love as a great spur to chivalric deeds, which honoured both man and

---

[76] *Le Tournoi de Chauvency*, ll. 954-9.
[77] Baudouin de Condé, ii, 178.
[78] BL MS Additional 21357 fos 1r-5r; BL MS Additional 21370 fos 1r-14r.
[79] Chrétien de Troyes, *Arthurian Romances*, ed. & trans. W. W. Comfort (Dent, 1975), pp. 32ff; *Aucassin et Nicolette*, ed. M. Roques (Paris, 1925), p. 2.

woman, but he warned against loving too much because this could lead to an idle life and fear of risking one's life in adventures, thus bringing shame to both parties.[80] Practical concerns could also be of overriding importance. It was all very well for Lancelot to achieve worldly success in the tournament through the inspiration of his love for Queen Guinevere, even at the expense of failing in his quest for the Holy Grail, but Louis de la Tremouille refused to commit adultery with the married woman whom he loved since he knew that public shame would, in reality, exclude him from joust and tournament.[81]

Despite the glorification of it in romances, the church always took the dimmest view of adultery. For this reason, therefore, both preachers and clerical authors were particularly harsh on courtly love. Love's inspiration was characterized as lechery by disapproving clerics like Jacques de Vitry and Robert of Brunne.[82] Edward III's series of tournaments in 1348, after the victory of Crécy and the surrender of Calais, which, as we have seen, were marked by extraordinary pageantry,[83] provoked a storm of chronicle criticism. Geoffrey le Baker noticed that they were attended by 'plurima dominarum comitiva', but the Meaux chronicler, echoed by Henry Knighton, denounced these women who were rarely accompanied by their own husbands but rather by their partners in lust, and blamed the spreading plague on their immorality.[84] Even if some ladies did resort to tournaments for innocent motives or, as in Chrétien de Troyes' *Le Chevalier de la Charette*, hoping to find a husband there, the risks of having their intentions misconstrued were great. It was for this reason that the wife of the Chevalier de la Tour Landry disputed with her husband who had advocated courtly love: as the mother of three daughters she warned them that such love easily turns to mortal sin and adultery, distracts the lovers from God's service and loses unmarried ladies their marriages because their free and easy manners would be despised by any man with serious intentions.[85] La Tour Landry himself told a story which clearly illustrated this point. A certain pleasure loving lady who was accustomed to attend jousts without her husband and joined in the

---

[80] Geoffroi de Charny, *Livre de Chevalerie*, p. 484.
[81] J. Bouchet, *Le Panegyric du Chevalier sans Reproche* (Poitiers, 1527), fos xxiiiir-v.
[82] Jacques de Vitry, pp. 62-4; Robert of Brunne, pp. 145-6.
[83] Nicolas, 'Observations', pp. 26-30, 39-42.
[84] Geoffrey le Baker, p. 97; *Chronica Monasterii de Melsa*, iii, 69; Henry Knighton, ii, 56-7.
[85] La Tour Landry, pp. 139ff.

singing, feasting and dancing was compromised by being seen in a corner with a knight after the lights had accidentally been put out; although she was innocent of any misdemeanour, her brother-in-law reported the incident to her husband who never after trusted her. 'And so there was never peace between them, but ever glooming, louring and chiding, and all her household went to naught for this cause.'[86]

The problem with courtly love was that appearances were deceptive. This was recognized even in the romances. In the *High Book of the Grail*, when King Arthur behaved in a courtly manner to his hostess,

> The king could have been quite sure of having a lover if he had wanted, but there was a great difference between his appearance and his mind: he was raising the maiden's hopes with his behaviour, but his thoughts, wherever he might be, were always with Queen Guinevere.'[87]

The tournament, because it was an ideal place for the exaltation of courtly love, was of central importance in the romances and consequently had great influence on courtly etiquette in reality.

In practical terms, one of the most striking examples of the feminine inspiration behind the tournament was the wearing of ladies' tokens by the participants. Since the granting of a token to a champion was symbolic of the granting of a lady's favour, even this seemingly innocent practice was liable to misinterpretation. Jacques de Vitry in the early thirteenth century condemned the custom of wearing these 'insignia quasi pro vexillo' simply to please unchaste women,[88] thus suggesting, incidentally, that this romantic practice had appeared as early as the twelfth century and enjoyed a longer tradition than is usually believed. This is also substantiated by the *chanson de geste* of Gui de Nanteuil which dates from *c.*1180-1200: Gui's mistress, Eglantine, sent him a gonfanon with a lion painted on it, and enjoined him to bear it 'par amours' for her sake and make the lion drink the blood of their enemies.[89] Usually, however, the token was a more intimate and personal one, such as an item of clothing. This is well displayed in *Le Tornoiement de l'Antéchrist*, an early thirteenth century allegorical poem by a knight from Champagne, in which Antichrist bears Proserpina's chemise as his

---

[86] *Ibid.*, pp. 29-30.
[87] *The High Book of the Grail*, p. 185.
[88] Jacques de Vitry, p. 64.
[89] 'Gui de Nanteuil', *APF*, vi, ll. 1154-8.

ensign, the King of the Firmament bears two sleeves from the chemise of the Virgin Mary and Religion a sleeve from the chemise of Mary Magdalen.[90] Sleeves and veils were the most popular favours, and in *Perceforest* the ladies at one tournament became so enthusiastic that they tore off their veils, sleeves, chemises, hats, mantles and other clothing to give to their champions, so that by the end of the tournament they were all bareheaded and dishevelled, though they were able to laugh at this embarrassing predicament because they were all in the same boat.[91]

The idea of giving tokens was intimately connected with the whole idea of service to a mistress. Just as the knights at Le Hem obeyed the dictates of love by wearing their ladies' sleeves and veils fastened to their lances and helms in the jousts, so outside the lists the ideals of courtly love were put into practice. William Marmion was thus obliged to defend the golden helm which his lady sent him in the most dangerous places of Britain, and therefore carried out this service in the Scottish marches.[92] Similarly, when James Douglas surprised and slew the English garrison of Douglas castle in 1307, a letter was found on the body of Sir John Webtoun, the captain, which declared that when he had guarded the adventurous castle of Douglas 'That to kepe so perelous was' for one year in time of war 'as ane gude bachiller', then he could justifiably ask for the love and reward of love from his mistress.[93] Even the religious atmosphere of the journey to the Holy Land to fight against the enemies of God was corrupted by doctrines of courtly love. It was a common complaint of crusading enthusiasts that knights went on crusade, not for God's sake, but in their ladies' service and in the hope of temporal, feminine rewards rather than the heavenly rewards offered by the church.[94]

Courtly love, like the other chivalric conventions which grew up on the tournament field, was carried over into other spheres of life and, like them, it enjoyed particular influence in the field of war. The tournament and joust, however, remained the supreme expressions of those ideals since they were the nearest that most knights could ever hope to come to the glorious pageantry of romance. For the ladies too, there was a strong attraction in thus imitating the heroines of romance, not only by providing the inspiration for the

[90] Huon de Mery, pp. 16, 38, 47.
[91] *Perceforest*, i, 155v.
[92] Sarrazin, e.g. p. 280; *Scalacronica*, pp. 145-6.
[93] J. Barbour, *The Bruce*, i, 195.
[94] *Les Chansons de Croisade*, ed. Bédier, pp. 32-3, 104, 109.

whole affair but also by playing an increasingly active role in the running of hastiludes.

Even from the earliest period they had acted as prizegivers. The pike which was eventually awarded to William Marshal as the prize of the Pleurs tournament had been presented by 'une dame de pris' and, similarly, a certain lady donated a bear as a prize for the best tourneyer in the baronial tournament between Hounslow and Staines in 1216.[95] By the fourteenth century, the prizegiving had become a more elaborate and formal ceremony in which the ladies actually participated. It was the ladies and girls who were to present the prizes each evening to the best jouster in each party at the Smithfield jousts in October 1390, and when the ladies at the court of Savoy rewarded the Count with the customary gold rings and kisses, his knights complained because he had passed on the rings to those who had jousted best, but had kept the more valuable kisses for himself.[96] By this period, prizegiving by ladies had become *de rigeur*.

Whether or not the ladies were actually allowed to judge the hastiludes is not clear. Though they are often referred to as the judges and are frequently implied to have chosen the prizewinner themselves, there are indications that this was merely formalized courtly ritual, and that in fact they had no part in the actual judgement. Honoré Bonet, when denying the right of women to judge wagers by battle, justified this on the grounds that women were excluded by common law from the deeds of men, that they were inferior to men and could not judge men unless they had that authority specifically delegated to them, as in the case of a queen regent.[97] These arguments were equally applicable to the tournament, though one fifteenth century treatise on the subject limited the right of ladies to judge only in hastiludes involving lances. In all other hastiludes judgement was made by specifically appointed judges on the advice of ancient knights, esquires, *preudommes*, kings at arms and heralds.[98] Indeed, the very presence of these men with their technical experience and, in the case of heralds, their organizational abilities, indicates that they, rather than the lady spectators, would be the judges in such matters. The same men, ancient knights and heralds, were appealed to in all questions concerning arms, even

---

[95] *HGM*, ll. 3024ff; Matt.Paris, ii, 615.
[96] BL MS Lansdowne 285 fos 46v-47r; E. L. Cox, *The Green Count of Savoy* (Princeton, 1967), pp. 97-8.
[97] Honoré Bonet, *The Tree of Battles*, ed. G. W. Coopland (Liverpool, 1949), pp. 193-4.
[98] B. Prost, *Traités du Duel Judiciaire* (Paris, 1872), pp. 213-4.

in cases of disputed armorial bearings, since they were repositaries of customary procedure and knowledge.

If they were not allowed the ultimate decision in the prizegiving, the ladies gradually acquired an important role in tournament ceremonial. The festival at Le Hem is outstanding in this respect for not only did the ladies play a large part in the dramatic elements, some of them having to be rescued by the *Chevalier au Lyon* and others accompanying their knights to the lists, but also the whole festival was directed by a 'Queen Guinevere'.[99] The most usual active role of women in tournament pageantry was that of leading in the *tenants* to the field. This was a common literary device, for no knight errant could accomplish his adventures without an accompanying damsel, who was often his mistress, though sometimes merely the messenger who brought him to the place where the adventure was to be undertaken. In *Perceforest*, two damsels clad in white led each of the twelve *tenants* to the lists by the bridle,[100] and in practice this was repeated with great regularity throughout the fourteenth century. In William Montague's 1331 hastilude, each of the *tenants* led a lady in the procession by means of a silver chain and in 1386 each of the lords going to the Smithfield jousts led a lady by her horse's bridle through the streets of London.[101] In 1374, when Alice Perrers rode from the Tower of London to Smithfield as 'Lady of the Sun' (probably a somewhat impertinent reference to her connections with Edward III, whose personal device was a golden sun), she was accompanied by ladies each leading a knight by his horse's bridle. Again, in 1390, the October jousts were preceded by a procession in which the ladies led their knights to the lists by means of a golden chain.[102] On each occasion the ladies wore the same livery as their knights to emphasize their involvement in the festivities. The use of a chain rather than a bridle was a particularly effective way of stressing the allegorical chains which bound the lover to his mistress and her service.

In this way women gained an important part in the opening ceremonial of hastiludes. Their presence as spectators throughout the combats, which were often spread out over several days, also ensured that the celebrations at the end of each day's sport were increasingly prolonged and more elaborate. In the twelfth century tourneyers appear to have enjoyed purely masculine gatherings at the lodgings of the great lords at which chivalric news could be

---

[99] Sarrazin, pp. 227ff.
[100] *Perceforest*, i, 107v.
[101] *Ann.Paul.*, pp. 354-5; Stow, ii, 30.
[102] Stow, ii, 29; BL MS Lansdowne 285 fo. 46v; *The Brut*, ii, 343.

exchanged and there could be feasting, drinking and singing.[103] By the end of the fourteenth century, however, hastiludes *à plaisance* were conducted in a totally different manner. The jousting was only a part, albeit an important and essential part, of the festivities. Feasting and singing were now expanded by the addition of dancing and playing of games in which the ladies enjoyed equal status with the men. At Chauvency, the ladies began and ended the daily jousting with songs and spent the night playing games such as the *robardel, le roi qui ne ment, chapelet* and *beguignage*.[104] Since many of the songs and games had amorous undertones they emphasized the importance of courtly love which inspired both martial sport and celebrations. Edward III's marriage festivities continued for three weeks, with great assemblies of knights and ladies celebrating with a mixture 'de jouster, de bouhourder pour l'amour d'elles, de danser, de caroller de jeus', and at the hastiludes to celebrate the birth of Prince Edward in 1284, the floor of one of the upper rooms gave way causing many injuries.[105] All these activities were encapsulated in the phrase 'mener joyeuse vie' which had considerable vogue in the late fourteenth century. According to the allegorical jousting challenge letters of 1401, Henry IV's court was renowned for its jousting, dancing and leading a joyous life, while in 1390 Richard II actually offered a prize not only for the best jousters of each day but also for the lady or damsel 'qui mieulx dansera ou qui menera plus joieux vie'.[106]

By the end of the fourteenth century the tournament *à plaisance* was no longer a purely male preserve, and had diverged considerably from the much more serious hastilude *à outrance*, which had more affinity with the traditional tournaments of the twelfth century. Though ladies were not specifically excluded from border tournaments of the late fourteenth century, their presence was unlikely because of the war setting. The attendance of ladies and the desire to imitate romance combined to produce an increase in pageantry and ceremonial. Hastiludes were parcelled up in the fancy wrappings of processions, elaborate costumes and activities more apposite to the courtier than to the knight. Indeed, the hastiludes in which role playing and masking were involved often bore more resemblance to the courtly *entremets* and disguisings than to the starkly simple organization of the twelfth century tournament,

[103] *HGM*, ll. 3013ff, 4329ff; Jocelin of Brakelond, pp. 55-6.
[104] *Le Tournoi de Chauvency*, ll. 1247-1384, 2438-613, 2950-072.
[105] Jean le Bel, i, 80; *Ann.Mon.*, iv, 489.
[106] BL MS Cotton Nero Dii, e.g. fo. 261v; BL MS Lansdowne 285 fo. 46v.

particularly as the popularity of small indoor hastiludes grew.[107] The attendant pageantry of thirteenth and fourteenth century hastiludes not only made them more attractive to spectators, but also to the participants, for the processions and display were calculated to gratify knightly pride and vainglory, which were endlessly castigated by clerical moralists. It is the atmosphere of romance, however, which pervades hastiludes of peace. Romance settings, adventures and characters provided an endless source of inspiration for medieval tourneyers, and the courtly ideals, of which the romances were the greatest exponents, dictated the behaviour of the participants. Moreover, chivalric interest in romance, and Arthurian romance especially, as a model for its own behaviour continued long after its provisions were no longer applicable. This is reflected very clearly in heraldic treatises of the fifteenth century. Roi René d'Anjou's treatise, *La Forme des Tournois au Temps du roy uterpendragon et du roy artus*,[108] used the romances to build up a picture of tournaments under King Arthur to impress their superiority on his contemporaries and encourage them to imitate ancient practices; Merlin de Cordebeuf's treatise *L'Ordonnance et Manière des Chevaliers Errants*[109] similarly detailed the armour and weaponry of Arthurian knights to enable his contemporaries to appear at tournaments in such roles. Both taught precepts and practices which were anachronistic and impracticable. The dream remained more powerful than reality.

---

[107] On *entremets* see: L. H. Loomis, 'Secular Dramatics in the Royal Palace, Paris, 1378, 1389', *Speculum*, xxxiii (1958), pp. 242-55.
[108] Printed in E. Sandoz, 'Tourneys in the Arthurian Tradition', *Speculum*, xix (1944), pp. 395-420.
[109] Printed in R. de Belleval, *Du Costume Militaire des Français en 1446* (Paris, 1866), pp. 78-83.

CHAPTER SIX

The Tourneying Society

The developments and changes which took place in hastiluding practice over the three centuries covered by this study have all tended to point in one direction – towards an increasingly exclusive tourneying society. The growing popularity of jousts at the expense of *mêlée* style tournaments immediately reduced the number of knights who could appear in the lists at one event. The increasing emphasis on pageantry and display in hastiludes *à plaisance*, which eventually accompanied most occasions for public and private rejoicing, further reduced the numbers; for few could afford to equip themselves and their retinues in suitable style, let alone patronize the celebrations. Not only did appearances dictate the expenditure of large sums of money, but also an interest in personal safety led to heavy investment in increasingly specialized armour which was no longer appropriate for war as it had been in the past. These factors all suggest that tourneying was effectively becoming a privilege available only to those with great wealth. The comparable situation in Germany, where only those with four noble grand-parents were admitted to tournaments and even narrower restric-tions were placed on those seeking to join one of the exclusive tourneying societies suggests that social qualifications were equally as important as financial ones. The romances too, with their constant reiteration of the theme of an unknown or incognito knight whose noble parentage is publicly proved by his skill in tourna-ments, point to a correlation between nobility and tourneying.

To discover to what extent English hastiludes did become as exclusive as these facts would lead one to expect, it is necessary to make a study of those men who frequented tournaments. As in the question of how often tournaments were held, there is a problem of identification which is dependent on the whim of chroniclers, the vagaries of royal and seigneurial household accounts and the expertise of heralds. Therefore, although only about a thousand men can be positively identified as attending hastiludes over the period 1100 to 1400, this is clearly only the tip of the iceberg, and many thousands more must have been tourneyers. The existence of the two Dunstable tournament rolls of arms of 1309 and 1334 emphasizes this point, for between them they identify almost four hundred tourneyers, the majority of whom could not have been so identified from other sources. A quirk of fate preserved these two uniquely detailed records of tourneyers' names and their lesson warns us against drawing oversharp conclusions as to the number of active tourneyers in England at any one time. Similarly, the preservation of a great deal more source material for the fourteenth century, in the form of financial and administrative accounts, together with heraldic records and secular chronicles, tends to further distort the picture of a typical tourneyer, since far more information can be gleaned about the fourteenth century knight than about his twelfth or thirteenth century counterpart. Bearing in mind these limitations, it is still possible to draw some conclusions as to the composition of the tourneying society during this period.

At least in the early days, the most obvious common feature shared by tourneyers was their knighthood, which acted as a form of common bond between them. The French *fabliaux* never refer to tourneyers by that name but rather term them *chevaliers estranges* or *chevaliers d'estranges terres*, while in the twelfth century German *Liet von Troye* the phrase *ein gut ritter* is synonymous with *ein gut turnierer*.[1] Knightly rank and tourneying abilities were thus often regarded as being identical, or at least inseparable. The same view appears to have been taken by those responsible for English legislation on tournaments, for the landless knight is the lowest category of tourneyer envisaged by Richard I's decree of 1194, and only knights are presumed to tourney by the *Statuta Armorum* of 1292.[2] When Geoffrey of Anjou married Matilda of England in 1127, Count Fulk of Anjou begged Henry I to knight his son so that he could take part in the celebratory hastiludes,[3] the implication being that unless he was a belted knight he would be excluded. This highlights the important distinction between those knights who were distrained to knighthood so that they might perform administrative services, and the belted knights who performed the military

---

[1] Chênerie, ' "Ces Curieux Chevaliers Tournoyeurs" ', p. 328; W. H. Jackson, 'The Concept of Knighthood in Herbort von Fritzlar's *Liet von Troy*', *Knighthood in Medieval Literature*, ed. W. H. Jackson (Cambridge, 1981), pp. 45-6.
[2] *Foedera*, i, 65; *Statutes of the Realm*, i, 230-1.
[3] Honoré de Ste Marie, *Dissertation viii*, p. 183.

services traditionally due to the crown. It was from the ranks of the latter class that tourneyers were almost exclusively drawn. In the mid fourteenth century an English esquire, Miles Windsor, was knighted by the Soudan de la Traue on the morning before he was due to perform three courses à outrance against the French knight, Sir Tristan de la Roye.[4] On this last occasion the knighting was not to qualify the esquire to undertake the challenge, but to reward him for his bravery in accepting a challenge from one of the most renowned jousters of his day. As so often happens in chivalric literature, courage and prowess were rewarded with admittance into the ranks of the social group which laid exclusive claim to the possession of these virtues.

As the examples of Geoffrey of Anjou and Miles Windsor have suggested, tourneying was often associated with the ceremony of knighthood. It was common practice for new knights to display their worthiness of elevation by taking part in hastiludes which almost invariably followed the dubbing ceremony. Geoffrey of Anjou himself, with his fellow tiros, celebrated their new knighthood by tourneying, as did the sons of Frederick Barbarossa at Mainz in 1184.[5] More elaborate Round Tables were the setting for conferring knighthood on Baldwin and Balian Ibelin on Cyprus in 1223 and, nearer home, on the three sons of Roger Mortimer at Kenilworth in 1279.[6]

Frequently, the idea of tourneying immediately after the dubbing ceremony was taken a step further, and the new knight, usually accompanied by a large group of young men who had been knighted at the same time, would undertake a form of intensive military training by following tournaments for a few years. Baldwin of Hainault in 1168 and Arnold of Ardres in 1181-2 both left their patrimonies in order to join the tourneying circuit of northern France after they had been knighted and thus accepted into adulthood.[7] Their example was followed by many English knights: the Young King, Geoffrey of Brittany and the semi-legendary Fulk FitzWarin all travelled to northern France to attend a constant round of tournaments in the later years of the twelfth century. Similarly, in 1260, the lord Edward took a large company of new

[4] Froissart, ix, 491.
[5] 'Historia Gaufredi Ducis Normannorum et Comitis Andegavorum', Chroniques des Comtes d'Anjou, ed. L. Halphen & R. Poupardin (Paris, 1913), p. 180; Gislebert of Mons, pp. 151-2, 157.
[6] Philippe de Novare, p. 7; The French Chronicle of London, ed. G. J. Aungier (Camden Soc., 28, 1844), p. 16.
[7] Gislebert of Mons, p. 97; Chron.Ghisn., p. 203.

made knights, including John of Brittany, Henry of Almain, two sons of Simon de Montfort, Roger Clifford, James Audeley, Hamo Lestrange and Warin Bassingbourne with him on a tourneying tour of Europe which lasted for two years.[8] Even after such extended tourneying tours fell into desuetude, their inspiration lingered in that new knights conceived themselves under an obligation to prove themselves worthy of their new honour and to win renown, particularly in the lists. Thus, at least nine out of the sixteen knights who left the inactivity of the king's army in Scotland in 1306 to attend prohibited jousts in England had only been knighted five months before at the Feast of the Swans which had preceded the campaign and the thirty Englishmen in the middle of the century who went to the gates of Paris to challenge the French were also new knights anxious to prove themselves.[9]

There was clearly a connection in chivalric minds between the assumption of knighthood and participation in hastiludes, and it was perhaps natural that new knights should seek tournaments which not only trained them for their accepted vocation but also gave them a public opportunity to display their efficiency in that vocation. It does seem, however, that knighthood in itself was not an absolute prerequisite of tourneying; *behourds* seem to have been the prerogative of esquires only,[10] albeit they were an inferior form of hastilude to the tourney. Moreover, there are several early examples of non-knights tourneying. In 1182, for instance, the Duke of Brabant's son fought in a tournament although he had not yet been knighted, and in 1219-22 Ulrich von Liechtenstein spent three years tourneying before he was knighted in Vienna.[11] In England, Thomas of Lancaster was attending jousts with his younger brother in 1292-3 although he did not receive knighthood till 1297-8, and at least two men knighted at the Feast of the Swans were tourneying before then: Humphrey de Bohun had held tournaments and celebrations lasting a week long at Foleham in 1305 and Warin de Bassingbourne was one of ten men arrested for tourneying within the prohibited five mile radius of Cambridge in 1305.[12] In all these cases, however, the tourneyers were of knightly rank and, indeed,

[8] Roger of Hoveden, ii, 166; *Legend of Fulk FitzWarin*, p. 325; *Flores Historiarum*, ii, 456; Robert of Gloucester ii, 735.

[9] *Cal.Fine Rolls*, i, 534-5; Bullock-Davies, *Menestrellorum Multitudo*, pp. 181, 185-6; Henry Knighton, ii, 111.

[10] See: *Foedera*, i, 332; Walter of Guisborough, pp. 224-5.

[11] Gislebert of Mons, p. 140; Ulrich von Liechtenstein, pp. 15, 57.

[12] Maddicott, *Thomas of Lancaster*, p. 4; Bullock-Davies, p. 185; *Ann.Lond.*, pp. 138-9; *CCR 1302-7*, pp. 299-300.

were shortly to be dubbed, so that they were knights in everything except in the technical sense of having undergone the dubbing ceremony.

In the fourteenth century there is a marked increase in the number of esquires being admitted to tournaments and jousts in their own right, rather than merely as servants of some great lord. The prohibitions are expanded to include esquires and men-at-arms along with the earls, barons and knights who were forbidden to hold hastiludes or tourney and, at the other end of the scale, licences to perform feats of arms were granted to esquires as well as to knights.[13] On one occasion in 1389, Richard II even granted the rank of esquire and a coat of arms to John de Kyngeston in order to ensure that he was honourably treated in the combat to which a French knight had challenged him.[14] The fact that the king felt it necessary only to promote him to the rank of esquire rather than that of knight is significant, for it illustrates the fact that esquires were now being accepted as tourneyers in their own right.

In the fourteenth century it became increasingly common for those of chivalric rank not to take up knighthood, partly because of the financial burdens imposed upon knights and partly because it was no longer necessary to be dubbed in order to enjoy the privileges usually associated with that rank. In the twelfth century, dubbing to knighthood had marked formal entry into the martial world of nobility, but in the fourteenth century noble birth alone qualified a man for the same advantages without him having to undergo the formality of a knighting ceremony. Esquires were certainly admitted to hastiludes on the same terms as knights, for jousting challenges were frequently issued to all knights and esquires who were willing to participate in feats of arms; even though a day was often set aside solely for esquires to tourney, the last day of a *feste* was usually their opportunity to mingle indiscriminately with the knights.[15] Both the jousts at St Ingelvert and Buckingham's expedition to France in 1380 were remarkable for the large numbers of esquires who took up jousting challenges and performed feats of arms against both knights and esquires from France.[16] By 1477, heralds were charging ten marks for an earl, four pounds for a baron, forty shillings for a knight and twenty shillings and eight

---

[13] e.g. *CCR 1302-7*, pp. 535-6; *CCR 1307-13*, pp. 155, 237; *Foedera*, vii, 580, 617.
[14] *Foedera*, vii, 630.
[15] e.g. BL MS Cotton Nero Dii fos 260v-262r; BL MS Additional 21357 fos 1r, 3r; BL MS Lansdowne 285 fo. 47r; Adam Murimuth, pp. 155-6.
[16] Froissart, xiv, 105-51; *Ibid.*, ix, 275-7, 323-30.

pence for an esquire as their admittance fee for the lists, so that esquires appear to have replaced the landless knights of Richard I's decree as the lowest category of tourneyer officially countenanced.[17] By this period, therefore, it was the social rank of the aspirant rather than his military status which qualified him to tourney.

To a certain extent, however, these were tantamount to the same thing, for knighthood had always been associated with nobility. Indeed, it was a continuing theme of romances from the twelfth century onwards that success in tournaments was the proof of noble birth in an unknown knight.[18] Likewise, the fenestration of arms, which was practised in an elementary way even in the twelfth century when the tourneyers' shields were hung outside their lodgings, assumed the nobility of tourneyers since they all had to be armigerous. Hastiludes were, therefore, both exclusive, in that only the chivalric classes could participate fully, and also a great equalizer, in that there was a tremendous divergence in wealth and social status within the chivalric classes and in hastiludes the simple bachelor could fight alongside and on equal terms with the highest princes, dukes and earls of the realm.

In England the tourneying society was a close knit one, dominated by certain comital families whose descendants are found at hastiludes in every generation. Not only did the main branches tourney but also the extended 'family' of dependants, retainers and all those, in fact, who moved in their household and social circles. As is to be expected from their wealth and influence, the comital families of England were prominent as tourneyers in almost every reign from the twelfth to the end of the fourteenth century. The Beauchamps, the Veres and the house of Lancaster were tourneying in the thirteenth century and they were still tourneying in 1400 and beyond. One such typical family was the Clares, whose history will serve as an appropriate example of comital commitment to tourneying.

The first Clare known to have been a tourneyer was that Earl of Gloucester who, in 1194, was one of the three earls put in charge of administering Richard I's tournament decree, so that he was in at the beginning of legitimate English tourneying. Another Earl of Gloucester headed the list of English tourneyers recorded as being present at the Compiègne tournament of 1238 on the roll of arms

---

[17] B. Barnard, *Illustrations of Ancient State and Chivalry* (London, 1840), p. xii.
[18] Chênerie, ' "Ces Curieux Chevaliers Tournoyeurs" ', p. 350.

produced for the occasion.[19] Their descendant, Richard, earl of Gloucester (1222-62), was deeply involved in the baronial and court party tournaments of the 1240s and appears to have presided over the Waltham Round Table for it was he who ordered the lance head to be extracted for examination from the fatal wound inflicted on Ernald Munteny because he suspected foul play.[20] In 1247 he planned a tournament to celebrate his brother William's knighting and in 1252 he was obliged to go to the continent to recover all the arms and horses which William had lost in the tournaments which he had frequented there since being knighted; a year later he travelled to Angoulême with William de Valence to celebrate the marriage of his son, but there he shared his brother's ill-luck and was so badly beaten up at the hastiludes held to mark the event that he had to spend some time in healing baths.[21] He was still tourneying in 1255 when he received a personal prohibition against tourneying at Blyth due to the withdrawal of the king's licence.[22] It was from him that Matthew Paris obtained his story of ghostly tourneyers in Yorkshire[23] and, indeed, it was probably due to his contacts with Matthew Paris that the latter devoted such an unprecedented amount of space to tournaments in his *Chronica Majora*.

Richard's son, Gilbert, earl of Gloucester (1243-95) was also a tourneyer. He shared his father's predilection for 'political' tournaments, for in 1265 he was involved in at least three which were connected with the baronial rebellion.[24] In 1278 he was one of the *digniores* to receive gilded leather armour from Edward I for the Windsor Park tournament and in 1292 he followed in his ancestor's footsteps by being appointed to administer Edward I's *Statuta Armorum*.[25]

His son, Gilbert, the last earl of Gloucester (1291-1314) was similarly deeply involved in the 'political' tournaments of Edward II's reign, even though he attempted to act as a mediator between the barons and the king; as the latter's cousin and a brother-in-law

---

[19] *Foedera*, i, 65; A. Behault de Doron, 'La Noblesse Hennuyère au Tournoi de Compiègne de 1238', *Annales du Cercle Archéologique de Mons*, xxii (1890), p. 87 no. 45.

[20] Matt.Paris, iv, 633; v, 83, 318-9.

[21] *Ibid*, iv, 649; *Ann.Mon.*, i, 151-2; Matt.Paris, v, 367.

[22] *CPR 1247-58*, p. 432.

[23] Matt.Paris, iii, 367-8.

[24] *Ann.Lond.*, pp. 65, 67; *Ann.Mon.*, iii, 238-9; *Foedera* i, 806.

[25] 'Copy of a Roll of Purchases made for the Tournament of Windsor Park, vi Edw.I', *Archaeologia*, 17 (1814), p. 303; PRO DL10/186.

of Gaveston, but also a supporter of the Ordainers, he had a foot in both camps and therefore was not exempt from prohibitions. He received at least five personally addressed prohibitions in 1309 and 1313, and defied a prohibition to attend the September tournament of 1309.[26] In 1308 he reputedly held a Round Table to celebrate his own marriage and the following year he attended the Dunstable tournament where his arms were the first to be recorded on the roll of arms.[27]

A cadet branch of the Clare family, whose main land holdings were in Ireland, included a further four tourneyers. Thomas de Clare (d.1288) was personally prohibited from tourneying at Dunstable in 1265. His two sons were also tourneyers: Gilbert (1281-1307) had his lands seized and his arrest ordered for leaving the king's army in Scotland to tourney without licence and Richard (1283-1318) was at the Dunstable tournament of 1309 with the Earl of Gloucester, whose arms he bore with an azure label. On that occasion he brought with him his brother's *valet*, Nicholas de Clare, who also bore the Gloucester arms with a difference.[28]

The same pattern of the main comital branch and the cadet branches producing tourneyers is true of all the ancient comital families of England, such as the Beauchamps, whose cadets were especially keen tourneyers, and the Bohuns who, as hereditary constables of England, had a military background conducive to the sport. Even in the case of less well established earldoms, or those which changed hands, those promoted still came from tourneying families and continued to produce tourneyers in after generations. The earldom of Pembroke, for instance, passed through several families, the Marshals, the Valences and the Hastings, and yet produced a tourneying earl in every generation from the first Marshal earl, William, right through to John Hastings, the last. Ironically, William Marshal owed his advancement largely to his tourneying skills which first brought him to royal notice, while the last earl died on the tournament field learning the same skills.[29] The three knights whom Edward III raised to earldoms, William Bohun (Northampton), William Montague (Salisbury) and Robert Ufford (Suffolk) similarly came from families with a long standing tourneying tradition. They remained addicted to the sport, which is interesting in view of the fact that they were all to display

---

[26] *CCR 1307-13*, p. 159; *CPR 1307-13*, p. 520; *CCR 1313-18*, p. 70; *Foedera*, iii, 437-8, 438-9; Phillips, *Aymer de Valence*, p. 65.
[27] *Vita Edwardi Secundi*, p. 6; *CTG*, iv, 63 no. 1.
[28] *CPR 1258-66*, p. 406; *Cal. Fine Rolls*, i, 543; *CTG*, iv, 64 nos 13 & 16.
[29] *The Brut*, ii, 344-5.

outstanding military capacity in the king's service in his war against France. Indeed, the correlation between a very active tourneying career and a very active military career is strong, especially among the higher *echelons* of English society which provided the natural leaders of the king's armies.

The attendance of the earls was of considerable importance in ensuring the success or failure of a hastilude, since each earl had a large retinue of humbler knights which accompanied him to war and tournament. In this context, the existence of retaining contracts which mention tournament service is extremely valuable, for they reveal not only the sort of men required but also the type of duties expected of them.

We have already seen how Humphrey de Bohun, earl of Hereford, issued retaining contracts containing standard terms to his retinue.[30] His knights were to receive hay and oats for four horses, wages for three *garçons* and the right to have their chamberlain dining in hall in times of peace. In times of war and for the tourney the obligations were doubled so that the retainer received hay and oats for eight horses, wages for seven *garçons* and the right to have his chamberlain dining in hall. On these occasions, the retainer's own horse was to be supplied by the earl or be replaced by the earl if he had brought his own horse and lost it in battle or tournament.

Where the contracting party was of a higher social standing than Bohun's retainers, the numbers involved could be much larger. Henry Percy, for example, retained Ralph Neville in 1332 to serve him for life in peace and war with twenty men-at-arms, five of whom were to be knights. In war he was to receive dining rights in hall for 'luy et ses gentiz gentz come affiert', hay and oats, horse shoes and nails for fifty-nine horses and wages for fifty-three *garçons* and sufficient mounture for Neville himself. For tournaments these numbers were reduced; Neville was to come with three other knights, himself making the fourth, thirty-seven horses and thirty-two *garçons*, and again he was to be given his own horse but to this was added replacement of any horses 'de ses compaignons priseez'. The numbers were further reduced when Neville was summoned to attend Percy at parliament.[31] The sheer numbers involved in this contract make it likely that, although Percy's demands were high, they were largely fulfilled by this contract, whereas most of the contracting earls such as Hereford, Pembroke and Lancaster preferred to make a larger number of contracts for

[30] See *supra*: pp. 11-12.
[31] *The Percy Chartulary* (Surtees Soc., 117, 1911), pp. 273-4.

less men and horses. The fact that Percy was deeply involved in the administration of the northern marches and that he was deeply committed to the war in Scotland does not explain why he should have required such a large entourage for tournaments, even if it does explain his requirements for war.

The contracts discussed so far have involved only knightly retainers, but at least two are extant which involve men of lesser rank. In 1309 Aymer de Valence, earl of Pembroke retained John Darcy for life in peace and war as a *valet* receiving his keep and suitable robes from the earl together with a horse and armour in wartime, when he was to serve as one of the earl's personal bodyguard. For this he was to receive 100/- from rents *per annum*, but provision was made to increase this to thirteen and a half marks and to upgrade his commitments when he became a knight, an advancement that was clearly anticipated by both parties. An unusual clause due, perhaps, to his *valet* status, allowed Darcy to choose his own lord for tournaments in times of peace; the earl had first claim on his services in the sport, but even then had to pay him the same rates he could get from another lord, rather than simply the usual rates of pay for one of the earl's *valets*.[32] Ten years later, Sir Ralph Basset of Drayton retained Philip Chetwynd for peace and war for a temporary period of one year in the capacity of an esquire. Chetwynd was to provide his own horse, except for the tourney, and to receive the costs of three horses and three *garçons* in times of war and two horses and two *garçons* in times of peace, together with a fee of one hundred marks sterling for the year. Again, provision was made for the service to continue if Chetwynd took 'le ordre de chivalyre' within the covenanted year.[33] In both these cases, therefore, the men retained were clearly of chivalric rank; even if they had not yet taken up knighthood, it was obviously only a matter of time until they did so. The ambiguity surrounding the differences in social status between esquires and *valets* is unimportant in this context, since the terms of the contracts ('com un des autres valets': 'selom ceo qe yl fet a ces altres esquiers') suggest that the distinction was simply one of equipment expected from the retainer, rather than anything of deeper significance.

The Basset/Chetwynd contract underlines the well-known fact that retaining relationships could be of a temporary nature, even if they were likely to be reviewed and renewed at the expiry date.

---

32 PRO E40/A11547.
33 Staffordshire County Record Office, H.M. Chetwynd Bundle I. I owe this reference to Dr J. R. Maddicott.

Temporary contracts appear to have been more lucrative than a lifelong retainership: Philip Chetwynd was to receive a hundred marks sterling for one year and an indenture between Aymer de Valence, earl of Pembroke and Sir Robert FitzPayn gave the latter a hundred pounds sterling for a year's service in tournaments only, even though the earl was to provide horses, robes and saddles for FitzPayn, his two bachelors and his son if he became a knight during the period, together with the keep of the knights, FitzPayn's three *valets* and two esquires for each knight. Unlike the other extant contracts which include tournament service as part of a more general and life-long commitment this indenture was solely concerned with tournament service, even though it was made at Dumferline during the Scottish wars; the only clause to expand the duties was one specifying the entourage required should FitzPayn decided to attend the earl to parliament.[34]

Another unusual contract is the one between Sir Stephen Segrave and Sir Nicholas Cryel,[35] which also belongs to the reign of Edward II. In it, Cryel promised life service as a bachelor with nine *garçons* and nine horses for tournaments, seven *garçons* and seven horses for war and five *garçons* and five horses for peace, including parliament service. Unlike most other indentures, larger numbers were required for tournament than for war; moreover, in a clause comparable to those allowing for the retainer's assumption of knighthood, the terms were altered to twelve *garçons* and twelve horses for war and tournament with the additional service of two extra bachelors and, in the case of war only, of a further seven esquires, if Cryel was advanced to the rank of banneret. Added to these unusual terms was a unique penalty clause. In most contracts, the penalty attached to non-performance was withdrawal of fees or reseizing the lands given to the retainer. In this case, however, defaulting on services incurred a fine of one thousand marks 'a la croyserye vers la tere seinte' and to ensure that such an enormously heavy fine was possible, Cryel was obliged to offer his manor of Walmere in Kent as security. No retaining fee is mentioned, and this, combined with the huge penalty, suggests that Cryel's service was perhaps intended as a means of repaying in kind a large loan made by Segrave. The fact that there is no known contact between the two parties bears this out, for most retaining contracts such as, for instance, that between Humphrey de Bohun and Bartholomew de Enefield, can be seen to be working in practice.[36] Cryel did not form part of Segrave's

34 PRO E101/27/11.
35 Berkeley Castle Muniments, Select Charter no. 490.

retinue on military campaigns, there is no evidence of him witnessing Segrave's charters and there seems to be no link in their careers which could suggest any ties of friendship or retinue; there is not even any correlation in their landholdings, for Segrave held nothing in Kent where all Cryel's lands lay.

Most retaining contracts exist in the form of indentures sealed interchangeably, though the Segrave/Cryel one took the form of letters patent issued and sealed by Cryel himself. The indenture itself was probably not enforceable at law, there being no evidence of a retaining contract being sued upon, even though some military indentures, which were drawn up in more precise terminology, were brought before the courts. The only method of forcing a retainer to perform his duties was to take a sum of money from him and hold it as a bond for his good service in much the same way as Cryel appears to have pledged his manor.

Though not all retaining contracts contained specific tourneying clauses, it is evident from the numbers of retainers attending hastiludes with their lords that attendance at tournaments was an important feature of service. At least thirty-eight of Aymer de Valence's retainers are identifiable as tourneyers, for example. Even though the earl himself was absent, having been sent abroad on a diplomatic mission at the last minute, thirty-two of them appear on the Dunstable tournament roll of 1309.[37] Likewise, at least twenty-seven of Gilbert, earl of Gloucester's retainers were tourneyers, and twenty-three of them accompanied him to the same Dunstable tournament.[38]

In a much smaller way, the same is true of many English baronial families. Nicholas Segrave, for instance, attended the Dunstable tournament with a retinue of seven knights, including his own

---

[36] Enefield went abroad with the earl's father in 1294 (twice) and 1297 (*CPR 1292-1301*, pp. 68, 84, 226); he served the earl in Scotland in 1299 and 1314 when he was captured at Bannockburn (PRO C67/14 m5; *Continuatio Nicholai Triveti*, p. 15). He received lands from the earl and at the earl's instance in 1294 and 1315 (*CPR 1292-1301*, p. 84; *CPR 1313-17*, pp. 278, 289), and he witnessed the earl's charter in 1315 (*CPR 1313-7*, p. 284). He followed the earl in politics, being pardoned his part in the murder of Gaveston in 1313 (*CPR 1313-7*, p. 24) and he served in the earl's retinue at the Dunstable tournament in 1309 (*CTG*, iv, 65 no. 29).

[37] See: Appendix II, table I.

[38] See: Appendix II, table II.

brother and nephew,[39] and his family tradition of tourneying was as extensive and as ancient as that of the earls. Stephen Segrave (d.1241), was considered responsible, among others, for the flaring up of hostilities between the northerners and southerners at the Blyth tournament of 1237.[40] His grandson, Nicholas (1238-95), who fought for the barons in the civil wars, received a personally addressed prohibition against tourneying at Dunstable in 1265, and two of his sons and his grandson are found on the Dunstable tournament roll of 1309.[41] His son Nicholas (d.1321) enjoyed a particularly colourful career dominated by martial pursuits. In 1305 he was summoned for trial to the Westminster Parliament because, having quarrelled with John Crumbwell when both were in the king's army in Scotland, he had challenged him to a duel, thus defying not only the king's prohibition on feats of arms but also the Constable of Dover's express prohibition on travelling to France where the duel took place, beyond Edward I's jurisdiction. Having been arrested on his return, he compounded his offence by escaping from his prison but, despite the king's anger, he was eventually pardoned in consideration of his good services in the king's wars, having submitted *de haut en bas*. By 1312 he was sufficiently restored to royal favour to be appointed marshal of the new king's household.[42] His brother, Henry (d.1318) and his nephew Stephen (d.1325) were, like him, extremely active knights serving in all the major campaigns from the 1290s onwards. Henry was chiefly remarkable for an acrimonious law-suit involving robbery, arson and armed companies against a fellow tourneyer, Walter de Bermingham, while Stephen's main claim to fame rested on his being held responsible to the tune of ten thousand marks for the escape of Roger Mortimer from the Tower while he was constable there.[43] It was also this Stephen who retained Nicholas Cryel for life in peace, war and tournament with the unusual penalty clause of a thousand mark fine payable to the cause of the crusade.[44]

Another typical tourneying family of baronial status was that of the Bassets, who were important marcher lords. Philip and Gilbert Basset were both strenuous knights who were personally prohibited from tourneying at Northampton, Canterbury or Royston in 1234

---

[39] See: Appendix II, table III.
[40] Matt.Paris, iii, 404.
[41] *CPR 1258-66*, p. 406; *CTG*, iv, 68 nos 117, 125, 126.
[42] *CCR 1302-7*, p. 335; Phillips, *Aymer de Valence*, p. 44.
[43] *CCR 1307-13*, p. 351; *CPR 1307-13*, pp. 360, 563; *CCR 1302-7*, p. 482.
[44] Berkeley Castle Muniments, Select Charter no. 490.

because they had joined Richard Marshal's rebellion.[45] Gilbert was also involved in the northerners versus southerners tournament at Blyth in 1237, and four years later he was to be found fighting in the court party at the Northampton tournament.[46] Ralph Basset of Drayton (d.1265), who was killed fighting on the baronial side at Evesham, received a personally addressed prohibition in the February before he died. Ralph (d.1343), his grandson, had his lands seized and his arrest ordered for leaving the king's army in Scotland without permission in order to tourney in England in 1306;[47] three years later he attended the Dunstable tournament and in 1319 he retained Philip Chetwynd to serve him as an esquire in peace, war and tournament, so he obviously envisaged a continuing commitment to the sport.[48] His son tourneyed as 'Monsieur Rauf Basset le filz' at the Dunstable tournament of 1334, but he died before he could inherit from his father.[49] Other members of the Basset family were also tourneyers: Adam Bernard was pardoned in 1305 for killing Thomas Basset accidentally in the Leicester jousts, Richard Basset of Weldon (d.1314) fought at the Dunstable tournament of 1309 and Simon Basset fought at the Dunstable tournament of 1334.[50]

A similar history of a long line of tourneyers could be repeated, with minor variations, for many of the knightly families in England. The point is that the Segraves and the Bassets were not unusual but rather typical of the sort of men who frequented tournaments both on their own account and in the company of the greater magnates. The vast majority of them lived unexceptional lives, serving the king on royal campaigns whenever the need arose, and in local administration as justices of the peace, sheriffs and special commissioners.

One notable feature, however, appears to be that those knights who were most strenuous or most actively and most often employed in military service were usually the ones most dedicated to hastiludes. The most outstanding example of this is Henry, duke of Lancaster, who fought in almost every one of Edward III's major campaigns in Scotland, Flanders, Gascony, France and Brittany, captained the king's army in Scotland in 1336 and was appointed the king's

---

[45] *CPR 1232-47*, pp. 68, 70.
[46] Matt.Paris, iii, 404; iv, 88.
[47] *CPR 1258-66*, p. 406; *Cal.Fine Rolls*, i, 543-4.
[48] *CTG*, iv, 67 no. 86; Staffordshire County Record Office, H.M. Chetwynd Bundle I.
[49] *CTG*, iv, 392 no. 65.
[50] *CPR 1301-7*, p. 313; *CTG*, iv, 69 no. 148; *Ibid.*, iv, 390 no. 16.

lieutenant in Aquitaine in 1346.[51] His first recorded appearance at a hastilude occurs surprisingly late, for he was already twenty-eight or nine when he attended a tournament at Blyth in 1328 with William, earl of Ulster; four years later he appears as one of the tourneyers on the Dunstable roll of 1334. In 1338 and 1341 he tourneyed several times against the Scots on the northern borders and in 1340, when he was being held as security for the payment of Edward III's debts in Flanders he obtained leave to attend the jousts at Le Bure on a solemn undertaking to return voluntarily to his prison as soon as they were over.[52] In 1342 he jousted in London at the *feste* for the Countess of Salisbury and also tourneyed at Dunstable with the other veterans of the Scottish campaign of that year. In 1344 he not only held hastiludes at Leicester to celebrate his daughter's marriage but also jousted at the Windsor Round Table where he became a founder member of Edward III's nascent order.[53] In February of the same year he had anticipated this foundation with the creation of an embryonic order or jousting society of his own. He received royal approval for his appointment as captain for life of a team of Lincolnshire knights who were to meet annually on the Monday of Whit week to hold jousts at Lincoln; they were to be allowed to joust regardless of general prohibitions or whether the country was at war or peace unless the king himself was holding a hastilude on that day and on Henry of Grosmont's death the order was to be perpetuated by the election of another captain by the jousters themselves.[54] As Henry was an unusually literate man, it is not impossible that the Lincolnshire order, which was also purely secular, may have served as a model or at least the inspiration for Edward III's own order of the Round Table.

Having had a major charge at the siege of Calais, during which there was daily jousting between the besiegers and the beleaguered, Henry returned to England where he participated in the king's celebratory hastiludes of 1348.[55] In 1354 he challenged Otto of Brunswick to a judicial duel in front of the French king which, however, he was not allowed to proceed with, even though he

[51] *CCR 1337-9*, p. 41; *CPR 1345-8*, p. 475; for a detailed study of his life and career see K. Fowler, *The King's Lieutenant* (London, 1969).
[52] PRO DL41/9/1; *CTG*, iv, 390 no. 16; Andrew of Wyntoun, vi, 103-115; *Scalacronica*, ed. & trans. H. Maxwell (Glasgow, 1907), p. 112; Henry Knighton, ii, 23; PRO DL25/983.
[53] Jean le Bel, ii, 2-4; Adam Murimuth, pp. 123-4; Henry Knighton, ii, 30; Adam Murimuth, pp. 155-6, 231.
[54] *CPR 1343-5*, pp. 196, 379.
[55] Henry Knighton, ii, 50; Nicolas, 'Observations', pp. 27, 42.

arrived fully prepared at the lists. The following year he was again tourneying, this time at Woodstock to celebrate the birth of Thomas, the youngest son of Edward III and Philippa of Hainault. In 1358, only three years before he died, he jousted at the Windsor feast where he was wounded in the leg, but he obviously intended to continue tourneying, for he accepted a gift of jousting armour from the Black Prince in this year.[56] His tourneying career had therefore spanned thirty years; he was nearly sixty when he fought in his last recorded hastilude and he was active in the lists for as long as he was active in the field on campaign.

Further down the social scale from one of the greatest captains of his day and the premier magnate of England, there is the same correlation between the habitually active soldier and the dedicated tourneyer. Sir Giles de Argentine, for instance, was not only accounted *un chevaler renome* but was also reputed to be the third best knight in the world.[57] He served as a *valet* in the Falkirk campaign of 1298, and seems to have been fighting in Scotland almost continually from at least 1302 to 1306: he was certainly present at the siege of Stirling in 1304 and had his arms painted on the roll of arms drawn up on that occasion.[58] In 1311 he went to the East as a crusader and two years later Edward II was canvassing all the eastern powers in an attempt to secure their aid towards obtaining his release from prison in Salonica, where he had been captured and confined by the men of Rhodes.[59] After his release, he spent some time fighting in the wars of Henry of Luxembourg before returning to England where he immediately joined the forces of the Bannockburn campaign as captain of the king's personal bodyguard. At that battle in 1314, he was personally responsible for ensuring Edward II's safety by leading him off the field of defeat. Then, in an action typical of the man and of the type, he refused to leave the field himself, saying that he had never yet incurred the shame of fleeing a battlefield, and, spurring his horse into the enemy ranks, fell in a hopeless but gallant gesture of courage and defiance.[60] It is illuminating to discover that even such an obviously dedicated

---

[56] *Chronicon a Monacho Sancti Albani*; *Register of the Black Prince*, iv, 124; *Eulogium Historiarum*, iii, 227; *Register of the Black Prince*, iv, 247.
[57] *Scalacronica*, p. 142; J. Barbour, *The Bruce*, ii, 317-8.
[58] H. Gough, *Scotland in 1298* (Paisley & London, 1888), p. 189; *CCR 1302-7*, p. 66; *Cal.Fine Rolls*, i, 543; *CPR 1301-7*, p. 242; College of Arms MS M14 fo. 269v (fo. 581 in new numbering).
[59] *CPR 1307-13*, p. 324; *CCR 1313-8*, pp. 71, 76.
[60] *Scalacronica*, pp. 142-3; J. Barbour, *The Brut*, ii, 317.

and strenuous knight, so deeply concerned to win renown and honour, should have considered it no disgrace to abandon the king's army to attend hastiludes. He did this not once, but twice: in 1302 his lands in Essex were forfeited and his arrest ordered because he had been found guilty of a contempt against the king (possibly the forcible entry into a royal clerk's house in Suffolk with a large number of armed men, where they consumed, destroyed and appropriated his goods and beat up his servants). He was committed to prison from whence he was released on condition of going to Scotland in the company of Sir John Segrave. By November he had left the king's army to take part in jousts at Byfleet held against the royal prohibition.[61] In 1306 he again left the king's army without permission in order to tourney in England with a large group composed mainly of royal household knights.[62] Three years later, he was able to tourney legitimately. In late March he left the family manor in Hertfordshire with his elder brother John so that they could both participate in the Dunstable tournament where Giles lost his horse fighting in the company of Guy, earl of Warwick. In May he held his own great tournament at Stepney in which he assumed the role of 'King of the Greenwood' and with a team of companions fought against all comers.[63] He even possibly fought in the lists against Saracens during his wanderings in the middle east, though it is more likely that he took part in three battles or campaigns against the heathen.[64] Although Sir Giles de Argentine enjoyed an unusually colourful career which took him to many far flung places, he was, in fact, typical of many of the strenuous knights of the period – men like Sir Roger Clifford, Sir Thomas Berkeley and later, Sir Piers Courtenay, who were equally at home on the battlefield and in the lists. Again this reinforces the conclusion that hastiludes and war were not incompatible, but rather complementary.

It was thus no coincidence that a very high proportion of the knights whose names and arms are to be found on the Dunstable tournament roll of 1309 are repeatedly to be found on the protection rolls for service in Wales, Gascony and Scotland in the 1290s.[65] Military preoccupations and hastiluding went hand in hand, and it was natural for Robert of Avesbury to state that the *solempne hastiludium* held in Cheapside in 1331 had been organized 'for all

---

[61] *CPR 1301-7*, p. 86; *CCR 1302-7*, p. 66.
[62] *Cal.Fine Rolls*, i, 543-4.
[63] Maddicott, *Thomas of Lancaster*, p. 95; *CTG*, iv, 64 no. 7; PRO SC6/1109/12; *Ann.Lond.*, p. 157; *Ann.Paul.*, p. 267.
[64] J. Barbour, *The Bruce*, ii, 318.
[65] PRO C67/9; C67/10; C67/13; C67/14.

the *strenuous* earls, barons, knights and other nobles of the realm.'[66] (my italics)

This did not mean, however, that those knights who had adopted a career in administration and never, or rarely, fought on military campaigns, never tourneyed. They did participate on occasion, but just as the more strenuous the knight the more often he tourneyed or jousted, so the less strenuous the knight, the less often he did so. Geoffrey Scrope, for instance, came from a long tradition of tourneyers, his ancestors and descendants being noted in the sport. William Scrope (d. by 1312) had been 'le plus noble tourneor en son temps'; Geoffrey's own son, Henry (d.1391) had tourneyed at Dunstable in 1342 to great applause from Edward III, and James and John Scrope both jousted and were unhorsed at St Ingelvert in 1390.[67] Geoffrey Scrope became chief justice of Common Pleas in 1324, served on innumerable local administrative commissions in Yorkshire and continually on judicial commissions throughout the country; from 1320 he was regularly employed on diplomatic commissions for the crown, treating with the Scots, French and Flemish.[68] Despite such heavy commitments to administration, and a striking absence from military campaign, he still managed to find time to tourney. He had, indeed, been one of four young men knighted at the Northampton tournament of 1323, and became a 'noble chevaler a to[u]rnea'; he was observed participating in tournaments at Guildford and Newmarket wearing his family coat of arms, and he also received robes for the hastiludes in 1332 at Woodstock to celebrate the birth of Prince William.[69]

Another chief justice, Sir William Thorpe (d.1361) who lost his office, lands and goods when he was convicted of receiving bribes in 1350, had also been a tourneyer for his arms and name are to be found on the Dunstable tournament roll of 1334.[70] Since he came from a chivalric background, his social position would have obliged him to conform to knightly expectations and attend tournaments, but Scrope seems to have had a genuine predilection for the sport and, indeed, a talent for it.

---

[66] Robert of Avesbury, pp. 285-6.
[67] *The Scrope and Grosvenor Roll*, i, 132, 133; Froissart, xiv, 141, 145-6.
[68] *CCR 1323-7*, p.74; *CCR 1318-23*, p.328; *CPR 1317-21*, p.504; *CPR 1321-4*, p.278; *CPR 1327-30*, p.399; *CPR 1330-34*, pp.188, 465; *CPR 1338-40*, p.39. For a review of his career see: E.G.L.Stones, 'Sir Geoffrey le Scrope (c.1285-1340)', *Eng.Hist.Rev.*, cclxx (1954), pp.1-17.
[69] *Scrope and Grosvenor Roll*, i, 143, 144-5, 133; BL MS Cotton Galba E111 fo.183v.
[70] *CPR 1350-54*, pp.30, 61-2; *CTG*, iv, 391 no.46.

Another feature of the link between the degree of activity of a knight in war and tournament is the length of service in each. As might be expected, particularly of strenuous knights, the tourneying career usually lasted as long as the capability of the individual to perform his military duties. This means that the romance concept of tourneyers being young, unmarried men who had not yet inherited their lands[71] is a distortion of reality. Similarly, Duby's concept of the *iuvenes*, who formed the vast majority of tourneyers in the twelfth century,[72] is also misleading, at any rate as regards thirteenth and fourteenth century England. Although it is true that many tourneyers did fit into this category because, as we have seen, they were younger sons, cadets or household knights, most of them were by no means young men. Where ages of tourneyers can be ascertained, the average seems to be about thirty years old. There are exceptions, of course, at both ends of the scale. Henry, earl of Lancaster (d.1345) tourneyed at Warwick, Dunstable, Croydon and Fulham in 1293 at the tender age of twelve or thirteen, in the company of his sixteen year old elder brother; the Black Prince was also only thirteen when he tourneyed at the head of the exterior party in the 'Pope and Cardinals' jousts at Smithfield in 1343.[73] For convenience's sake, since they provide the most complete list of identifiable tourneyers available, it is best to examine the two tournament rolls of 1309 and 1334 to find out at what age knights tourneyed. The average age of those knights whose ages can be ascertained at the earlier encounter was thirty and a half, the youngest, Ralph Perot, being eighteen, and the oldest, William Paynell, being fifty-five. Only thirty-six out of nearly two hundred and forty men recorded on the roll bore labels on their arms signifying that they had not yet inherited their fathers' lands and title, and some of these bore labels even though, like Thomas, earl of Lancaster, they had already inherited.[74] Likewise, the average age of the tourneyers at Dunstable in 1334 was thirty-one and a half years old, the youngest, John of Eltham, being eighteen and the oldest, Gilbert Talbot, being fifty-eight; again only eighteen out of one

---

71 Chênerie, ' "Ces Curieux Chevaliers Tournoyeurs" ', pp. 355-6; see also J. Flori, 'Qu'est-ce qu' un Bachelor? Étude Historique de Vocabulaire dans les Chansons de Geste du XIIe Siècle', *Romania*, 96 (1975), pp. 289-314.

72 G. Duby, *The Chivalrous Society*, ed. & trans. C. Postan (London, 1977), chapter 7.

73 'Account of the Expenses of John of Brabant', ed. J. Burtt, pp. xi-xiii, 4-7, 10, 12; Adam Murimuth, p. 230.

74 Perot's shield only appears on the fuller version of the roll in College of Arms MS 2nd G.3. fo. 45v; *CTG*, iv, 68 no. 128.

hundred and thirty-six bore labels.[75] There was, therefore, a wide disparity in the ages of tourneyers, reflecting the fact that as long as a knight was fit and able to participate he would do so, despite the literary conventions which ascribed tourneying to the period of youth.

Even though society was much more settled in the thirteenth and fourteenth centuries than it had been in the twelfth, when the *iuvenes* were wandering across the continent in search of hastiludes, the *chevalier d'estranges terres* was still a common figure in reality as in romance. Foreign knights, particularly Bretons and Hainaulters, frequently came to England to attend tournaments, especially in the fourteenth century when Edward III was anxious to foster his chivalric reputation in Europe and therefore ensured that his hastiludes were also proclaimed on the continent. Many foreign knights must also have remained in England after they had been employed in Edward III's armies in France and Scotland. Edward III's attitude was therefore very different from that of Richard I who, in his tournament decree of 1194, had actually prohibited foreign knights from tourneying in England.[76] The close links between England and Hainault which had been built up over the years were maintained by Edward III, especially after his marriage, and part of their shared culture was a chivalric interchange. The tournament held in London in 1342, for example, was proclaimed in Hainault, Brabant, Flanders and France and was attended by Count William of Hainault, his uncle, John Beaumont and the exiled Robert of Artois: William of Hainault then went on to the Eltham hastiludes where he was wounded in the arm while jousting.[77] Knights from Flanders, Hainault and Brabant were always prominent at the hastiludes celebrating Edward III's annual Garter feast on St George's day and on one occasion the Duke of Brabant came to the Garter feast specifically to obtain military aid against the Count of Flanders.[78] There was a similar tradition of chivalric links with Brittany. In the thirteenth century successive dukes came to England in their youth to attend tournaments in much the same way as young English knights went on continental tourneying tours. In the fourteenth century, Breton dukes still found it advantageous to

---

[75] *Ibid.*, iv, 389 nos 1 & 2; Ralph Stafford is omitted from the published version but is included between John Cleveden and Ralph de Chelton in BL MS Cotton Otho Div fo. 189v.

[76] *Statutes of the Realm*, i, 65.

[77] Jean le Bel, ii, 3-4; Froissart, iv, 124, 125; Adam Murimuth, p. 124.

[78] e.g. Froissart, iv, 213-4; Henry Knighton, ii, 98-9; *Scalacronica*, pp. 176-7.

attend English hastiludes and thus maintain English goodwill and support against their rival claimants to the duchy.[79] It is probable that links of this kind would also have grown up between England and Bohemia if they had not been cut short by the premature death of Queen Anne and Richard's own deposition, for Bohemian knights were not only present at the hastiludes to celebrate their marriage in 1382, but also remained behind in royal service where they inevitably became involved in the chivalric pursuits of the household. At least one Bohemian knight from the queen's household fought at St Ingelvert where he disgraced himself by an ill-placed stroke and by continuing his course without stopping.[80]

There was, therefore, a continual stream of foreign tourneyers into England, mainly from those areas with a traditionally close and amicable relationship with England. They were occasionally supplemented by French knights, particularly after the English victories at Crécy and elsewhere brought an influx of noble French prisoners who were allowed to participate in hastiludes with their captors' permission. An even greater number of English knights crossed the Channel in order to tourney abroad, however, so that this chivalric interchange was not purely one sided. We have already seen how many young men of noble birth who had just received knighthood would go to the continent, usually for a period of about two years, to attend tournaments with their following; we have also seen that many knights went to the marches of Calais and Scotland to fight hastiludes à outrance. On occasions of particular importance a very large proportion of the more prominent chivalry of England might be present at a foreign hastilude. At St Ingelvert, for example, the names of over a hundred English knights and esquires who participated have been recorded by various chroniclers.[81] In an earlier generation, English knights were present and highly regarded for their prowess at the Le Hem jousts, and the Round Table held at Bar by the Duke of Brabant to celebrate his marriage to Edward I's daughter attracted a large number of English knights, many of whom, no doubt, came over in the princess' entourage.[82]

Less prestigious events also attracted English knights who were anxious to win a more extensive reputation and to try their skills in

[79] PRO E101/351/12 m1, 5; *Records of the Wardrobe and Household*, ed. Byerly, pp. 5-7, 20, 22, 26, 34, 47; *Ann.Paul.*, p. 361; Robert of Avesbury, p. 286; *Issues of the Exchequer*, pp. 170, 172.

[80] *Chronicon a Monacho Sancti Albani*, pp. 332-2; Froissart, xiv, 142-3; *Chronique du Religieux de St Denys*, i, 676.

[81] Froissart, xiv, 105-51; *Chronique du Religieux de St Denys*, i, 676-81.

[82] Sarrazin, pp. 225-6, 231; *Ann.Mon.*, iii, 388-9.

less accustomed places against unknown opponents. The earls of Gloucester and Lincoln led an impressive company of ten knights to a tournament at Compiègne in 1238, (or 1270: the date is disputed); Hugh Courtenay, Ralph Dacre (?Ravons Daser), John Vescy, Roger Clifford, Thibaut Meletun, Hugh Despenser, Otto de Grandison, Philip Daubigny (?Philippe de Begny), William de Say and John Comyn all came from families with a tradition of tourneying which was also to extend to their descendants, and their names were all recorded on the roll of arms drawn up there.[83] Similarly, in 1310, a later Hugh Despenser attended a tournament at Mons with Robert d'Enghien, where their names and arms were recorded on another roll of arms.[84] In the context of this latter tournament, it is interesting to note that Edward II had felt it necessary on 31 December 1309 to order all the wardens and bailiffs of the ports to prohibit and prevent any man-at-arms of any rank from going abroad without the king's especial order, 'as the king understands that some persons purpose to go to parts beyond the sea to tourney or do other feats of arms there.'[85]

This was by no means a unique prohibition,[86] which suggests that some inveterate tourneyers were slipping abroad to indulge in their favourite sport when hastiludes were prohibited in England. As prohibitions were often issued to ensure that the chivalry of the realm were all together in one place, whether for council or war, such an obvious loophole as going abroad to tourney had to be removed; hence the orders to blockade the ports against potential tourneyers. If some knights had to be physically prevented from going abroad to tourney, others tourneyed abroad simply because they were prevented from returning to England, and it was for this reason that political exiles were often to be found on the tournament fields of Europe. Two of the most notorious, Piers Gaveston and Robert de Vere, were both accepted into tourneying circles in Europe during their banishments. Gaveston tourneyed abroad while exiled from England in 1307 and de Vere was similarly involved in French royal hastiludes in 1388-9; one of the latter's knights performed a feat of arms against a French knight in the presence of the king, and de Vere personally jousted at the hastiludes held by

---

[83] Behault de Doron, 'La Noblesse Hennuyère', pp. 87-8 nos 45-56.
[84] A. Behault de Doron, 'Le Tournoi de Mons de 1310', *Annales du Cercle Archéologique de Mons*, xxxviii (1909), pp. 224-5 nos 121 & 122.
[85] *CCR 1307-13*, p. 237.
[86] See, for example, *Cal.Fine Rolls*, i, 544; *Foedera*, iii, 108.

'the Knights of the Golden Sun' to welcome Queen Isabella to Paris in 1389.[87]

Although English exiles made their presence felt on the continental tourneying society, the vast majority of English tourneyers abroad were the ordinary knights who were devotees of the sport at home. Just as they were prepared to come from all corners of the kingdom to attend hastiludes, those knights who valued their reputation were willing to go abroad in pursuit of them. The wandering spirit which had been so strong in the twelfth century *iuvenes* still lingered on even into the late fourteenth century, and the same values, such as the seeking after *los et pris*, which had animated the bachelors of the twelfth century continued to stimulate knights and esquires of following generations to pursue excellence in the lists.

If the inspiration to tourney changed remarkably little over the period 1100 to 1400, the same is true of the men who practised the sport, for the tourneying society also remained remarkably static. Most tourneyers were the people who moved within a fairly limited circle; they were either the members or cadet branches of the comital and great baronial families of England or men of their households and retinues. They were, therefore, a close knit society, reliant to a large extent on the patronage of the magnates and the king, even though they were themselves of noble rank. The growing cost of tourneying and jousting, particularly in relation to improved armour and increased pageantry, meant that as time went by patronage became even more important, and many knights whose ancestors had been able to afford to tourney in their own right wearing the same armour that they wore for war, found that they had to seek patronage in order to bear the cost of providing themselves with the two completely different suits of armour which had become requisite for war and hastilude. Although it was still possible in this later period to rely on royal or aristocratic patronage for the basic equipment, as indeed William Marshal had done at the start of his career in the twelfth century, it was no longer possible to make one's fortune in the lists as he had done. In hastiludes fought *à plaisance* winnings were limited to formally awarded prizes; it was no longer the object to hold captured knights to ransom, nor did the victor have any claim against the defeated man's horse and harness. In these circumstances, patronage became more important than mere valour or skill in tourneying, hence the importance of having aristocratic connections. As patronage became more expensive,

---

[87] BL MS Additional 22923 fo. 10v; Froissart, xiii, 99, 145; *Chronique du Religieux de St Denys*, i, 496–8.

tourneying became more court centred, simply because the king had most resources at his command.

The costs could be prohibitive. John of Brittany spent nearly a hundred pounds on attending tournaments for only four months in 1285-6, and at the same period Edward I still owed over sixty-eight pounds for horses killed, captured or replaced for his following when tourneying abroad over twenty years before.[88] In 1307 Prince Edward spent over sixty-six pounds on preparations for a tournament for his household at Wark which, in the end, never took place because Edward I prohibited it, and in just over four months in 1329 lord Berkeley spent over fifty pounds on jousting at hastiludes which were so unremarkable as to attract no chronicle attention whatsoever.[89] When such heavy expenses were incurred merely by the incidentals of tourneying at minor events, it is not surprising that only the greatest aristocrats could afford to tourney in their own right, let alone sponsor the game, particularly when their following looked to them to make good any of their own losses. Despite the necessity for wealth, it is interesting to note that in England, unlike the Low Countries,[90] the rich citizens and burgesses, who were often spectators at hastiludes, were not admitted to the ranks of the tourneying society until long after the period covered by this study. Wealth alone was not considered a sufficient qualification to be included in the ranks of tourneyers, and although there were no hard and fast rules about the length of noble ancestry requisite for admittance, as there were in Germany, birth played an important part in determining whether or not a man tourneyed. Indeed, it was expected that a man of high birth would tourney, and if he did not do so, he failed in his social duty.

The average tourneyers in the twelfth and in the fourteenth centuries were, therefore, almost identical, though their numbers were more restricted in the later period. They were consistently of chivalric, and hence noble, rank and moved within the same royal and aristocratic circles; for this reason they were well versed in chivalric lore, romances and courtly ethics as expounded by heralds, *jongleurs* and minstrels, who were the inevitable hangers-on in such society. They were motivated by the same desire to win praise and renown and particularly to shine in front of the ladies. Though their

---

[88] *Records of the Wardrobe and Household*, ed. Byerly, pp. 5-7, 20, 22, 26, 34, 47; *Ibid.*, pp. 63, 244.
[89] BL MS Additional 22923 fos 1v-2v, 7v, 8r, 10v, 15r; Berkeley Castle Muniments, Select Rolls no. 60.
[90] J. Vale, pp. 25-41.

ages, wealth and social status varied tremendously, they were all equals in the lists, which publicly underlined not only the exclusiveness of what was essentially a very elite society, but also the cohesiveness of that society regardless of the differences between its members. Even if a very large proportion of tourneyers were at one time rebels against royal authority, this was because tournaments were easily manipulated for political purposes, and rebellion did not exclude a man from the tourneying society any more than it altered his social status. Given such a close knit society, it is not surprising that tournaments were such important centres for the exchange of cultural values and the spreading of chivalric customs which were to have a much wider impact outside the tournament field.

CHAPTER SEVEN

The Forms of Combat

Having examined in some detail the more general aspects of the tournament throughout the period 1100 to 1400, it is now time to turn to the technical side of the conduct of the tournament. In the next two chapters, therefore, we shall look first at the different forms of hastilude which emerged over the period, and then at the development of a specialized armour designed for sport as distinct from war.

It is important to begin with an attempt to distinguish between the different types of hastilude, as far as this is possible. This is essential, not only because informed contemporaries made the distinctions, but also to avoid making historical blunders by confusing the rules and practices of one game with another.[1] There are many pitfalls in such an attempt, mainly due to the fact that at the period when hastiludes were flourishing the chronicles, which are the best source, made no attempt to describe or define what was happening in the lists. It was only once they had fallen into desuetude that heraldic authors in particular became intrigued by the obsolete terminology and self-consciously endeavoured to distinguish between and define the different forms of hastilude. For this reason, their attempts are frequently unreliable and it is to romances and chivalric literature that we must often turn for invaluable descriptions of the games.

There were obviously basic similarities of practice in all martial sports which sometimes caused chroniclers to confuse them. It was a confusion which some tourneyers exploited to their own ends as,

---

[1] e.g. T. Jones, *Chaucer's Knight: portrait of a medieval mercenary* (London, 1980), p. 183, where the author's central thesis is sustained by erroneously attributing the rules prescribed in the Duke of Gloucester's *Ordinances for Combat Within Lists* (which was intended for chivalric combats and feats of arms) to a *mêlée* style tournament.

for instance, in deliberately trying to avoid the penalties of prohibitions on hastiludes by proclaiming them under other names. This disingenuous ruse was used by the tourneyers at Hertford in 1241: Henry III temporarily withheld Walter Marshal's inheritance on the ground that he had contravened the spirit, if not the letter, of a general prohibition by attending the tournament which 'sophistice illud fortunium appellasti'.[2] It was in an effort to make such evasions impossible that the writs forbidding hastiludes became more prolix and more precise in their terminology. A year after the Hertford *fortunium*, for example, Henry III issued a general ordinance for keeping the peace which included a clause prohibiting anyone from meeting 'ad turneandum vel ad burdiandum vel ad alias quascumque aventuras':[3] similarly rigorous definitions became a standard feature of subsequent prohibitions.

Although tourneyers were able to hold hastiludes under other names to evade prohibitions, there were technical distinctions which must have been clear enough to contemporary eyes. Edward II, for instance, in an unusual prohibition issued on 12 May 1309 forbade all tournaments, *behourds* and other feats of arms until 8 September 1309, but he specifically, and without explanation, excepted jousts from the ban.[4]

The commonest term in use throughout the period 1100 to 1400 was the Latin *hastiludium*, which was also gallicized as *hastilude*. Its widespread usage was due to the fact that it was a generic term applicable to all martial games indifferently, because it simply meant a 'lance game'. It could thus be used in conjunction with other terms which were more precise. Matthew Paris, for instance, described how the French invaders fought their erstwhile baronial allies near London in 1216 'ad equestrem ludum, quod hastiludium vel torneamentum dicitur' and when quoting a letter of William d'Albini proroguing a baronial *torneamentum* from Stamford to between Staines and Hounslow, Paris refers to the same event as a *hastiludium*.[5] Likewise, the Nefyn Round Table of 1284 was celebrated 'in choreis et hastiludiis'; while the licence granted to Richard Redmane and three other English knights 'de guerra hastiludiare' against four Scots at Carlisle in 1393 was intended to give the challengers a certain amount of latitude in their choice of the particular form of combat.[6]

[2] Matt.Paris, iv, 157-60.
[3] *CCR 1237-42*, p. 483.
[4] *CCR 1307-13*, p. 155.
[5] Matt.Paris, ii, 650, 614-5.
[6] *Ann.Mon.*, ii, 402; iii, 313; iv, 491; *Foedera*, vii, 745.

By the fourteenth century, although *hastiludium* remained a generic term, it no longer seems to have included tournaments but only other types of game. Thus, the *Modus Armandi*, a manuscript treatise on the armour required for various kinds of combat dating from c.1300, clearly sets out different armour for war, for tournaments and for hastiludes, while Edward III is described in another source as a king who much delighted both 'in torneamentis et hastiludiis'.[7] This distinction suggests that the declining popularity of the *mêlée* style tournament in favour of more individualistic games which were fought with lance only caused the association of the term 'hastilude' with the latter groups. The more distinctive tournament, which involved greater numbers of men and the use of other weapons, therefore required a separate identification.

The tournament was the most dangerous of all the military games, so in later years it acquired greater prestige than other hastiludes. It was fought over a wide area of countryside, often in a plain – though of the five places named in Richard I's decree only one, Salisbury/Wilton, was in a river valley, the others all being set among hills which provided greater opportunities for a variety of fighting, including the ambush. The knights fought under the banner of their leader in companies which could be as large as two hundred though smaller numbers were more usual: Baldwin of Hainault attended tournaments at Bussy-le-Chateau and Rougemont in 1172 with companies of eighty and a hundred knights respectively, while the Young King also brought companies of eighty and a hundred knights to tournaments at Lagny and Eu in 1176-80.[8] Even a comparatively unimportant leader like the Chamberlain of Tancarville could fight with thirty knights under his banner.[9] Nor were tournaments much smaller in the fourteenth century; in 1307 Gaveston, who had declared that his company would consist of sixty knights, appeared on the field at Wallingford with two hundred; in 1309 and 1334 at least two hundred and thirty-six and a hundred and thirty-six respectively took part in tournaments at Dunstable, which was again the site of a tournament fought by between two hundred and thirty and two hundred and fifty knights returning from a Scottish campaign in 1342.[10] It was not the case, therefore, as some historians of the supposed 'decline of chivalry'

---

[7] BL MS Additional 46919 fos 86v-87r; *Ann.Paul.*, pp. 352-353.
[8] Gislebert of Mons, p. 108; *HGM*, ll. 3197-201, 4750-53.
[9] *Ibid.*, ll. 1314-5.
[10] *Ann.Paul.*, p. 258; *CTG*, iv, 63-72 with additions from College of Arms MS 2nd G.3. fos 42-49v; *CTG*, iv, 389-95 with addition of Ralph Stafford from BL MS Cotton Otho Div fo. 189v; Geoffrey le Baker, p. 75.

have suggested, that the tournament became debased by decreasing in size but rather that other smaller types of hastilude increased in popularity at the expense of the more cumbersome tournament in which there was less opportunity for the individual to shine. The Dunstable tournament of 1342 is indeed the last recorded occasion of its kind in England.

Once the companies were assembled at a tournament, they were divided into two teams, according to the region or heraldic march of their origin or their political allegiance. Sometimes there would be hastiludes on the evening preceding the tournament, which were known as the 'vigils' or 'vespers' of the tournament. In fifteenth century heraldic sources these were variously described as occasions on which the tourneyers paraded through the streets in their richest clothing to the lists where they made their horses leap and flourished their swords to get themselves in the mood for the next day, or occasions at which new made knights tourneyed with shields of the same colour and courtesy lances of yew, but without swords.[11] However, apart from the fact that the vespers were considered to be a non-serious trial for the next day, there is not much evidence from contemporary sources to suggest that the fifteenth century explanations are apposite to an earlier period. It was at the vespers of the tournament between Maintenon and Nogent-le-Roi in 1180 that Renaut de Nevers captured two of the Young King's household knights, for this was the combat for the young men only:

> ... li baron e li halt home
> As vespres pas ne torneierent,
> Mais de lor genz i enveierent.[12]

In Wolfram von Eschenbach's *Parzival*, the vespers began in the morning of the day before the tournament and involved all those who were going to participate then. During the skirmishing, tempers were lost and the vespers became a full scale combat, with knights keeping their winnings regardless of knightly etiquette and breaking so many spears that it could well be considered a tournament proper. As a result, the tournament for the next day was called off because too many knights had been captured and the rest

---

[11] B. Prost, *Traités du Duel Judiciaire* (Paris, 1872), pp. 208-9; Vulson de la Colombière, *Le Vray Théâtre d'Honneur et de Chevalerie* (Paris, 1648), i, 41; Sainte Palaye, *Mémoires sur l'Ancienne Chevalerie* (Paris, 1759), i, 32-3.
[12] *HGM*, ll. 3716-8.

were too exhausted to fight again. The prize was therefore awarded to Gahmuret, and when he protested that a tournament prize could not be won at the vespers, a judge was called in who gave as his opinion that it could indeed be won by any knight who came with his helm fastened on his head for the purposes of chivalric combat, regardless of whether or not the tournament itself had taken place.[13] As late as 1405, the French still held trial jousts before the actual day, everything being exactly as it would be at the festival except that surcoats and crests were not worn and that certain knights took part in the trials who did not actually take part on the day.[14]

The tournament proper was generally introduced by *commençailles* in which individual knights fought together before their companies joined in the action.[15] This had its parallel in warfare when battles were frequently preceded by the joust of two champions and also in literature when it is the great romance heroes who begin the tournament by their encounters.[16] The general *mêlée* started when one of the companies charged another, the knights riding in serried ranks with their lances couched in rest and the combat continuing till the lances were broken; then the close hand-to-hand sword fighting of the *mêlée* began. The knights were supposed to act as a unit, leading attacks and making defences and rescues, though inevitably in the excitement of the fight the cohesion of the company was often lost and if the tourneyers got carried away too early by their desire to win ransoms and booty this could be fatal for the success of the company manoeuvre. It was those companies who rode 'sereement & sans desrai'[17] who usually won the day, and once the opposing knights had been scattered individuals could seek to make their gains. Those knights who had been captured were required to go outside the lists to arrange terms with their captors, while those who wanted time to rearm or merely to rest could take refuge in the *recets* which were areas of neutral ground in which no-one was allowed to harm them. Victory was won by the party which held the field at the end of the day or by the party with most booty. Though these were usually one and the

[13] *Parzival*, pp. 40-46, 54-5. See also Ulrich von Zatzikhoven, *Lanzelet*, trans. K. G. T. Webster (Columbia University Press, 1951), pp. 64ff.

[14] Gutierre Diaz de Gamez, *The Unconquered Knight*, ed. & trans. J. Evans (London, 1928), p. 144.

[15] *HGM*, ll. 3499ff, 5517ff, 6057.

[16] See *supra*: pp. 25-6. For literary *commençailles* see K. T. G. Webster, 'The Twelfth Century Tourney', *Anniversary Papers presented to G. L. Kittredge* (Boston & London, 1913), p. 232.

[17] *HGM*, l. 1308.

same thing, there could be problems when, as at the Wallingford tournament of 1307, Gaveston's party won most booty but the barons held the field.[18] On other occasions when there was no clearcut winner, as in the tournament between Gournai and Ressons in 1180, the sport had to be ended by agreement.[19] This reinforces the idea that, even in the twelfth century, there were rudimentary rules to be observed in the tournament,[20] though how far these were *ad hoc* arrangements rather than a formalized code of conduct is difficult to assess.

Until the end of the thirteenth century there were apparently no restrictions on who could take part in tournaments: foot soldiers therefore appear regularly. Sir Symons de Neaufle, for example, brought

> Treis cenz serjanz de pie o armes,
> O ars, o glaives, o gisarmes,

to a tournament between Anet and Sorel; the Count of Flanders similarly brought large numbers of foot soldiers to a tournament at Eu, where they would have been completely overwhelmed by the Young King's knights if they had not stayed so near their *recet* and guarded themselves so well.[21] The suggestion that Symons de Neaufle's men were armed with bows and arrows is substantiated by the monk of Montaudon who, at the end of the twelfth century, complained that he hated to see 'dart e quairel' in tournaments and by Knighton's account of the tournament which turned into the 'little battle of Chalons' in 1272 at which Edward I's company of a thousand knights and foot soldiers were obliged to resist the Duke of Burgundy's men 'cum fundis et arcubus'.[22]

There was evidently no limitation on weapons at this period for knights fought with lances, swords and maces as they did in war,[23] nor were there any prohibited strokes as yet. Though later it was to become an offence to strike an unhelmed knight, the fact that William de Preials was clad in only in a hauberk and *chapel de fer* when attempting to rescue the Young King did not prevent his

---

[18] *Vita Edwardi Secundi*, p. 2.

[19] *HGM*, ll. 5577-80.

[20] The tourneyers must have met beforehand to decide the limits of the field, the form of combat and whether the sport was to be *à outrance* or *à plaisance*, which implies some sort of formal arrangements with regard to the tournament.

[21] *HGM*, ll. 2827-30, 3243-50.

[22] *Florilège des Troubadours*, p. 360; Henry Knighton, i, 265; *Flores Historiarum*, iii, 30-1.

[23] *HGM*, ll. 2510, 2966, 3797.

opponents from attacking him at Lagny in 1180.[24] The Count of Flanders was unhorsed and captured in 1168 when he was struck on the chest by a *fautre* flung at him by another tourneyer, and tempers were lost at the 'little battle of Chalons' when the Duke seized Edward I round the neck with his arm and tried to drag him from his horse.[25] There was no rule to prevent several knights or foot soldiers from banding together against one knight, which was a much practised, if unchivalrous means of securing prisoners. Nor was it against regulations to arrive at and participate in a tournament which had already begun. William Marshal himself arrived at one tournament to find that most of the knights were already armed and the companies were beginning to charge, but this did not prevent him joining in. Another time he captured a knight who fell off his horse and broke his leg during a tournament outside the inn where Marshal, who was not even participating, was having dinner with some friends.[26] Philip, Count of Flanders, whose chivalric reputation was second to none, had a policy of holding his men aloof from the tournament until the other companies had worn themselves out with fighting and were in disarray, and then delivering his charge so that he had an easy victory. Having been a victim of this tactic several times himself, the Young King also adopted the same policy on the advice of William Marshal and thereafter enjoyed a similar success.[27]

The only rules which existed in the twelfth century to distinguish the tournament from real battle were, firstly, the provision of *recets* which were inviolable; (tourneyers could also withdraw from the field which was bounded by palisades and ditches, but this carried with it notions of shame and dishonour which were not applicable to taking refuge in a *recet*.); secondly, the recognition that unhorsing and capturing knights, not killing them, was the object of the game; and thirdly, the codes of conduct concerning prisoners. Anyone captured in a tournament had to be released, although he was obliged to pay a ransom. When Gawain announced that he would send a knight he had captured in a tournament as a prisoner to the lady who was his captive's greatest enemy, the knight replied:

> That is not yours to do, sire. A tournament is not warfare, and I will not be taken back to the castle. I am quite able to pay my ransom.[28]

[24] *Ibid.*, ll. 4871ff.
[25] Gislebert of Mons, pp. 97-8; Henry Knighton, i, 265; N. Trivet, *Annales*, ed. T. Hogg (London, 1845), pp. 285-6.
[26] *HGM*, ll. 1425-7, 5008-9, 1410ff, 7209-32.
[27] *Ibid.*, ll. 4871ff.
[28] *The High Book of the Grail*, p. 48.

On the other hand, Renaut de Nevers refused to release two members of the Young King's household whom he had captured because he wished to revenge himself for not being accepted into the Young King's *maisnie*. As soon as he had given his promise to pay the ransom to his captor a prisoner should have been released and could even rejoin the sport, as William de Preials did when he saw the Young King was about to be captured.[29] The reckoning was made at the end of the day when the tourneyers paid courtesy calls at the lodgings of the great lords and sorted out among themselves the value of the ransoms.

It was also to these great lords that knights who felt themselves mistreated in the tournament went for redress.[30] This role of advising on chivalric disputes had not yet been adopted by heralds, whose role in the twelfth century hastilude seems to have differed little from that of the minstrels with whom they were classed. It was not until attempts were made to formalize the rules and render the game less dangerous that heralds emerged in their more familiar organizational roles.[31]

The gradual accretion of customary rules of combat for the tournament in the thirteenth century is perhaps best illustrated in the early fourteenth century romance, *Perceforest*, where King Alexander is credited with the invention of tournaments. To prevent them becoming an opportunity for treason and disloyalty he prohibited the use of any weapon intended to deliver the *estoc*, a thrusting blow which pierced the armour and gave the *coup de grâce*. Instead, he allowed only the sword, shield and lance: striking from behind and attacking an unhelmed knight were also strictly forbidden.[32] These were the essence of the rules that fifteenth century treatises also set out, by which time the weapons were all blunted and of a standard length to avoid giving advantage to one opponent.[33] Tournaments *à plaisance*, that is with blunted weapons, were not unknown even in the twelfth century. The author of the history of William Marshal often states that his hero was fighting in tournaments that were not *à plaisance*, with the implication that if

---

[29] *HGM*, ll. 3741ff., 4871ff.

[30] *Ibid.*, ll. 4083ff., 3225ff., 3309ff.

[31] The role of heralds at tournaments is a huge subject and one that has only been glanced at in this study because of its complexity.

[32] *Perceforest*, i, 22r.

[33] Prost, *Traités du Duel Judiciaire*, pp. 212, 215-6; René d'Anjou, 'Traité de la Forme at Devis d'un Tournoi', *Verve*, iv, no. 16 (1946), pp. 47-8; Bodleian MS Ashmole 764 fos 32r, 33r.

they had been *à plaisance* then no taking of booty or ransoms would have been allowed.[34] By fighting with sharp weapons (*à outrance*) the tourneyers were theoretically putting their lives at stake, though this was redeemable by payment of ransom.

Because of the dangers of the tournament and because it was the nearest *simulacrum* of battle of all hastiludes, it was considered to be the most honourable of all the feats of arms, after warfare:

> Et vraiement ils sont bien a loer et priser; car il convient grans mises, grans estofes et grans despens, travail de corps, froisseures et blesseures et peril de mort aucune fois.[35]

For the same reasons, Sicily herald proclaimed that the *bienvenue*, a payment made by a knight the first time that he took part in a hastilude, was payable only once if he tourneyed first of all, but if he jousted first and then tourneyed it had to be paid on both occasions for the tournament enfranchised the joust but not *vice versa*.[36]

If the tournament was an imitation of battle, the joust was an imitation of the judicial duel which occupied such a large place both literally and allegorically in the medieval romance.[37] It swiftly gained popularity with knights to whom it offered a greater opportunity of revealing their individual prowess and with ladies to whom it offered a more interesting spectacle since everything occurred within view. Secular authorities also seem to have preferred jousting to tourneying, perhaps because jousts were less destructive of lives and property. It is noticeable, therefore, that the only hastiludes to be excluded from general prohibitions in England are jousts, albeit even this occurs on only three occasions.[38]

The joust was fought between individuals, the knights riding from opposite ends of the lists to encounter each other with lances in rest. Skilled horsemanship was essential as there was nothing to prevent the horses crashing together, for the barrier was not introduced until the 1420s. In fact, it was the crashing of horses, or their swerving to avoid the encounter, that frequently caused the combatants to completely miss each other.[39]

---

[34] *HGM*, ll. 1310-2, 2502.
[35] Geoffroi de Charny, 'Le Livre de Chevalerie', p. 464.
[36] A. Wagner, *Heralds of England* (London, 1967), p. 103.
[37] W. R. J. Barron, 'Knighthood on Trial: the acid test of irony', *Knighthood in Medieval Literature*, ed. W. H. Jackson (Cambridge, 1981), p. 92.
[38] *CCR 1307-13*, p. 155; *CCR 1323-7*, p. 133; *CCR 1341-3*, p. 100.
[39] This occurred with monotonous regularity at the St Ingelvert jousts in 1390. See Froissart, xiv, 105-51.

There were several different methods of fighting in the joust which had evolved by the end of the fourteenth century. Like the tournament, they could be fought *à outrance*, though this was generally restricted to jousts against national enemies such as the French or Scots, or *à plaisance*. The latter were particularly common as a means of celebrating noble births and marriages, at which times they were usually referred to by chroniclers as *solempne joustes*.[40] There were also varying degrees of formality associated with jousts; usually they were declared in the name of one knight, the *tenant*, who, perhaps with a chosen team of fellows, would proclaim his intention of holding the field against all comers. Sometimes this meant that each of the *venants* chose his opponent beforehand, as at St Ingelvert where each *venant* had to touch the shield of whichever of the three *tenants* he wished to encounter, and then the jousts would take place in the lists which were otherwise empty of combatants. At other times the assignment of opponents was much less formal: all those wishing to fight would be within the lists and whenever he felt ready one knight would start forward with his visor down and his lance in rest. He could either pick out one of the opposing team to joust against or he could wait to see if one of them would take up his challenge. In their enthusiasm, it often happened that several knights would come forward against one knight though courtesy usually ensured that the superfluous knights would drop out. Occasionally, accidents happened, as when Pero Niño, a Castilian noble sampling this French method of fighting for the first time found himself struck by two knights at the same moment, or when Henry, duke of Lancaster, was seriously wounded while jousting against one man by a jouster who attacked him from the side.[41]

There were also several different techniques of fighting the joust, some of which Pero Niño experienced in Paris. One French champion was an exponent of the somewhat crude, but nevertheless effective, 'French method' of running full tilt at his opponent to overthrow him by the combined weight of heavily armed man and horse. To avoid him, Pero Niño reined in his own horse then gave it the spurs when the Frenchman was about to hit him, planting his lance on his adversary's shield so that with the shock his lance broke, the horses crashed and his opponent was thrown to the ground with his mount. A second adversary of German origin was a skilled horseman who jousted with great dexterity, never waiting for

---

[40] e.g. *The French Chronicle of London*, ed. Aungier, p. 62; *The Brut*, i, 308-9.
[41] *The Unconquered Knight*, p. 143; *Scalacronica*, p. 176.

the shock and avoiding the encounter but making great play with his bridle, wheeling round to reach Pero Niño with his lance whenever he could or using the horse's petrel sideways as a ram with which to knock him off balance.[42] Another German jouster in a much earlier age who enjoyed a considerable chivalric reputation, Ulrich von Liechtenstein, demonstrated a different method of fighting for he used swingeing sideways blows to unhorse his opponents and, unlike Pero Niño, he emerged successfully from an encounter with two knights who charged at him simultaneously by avoiding the first and breaking his lance on the one behind.[43] Though German hastiludes tended to be out of step with French practices which were predominant in England and the Low Countries, it must be noted that, according to Wolfram von Eschenbach's *Parzival* written c.1200, there were five different methods of jousting but he offers no explanation for what took place.[44] Two German jousts of the fourteenth century do seem to have been practised in England and France: the *Hohenzeuggestech* and the *Scharfrennen*. The former had as its objective the splintering of lances only, so that the knights used light lances and rode in a standing position in a saddle which had a waist high front support extending downwards to completely cover the legs which were held in place by bars around the thighs. The main object of the *Sharfrennen* was unhorsing, so that a heavy lance was used and there were no front or rear saddle supports so that the rider's fall was unimpeded.[45] It was important when trying to unhorse a knight always to drop the lance on impact to avoid injury to either party although it was when Sir John Saint-John did this carelessly that he mortally wounded the young earl of Pembroke whom he was instructing in the art of jousting.[46]

The joust was much more of a spectator sport than the tournament because it was fought within a confined space, often a market place which had been strewn with sand and surrounded by a wooden palisade;[47] wooden *berfrois*, or stands, were also built from which the nobles and especially the ladies could watch in comfort and safety. Although it was regarded, like the tournament, as an honourable feat of arms, it came lowest in the scale of values beneath war and tournament because it offered only the one form of

[42] *The Unconquered Knight*, pp. 146-7.
[43] Ulrich von Liechtenstein, pp. 114, 115.
[44] *Parzival*, ed. A. T. Hatto (Penguin Classics), p. 403.
[45] C. Blair, *European Armour: c.1066-c.1700* (London, 1958), 160; R. C. Clepham, *Defensive Armour and Weapons* (London, 1900), pp. 86-9.
[46] *The Brut*, ii, 344-5.
[47] e.g. Smithfield 1363, see: PRO E101/571/26.

combat, with the lance, and therefore it was regarded by authors of chivalric courtesy books as only the first step of a knight up the ladder of military accomplishments.[48] That such valuations did have an effect in reality is clearly illustrated by the festival of Chauvency where, after several days' jousting, a council of knights decided that to prevent anyone being injured and thus being forced to absent himself from the tourney, the jousts on the day before were all cancelled;[49] the jousts thus had to give way to the more prestigious tournament.

If the joust was the first chivalric activity of the newly dubbed knight, the *behourd* was one of the most popular means of training him before he attained knighthood. The *behourd* was one of the most enigmatic of the hastiludes. It appears in the twelfth century, for when Arnold of Ardres had grown to man's strength he frequented 'behordicia' and tournaments, while Henry, son of Bernier, in the *chanson de geste* of Raoul of Cambrai was taught from the age of seven and a half to bear arms and to 'behorder'.[50] The association of *behourds* with young men training to be knights is one that continues to the end of the period and for that reason we hear much of esquires in their context. As early as 1234 Henry III prohibited a *behourd* between the esquires of H[enry?] FitzMatthew and Walter Clifford.[51] It was also esquires who held 'quoddam hastiludium quod burdice dicitur' at Boston fair in 1288.[52] Before he was knighted William Scrope was considered 'un dez pluis noblez bohordurez q[ue] hom[m]e troverait en un paiis', while Robert of Brunne included 'these bourdys of these squyers' in his general condemnation of all hastiludes because they embroiled their participants in the seven deadly sins.[53] *Behourds* were not totally limited to esquires, however, for they were often held in conjunction with knighting ceremonies, coronations, royal marriages and similar gatherings of the chivalric classes, and their prohibitions were addressed to knights and esquires indifferently.[54]

From the fifteenth century onwards, attempts have been made to

---

[48] Geoffroi de Charny, pp. 472-4.
[49] *Le Tournoi de Chauvency*, ll. 2708-15.
[50] J. Flori, 'La Notion de Chevalerie dans les Chansons de Geste du XIIe Siècle', *Moyen Age*, lxxxi (1975), p. 230.
[51] *Foedera*, i, 332.
[52] Walter of Guisborough, p. 244.
[53] *The Scrope and Grosvenor Roll*, i, 133; Robert of Brunne, l. 4628.
[54] For prohibitions addressed to esquires see: *CCR 1307-13*, p. 159; *CCR 1327-30*, p. 547; *Foedera*, iv, 698.

explain what happened in the *behourd* with varying degrees of success. One heraldic manuscript describes it as a diminutive tournament, fought in an enclosed park, which was not published or officially proclaimed, nor fought with pennons or blazonry. It was held for the pleasure of the lords who jousted in equal numbers, one against one, or a hundred against a hundred, and whoever broke most lances was awarded a prize which was customarily granted to the heralds in the form of *largesse*, because they received none of their usual dues in the 'buhort'.[55] The idea that it was a small scale informal tournament receives backing from a fifteenth century treatise on Arthurian *cries des joustes*, which specified the same defensive armour for both *behourd* and tourney, though the offensive weapon for the former was a two and a half foot long cudgel attached to the hand and for the latter, a rebated sword.[56]

However, by the fifteenth century it is clear that *behourd* was being used as a generic term for all hastiludes; Anthoine de la Salle in his treatise *Des Anciens Tournois et Faictz d'Armes* refers to all tournaments, jousts and *pas d'armes* as *behourds* indifferently.[57] What can be gleaned from the sources is that the *behourd* during the period 1100 to 1400 was an informal sport frequently occurring on the spur of the moment so that there was no need for a specific field or lists of any kind. It seems to have been fought with lance and shield only,[58] and almost always *à plaisance*, although this did not prevent it being included with other hastiludes in prohibitions throughout the thirteenth and fourteenth centuries; as early as 1226 Matthew de Berghefeld had been accused of breaking the king's peace by holding a 'buhurdicium'.[59] The informal nature of the *behourd*, combined with the fact that it was fought *à plaisance*, meant that it was a particularly suitable hastilude not just for training knights but also for celebrations, hence its association with occasions of rejoicing.

Another hastilude which also served as a means of teaching tiros to joust was the quintain, which was sometimes called the peacock (*pavo*) or the pile. The term 'peacock' inevitably brings to mind the *Vows of the Peacock*. In the *Romance of Alexander*, a peacock was served up at a banquet and all the knights present swore on the bird

---

[55] BL MS Harleian 6069 fo. 106v.
[56] Bodleian MS Ashmole 764 fo. 32r.
[57] Prost, *Traités du Duel Judiciare*, pp. 204-21.
[58] 'Gui de Nanteuil', *APF*, vi, l. 1813; *Parzival*, p. 329.
[59] *Curia Regis Rolls 1225-6*, xii, p. 451 no. 2247.

to perform certain feats of arms.[60] Whether there was any link between the game and the chivalric vows of the romance is pure supposition, though given the ideological links between chivalric vows and hastiludes this would not be unlikely.

There were many variants of the game, but essentially it consisted of an object, usually a shield, fixed to the top of a pole at which the horseman aimed his lance; it could also be used by men on foot attacking a mannikin on top of a pole with swords and clubs. The fifteenth century treatise, *Knyghthode and Bataile*, which is a verse paraphrase of the classical *De Re Militari* by Vegetius, says that young men should first be taught to fight by means of the quintain which the versifier urged him to imagine to be a Turk for 'though he be slayn, noon harm is'.[61] The apprentice should also use a shield and mace of double weight to accustom him to bearing the weight of arms. Practice at the quintain was a vital part of a knight's education:

> And noo man (as thei seyn) is seyn prevaile
> In felde or in gravel though he assaile
> That with the pile nath first gret exercise,
> Thus writeth werreourys olde & wise.[62]

Even the doyen of French chivalry, Bertrand du Guesclin, began his spectacular military career at the quintain, and Robert the Monk records that during the First Crusade the knights in the army set up shields on posts outside their tents so that they could practice at it.[63]

It was also a sport popular among the non-knightly classes. In 1253 the young men of London proclaimed that they were going to hold a *pavo* and therefore set up a 'stadium quod quintena vulgariter dicitur'. This attracted some of the youths in the king's household who, having mocked the Londoners, were soundly thrashed for their pains.[64] It was perhaps with this riot in mind that two years later Henry III prohibited anyone from tourneying 'vel ad papilionem carrum aut pavonem vel alio modo justeare' without special

---

[60] *The Buik of Alexander*, ed. R. L. Graeme-Ritchie (Edinburgh, 1925-9), i, xxxvi-xlvii.
[61] *Knyghthode and Bataile*, ed. R. Dyboski & Z. M. Arend (EETS, cci, 1935), l. 375.
[62] *Ibid.*, ll. 358-61.
[63] Cuvelier, *Chronique du Bertrand du Guesclin*, l. 214; Robert the Monk, *Historia Hierosolymitana*, quoted by Du Cange, *Dissertations sur la Vie de Saint Louys*, p. 25.
[64] Matt. Paris, v, 367-8.

licence.[65] A similarly disorderly gathering of townsmen is recorded in 1257 when John Loterich received pardon for the death of Lauretta Portur, who was trampled under the feet of his men and horse while he was running with a lance at a standard during the celebrations of a wedding at Romney.[66]

Among the variants of the quintain which had a large following, particularly in towns, was water jousting. William FitzStephen described how, during the Easter holidays in the twelfth century, the young Londoners would go out in rowing boats on the Thames and while several rowed, one would stand in the prow with a lance which he aimed at a shield fixed on a pole in the river; if the lance broke he escaped unscathed, but if it remained whole he was precipitated into the river by the shock.[67] There was also water jousting involving two such teams encountering each other, the jouster on the prow attempting to dislodge his opposite number on the prow of the other boat. Other variants, according to fourteenth century manuscript illuminations, included running at the quintain on a wooden horse on wheels pulled by two esquires, jousting on barrels, running on foot with a lance at a knight who wore his helm and breastplate and sat on a stool and foot jousting in which one combatant sat on a stool, the other on a swing, and using one leg extended as a lance each tried to displace the other.[68]

It is possible that the *tupinaire* was a similar sort of game, though it is rarely heard of and almost impossible to elucidate. It received no chronicle notices and, indeed, is only known from prohibitions. In 1312 Philip of France prohibited all tournaments, jousts, 'tupineiz' and other feats of arms, adding that many French knights had already disobeyed his former veto on such hastiludes.[69] In England three writs in 1328, 1329 and 1331 variously prohibited 'tupinaire', 'tupinas' and 'turpine'.[70] In the first case, the term appears to be replacing the usual *behourd*, but in the other cases they are included with tournaments, jousts and *behourds*, so that they cannot be seen as an alternative name for any of these hastiludes. That they were a distinct form of wargame is suggested by Geoffroi de Charny's

---

[65] *CCR 1254-6*, p. 376.

[66] *CCR 1247-58*, pp. 607-8.

[67] FitzStephen, *Descriptio Civitatis Londoniae*, p. 31.

[68] J. Strutt, *Sports and Pastimes of the People of England*, enlarged & corrected by T. C. Cox (London, 1801), p. 127. It is possible that these illuminations, which are mainly taken from Bodleian MS Bodley 264, may be caricatures rather than true representations. See: Bodleian MS Bodley 264 fos 56r, 78v, 82v, 89r, 100r.

[69] *Ordonnances des Roys de France*, i, 509.

[70] *CCR 1327-30*, pp. 389, 544-5; *CCR 1330-33*, p. 397.

Book of Questions in which he asks 'Comment se font toupineures a estres dites toupineures et non autrement?'[71] He also poses the same question about tournaments and *encommensailles* but as he offers no answer, no light is shed on the matter. One explanation offered by a late heraldic source is that the term is a derivation from 'toupin', an earthenware pot used to cook meat in Burgundy, Lyonnais and Dauphine, with the presumption that the pot replaced the shield on the quintain.[72] As there is no evidence to support such a hypothesis, the derivation seems spurious like most heraldic attempts at etymology. As the case stands there is not enough evidence to attempt a definitive explanation of what was involved.

There is much more positive material relating to the term 'seeking adventures' (*aventuras quaerare*) which is also to be found mainly in royal prohibitions throughout the thirteenth and fourteenth centuries.[73] Sometimes it appears as a generic term, as when Henry III in 1242 prohibited anyone from meeting to tourney, *behourd*, 'vel ad alias quascumque aventuras', or when, with the consent of his magnates a decade earlier, he forbade the holding of any hastiludes 'neither under the name of tournament nor under the name of an adventure'. More usually, however, it appears as a specific form of hastilude included in a list of forbidden martial sports. The explanation can be found in the great popularity of the romances and their inevitable hero, the knight errant, who rode out to seek adventures and undertake whatever chance combats fell his way. A historical prototype of this literary knight errant is briefly glimpsed in the pages of Anna Comnena's *Alexiad*.[74] When the First Crusaders arrived in Constantinople and their lords were brought to swear allegiance to the emperor, one of the Frankish noblemen sat down on the Imperial throne. When reproved for his arrogance, he replied:

> at a crossroads in the country where I was born is an ancient shrine; to this anyone who wishes to engage in single combat goes, prepared to fight; there he prays to God for help and there he stays awaiting the man who will dare to answer his challenge. At

[71] C. Leber, *Collection des Meilleurs Dissertations ... Relatifs a l'Histoire de France* (Paris, 1838), xii, 163.

[72] *Ibid.*, xii, 162; Honoré de Ste Marie, pp. 191-2.

[73] e.g. *CCR 1237-42*, p. 483; *CCR 1261-4*, p. 133; *CCR 1296-1302*, pp. 373, 408, 583; *CCR 1307-13*, p. 159; *CPR 1232-47*, pp. 20, 48, 188; *CPR 1266-72*, p. 611; *Foedera*, iii, 6.

[74] Anna Comnena, *The Alexiad*, p. 326. He was later seriously wounded with forty of his men when he broke ranks to lead a charge against the Turks in contravention of the Emperor's advice: *Ibid.*, p. 341.

that crossroads I myself have spent time, waiting and longing for
the man who would fight – but there was never one who dared.

This knight was clearly a seeker after adventures, desirous of
proving his prowess in chance encounters. That the crossroads was
the customary place for such knights to go suggests that this pastime
was not unusual despite the silence of other, non-literary sources.

Ulrich von Liechtenstein's *Venusfahrt* of 1227 was based upon
similar ideas. His general challenge, which preceded his setting out
on a jousting tour dressed as the Lady Venus, listed the places he
intended to visit and the dates he would be there, so that any knight
who wished to fight him knew when and where he could encounter
'her'.[75] Again, the motivation appears to have been a desire to test
his strength against an unknown opponent in chance encounters.
This interpretation also elucidates the royal writ of 1228 which
ordered the sheriffs of Norfolk and Suffolk and Essex to arrest any
knights found travelling through their counties 'ad querendum
ibidem casus fortuitos'.[76]

This seeking of chance encounters could take the form of
attending hastiludes, but it could also be a much more dangerous
occupation involving temporary involvement in real wars. A man
like Marshal Boucicaut dedicated his whole life to seeking 'advan-
ture d'armes' both in peace and war, and never lost an opportunity
of taking part in some martial exploit.[77] Others enjoyed a brief but
more memorable moment of glory. In the 1320s, William Marmion
was the hero of an adventure which, apart from its inglorious
ending, could have come straight from the pages of romance. At a
great feast of knights and ladies in the county of Lincoln a lady sent
him a gilt crested war helm and a letter commanding him to make
the helm famous in the most dangerous place in Britain. The
consensus of knightly opinion was that Norham castle on the
Scottish borders was 'le plus perillous aventurous lieu du pais'. The
reputation was quickly justified, for within four days of his arrival
the castle was under siege. Marmion therefore armed himself and set
out against the Scots on foot, but he was recalled by the castellan
who told him that, as a knight errant, he ought to perform his
chivalrous deed on horseback, not on foot. With the castellan's
backing, Marmion spurred his horse alone into the Scottish ranks,
where he was swiftly wounded and unhorsed but was rescued

---

[75] Ulrich von Liechtenstein, p. 100.
[76] *CCR 1227-31*, p. 106.
[77] *Livre des Faits ... du Boucicaut*, p. 38.

before he suffered any mortal hurt.[78] This was not an isolated incident, for when the English garrison of Douglas was surprised and massacred by the Scots, a letter was found on the body of Sir John Webtoun, the captain of the garrison.

> A letter, that him send ane lady
> That he lufit per drowry.

The letter informed Webtoun that when he had spent a year in war as governor of

> The aventurus castell off douglas
> That to kepe so perelous was

then he might justifiably ask for and receive the love and reward of his mistress.[79]

Seeking adventures, therefore, covered a wide spectrum of martial exploits from the peaceable hastilude to acts of war, but essentially it involved the chance encounter against unselected opponents. It also embodied the idea of knight errantry, with combatants coming from afar to participate, which was indeed a common feature of hastiludes in this period.

If seeking adventures was inspired by romance literature, Round Tables were a direct attempt to imitate romance. They enjoyed the same patrons and both had links with Wales, which was the centre of Arthurian legend. There could even be a certain element of role playing, as we have seen, in which knights adopted the blazonry and, in some cases, the characters of Arthurian heroes. This happened at what appears to be the first Round Table on record. In 1223, those present at the knighting of the Ibelin brothers in Cyprus celebrated with festivities in which they also 'contrefait les aventures de Bretaigne et de la Table Ronde'.[80]

Within a decade of this celebration Henry III had prohibited those meeting at a Round Table at an unspecified place in England from tourneying there.[81] This, and other references, suggests that the Round Table was not a specific type of hastilude, but rather a chivalric gathering at which hastiludes took place. Although feasting was a regular feature of most hastiludes, if only because they were

---

[78] *Scalacronica*, pp. 145-6.
[79] J. Barbour, *The Bruce*, i, 195.
[80] Philippe de Novare, p. 7. For more detailed discussion of role playing, see *supra*, pp. 6ff.
[81] *CPR 1225-32*, p. 492.

held on occasions of celebration, a banquet seems to have been of central importance at the Round Table. When Roger Mortimer held one in 1279 at Kenilworth to mark the knighting of his sons it was described as a 'convivium ... quod rotundam tabulam milites vulgare nomine consueverant appellare'.[82] In 1344, after the jousts at Windsor were finished, Edward III 'made a grete soper, in the wiche he ordeyned feest, & bygan the Rounde Table'.[83] Marshal Boucicaut, at the St Ingelvert jousts in 1390 laid in a huge stock of provisions at his own expense for the consumption of all the *venants* 'si plantureusement comme pour tenir table ronde'.[84] The banquet and sumptuous hospitality to all who attended were, therefore, a prerequisite of the Round Table, a fact emphasized by the disparaging remarks made by chroniclers, as to the profuse but futile expenditure on such occasions.[85] In many respects, Round Tables were similar to Tables of Honour which were an important part of chivalric ideology, not least because they provided an ideal opportunity for public acclaim which was so vital to those knights who sought *los et pris*.[86] The Round Table, though more informal and more open than Tables of Honour, was similarly a prestigious occasion celebrating knightly values and glorifying those who had participated successfully in the lists.

The Round Table enjoyed a similar reputation to Tables of Honour partly because of its Arthurian origins and, like them, it attracted large numbers of foreign knights. Their presence was particularly noted at several English Round Tables, as, for instance, at Waltham (1252), Warwick (1279), Nefyn (1284) and Windsor (1344). On the last occasion, Edward III sent heralds to France, Scotland, Burgundy, Hainault, Flanders, Brabant and the Empire, inviting knights of all nationalities to attend, in a deliberate attempt to make the event as international as possible.[87]

As was natural at such military gatherings, hastiludes featured prominently among the activities, but because it was also essentially a celebration, these were fought *à plaisance*. Jousting seems to have been the most popular hastilude at Round Tables. Although Matthew Paris gives the impression that the Round Table was a

[82] *Ann.Mon.*, iv, 281.
[83] *The Brut*, ii, 296.
[84] *Livre des Faits ... du Boucicaut*, p. 65.
[85] *Ann.Mon.*, iv, 281.
[86] For Tables of Honour see: A. S. Cooke, 'Beginning the Board in Prussia', *The Journal of English and Germanic Philology*, xiv (1915), pp. 375-88.
[87] Matt.Paris, v, 318; *Ann.Mon.*, iv, 477; Trivet, *Annales*, p. 300; *Ann.Mon.*, ii, 402, 491; iii, 313; *The Brut*, ii, 296; Froissart, iv, 204, 206; Adam Murimuth, pp. 155-6.

martial game in its own right, and although many authors have thought that it took its name from being fought within a circular field,[88] there can be little doubt that the hastiludes took their usual form. Paris himself says that the knights at the Waltham Round Table jousted together for several days 'secundum quod constitutum est in illo ludo martio', and Clement V in his bull of 1314 prohibited all tournaments and jousts on the basis of dangers to body and soul which arise 'etiam in faciendis justis praedictis quae "Tabulae Rotundae' in aliquibus partibus vulgariter nuncupantur'.[89] Since the presence of ladies was also an important part of the Round Table gatherings, the celebrations had to include singing and dancing to occupy the evening and night, once the hastiludes had ended.[90]

The pageantry and imitation of romance which feature so strongly in Round Tables, were echoed in the fifteenth century by the *pas d'armes* in which the hastiludes were given a specific setting such as Jacques Lalaing's *Pas de la Fontaine des Pleurs* in 1449, for which a pavilion was set up near a 'fountain of tears' in Burgundy, where those desiring to fight could enrol their names. Even the three shields which had to be touched to indicate the choice of hastilude bore the device of tears.[91] Three years earlier, King René d'Anjou borrowed more directly from romance in setting up the *Pas du Chateau de la Joyeuse Garde* near Saumur, for he actually built a wooden castle in imitation of that of Lancelot.[92]

The *pas d'armes* seems to have originated in a challenger proclaiming his intention to defend a pass or narrow defile, which could be a natural one, or alternatively an artificial one created solely for the purposes of the hastilude. Any knight who wished to travel through the pass had first to fight the challenger and was only allowed to go through if he acquitted himself well. Sometimes the knight had to be accompanied by a lady, which further increased the possiblities of pageantry.[93]

This form of the *pas d'armes*, however, belongs firmly in the fifteenth century. When the term first emerged in the fourteenth

---

[88] J. Smyth, *The Lives of the Berkeleys*, ed. J. Maclean (Gloucester, 1883-5), i, 147; R. Cline, 'The Influence of Romances on Tournaments in the Middle Ages', *Speculum*, xx (1945).

[89] Matt. Paris, v, 318; D. Wilkins, *Conciliae Magnae Brianniae et Hiberniae 1268-1349* (London, 1737), ii, 437-8.

[90] e.g. *Ann. Mon.*, ii, 402, 491; iii, 313.

[91] Georges Chastellain, *Oeuvres*, ed. K. de Lettenhove (Brussels, 1866), viii, 189-247.

[92] Colombière, *Le Vray Théâtre d'Honneur*, i, 82ff.

[93] *Ibid.*, i, 81-2.

century it was merely used as an alternative to 'feat of arms'. At this period it was a much more sombre affair, usually lacking the romantic trimmings it later acquired. The feat of arms could be fought on horseback or on foot, though more often than not it was a combination of both. Equally, it could involve only one challenger and a defender, or a group of knights on each side. The desire to excel under conditions so difficult as to be almost farcical, is clearly shown in a French knight's challenge which John Cornwall accepted at the turn of the fifteenth century. They were to exchange ten lance blows in low saddles, shields without protective iron, arms bare of armour and the bascinet without a visor, followed by twenty sword blows in low saddles clad only in a haubergeon, twenty dagger blows on foot also in the haubergeon, and then ten axe blows on foot in their own choice of harness.[94] John Cornwall was also involved in a similar challenge with the Senechal of Hainault; the latter had originally sought to undertake a feat of arms on his own against all the knights of the Garter, but Henry IV had refused his permission, offering him one Garter champion in their place. This the Senechal accepted on condition that the number of courses was increased from the original twelve to thirty-six in each type of combat. At the same time the Senechal was also challenging John Cornwall to a feat of arms *à outrance* on foot, each being accompanied by three of his fellow countrymen all armed with lances, swords, daggers and battle-axes, but this fell through due to difficulties in remitting the letters. Instead, John Cornwall offered to fight alone against the Senechal *à outrance* which was accepted, though again there followed a long exchange of letters quibbling about the choice of judge in the affair.[95]

Although national hostility was the primary motivation in the choice of opponents, feats of arms were nominally undertaken for purely chivalric reasons. Often the challengers bore a device which their opponents had to endeavour to win from them. Chivalric terminology posed the wearer of the device as undergoing a penance from which he sought deliverance, as in the case of Michel d'Oris who bore a piece of leg armour until he was 'delivered' by an English knight.[96] At about the same time, the beginning of the fifteenth century, five French knights challenged five Englishmen to relieve them of a garter which had a lace and stick attached to it which they had adopted as their device. To win the gold stick they

---

[94] BL MS Additional 21357 fo. 4r.
[95] BL MS Additional 21370 fos 1r-14r.
[96] E. Monstrelet, *Chronique*, ed. Douet d'Arcq (Paris, 1857), i, pp. 11ff.

had to undergo nine courses with lance, sword, axe and dagger; for the lace, twelve lance courses on horseback and twenty-six sword blows on foot; and for the garter itself, all five had to fight together *à outrance* each aiding his companions.[97]

Such bands of challengers were not rare and it seems that once such a companionship had been formed it remained open to challenges for years afterwards. The seven French knights bearing the device of a diamond, who challenged the English to raise a similar group of seven to undertake feats of arms against them *à outrance* in 1398-9, did not actually fight their combat until 1402. Then, the defeat of the English and the death of lord Scales became the subject of several ballads by Christine de Pisan, who saw the triumph of French chivalry in terms of their international struggle.[98] It was a sign of the times, therefore, when in 1405-6 the same French victors, this time as champions not of the French cause but of the house of Orleans, were prepared to undertake a similar feat of arms against seven champions of the house of Burgundy.[99]

The feat of arms was a much more serious form of hastilude than those already discussed; it was almost invariably fought *à outrance* and the choice of opponents was deliberately those for whom political or patriotic loyalties would conflict and therefore embitter the contest. Here was no game fought 'nullo interveniente odio, sed pro solo exercitatio atque ostentatione virium'.[100] It must be included among the hastiludes, however, since it was fought within enclosed lists, was subject to stringent rules prohibiting one combatant from using unfair advantages such as in the length of his weapons, and was fought before a judge who could decide the outcome either way and intervene if necessary.

The prearranged combat fought between parties of equal numbers was an extension of these practices and ideas, although it predated the feat of arms (which only became really popular in the last decades of the fourteenth century) by many years. As early as 1194 the French king had proposed a combat of five knights from each country to end the Anglo-French wars and avoid the spilling of more blood.[101] The same offer was made by Charles, king of Naples and Sicily, to the King of Aragon, for a hundred against a hundred

---

[97] BL MS Additional 21357 fo. 3r.

[98] *Ibid.*, fos 1r, 2r; Christine de Pisan, 'Ballade ... sur la Combat de Sept Français Contre Sept Anglais', *Recueil de Chants Historiques Francais*, ed. Leroux de Lincy (Paris, 1841), i, 281-7.

[99] *The Unconquered Knight*, pp. 149-53.

[100] William of Newburgh, ii, 422.

[101] *Flores Historiarum*, ii, 110.

at the end of the thirteenth century, and by the Duke of Bourbon to the Earls of Pembroke and Cambridge who were besieging him a century later. Edward III proposed a combat of a hundred against a hundred to decide the rights to the French crown in 1340 – an offer which was repeated by Philip de Valois to the Duke of Lancaster during the siege of Calais.[102]

None of these challenges was taken up but some combats of equal numbers were fought out with lesser issues at stake. The most famous of these was the combat of thirty against thirty at Ploërmel in Brittany in 1351. The combatants were the garrisons of neighbouring castles, one of which was attached to the party of Charles de Blois and the other to the party of Jean de Montfort. The combat was arranged after it was decided that this would be a more honourable encounter than mere jousting, even though it was to be fought on foot. Weapons were *à outrance* and unlimited so that maces and battleaxes were also used, with resultant heavy casualties on both sides, including the leader of the Montfortians. The combat continued for so long that through sheer exhaustion it was agreed to have a break during which the participants could rest, dress their wounds, and take some refreshments.[103]

Thirteen years before this, Henry, earl of Derby arranged a similar event at Berwick. The combatants were all knights rather than mercenaries, as in Brittany, and it was agreed to have twenty English against twenty Scots, each man jousting three courses *à outrance* in war harness. Interestingly, when Alexander Ramsay, who led the Scots, suggested that the combatants should joust with plain shields, the earl rejected this because then no-one could win honour if they were not identifiable. The jousts continued for three days, with several mortalities, and prizes were awarded on each side to the knights who had struck the fatal blows.[104] Though combats involving such large numbers were less common than the feats of arms between small bands of knights, they were fought in much the same circumstances and in much the same spirit.

The chivalric combat went one stage further than feats of arms. The latter were hastiludes, however bitter the animosities which had prompted them. The chivalric combat was not a hastilude even though it shared many of the characteristics of feats of arms. It was a form of judicial duel fought out between men of chivalric rank,

---

[102] M. Amari, *La Guerra del Vespro Siciliane* (Milan, 1886), ii, 19-21; Froissart, vii, 473; Adam Murimuth, pp. 110-11; Henry Knighton, ii, 50-1.
[103] Jean le Bel, ii, 194-7; H. Brush, 'La Bataille de Trente Anglois et de Trente Bretons', *Modern Philology*, ix (1912), 511-44; *Ibid.*, x (1912), 82-90.
[104] Andrew of Wyntoun, vi, 103-15.

only allowable when a case could not be settled at law. Usually it involved some accusation of treason which neither accuser nor defendant could prove. The combat would be fought in the same lists as a feat of arms, sixty foot long and forty foot wide, and, as in all later hastiludes, the weapons had to be of standard length so that the parties stood on equal terms. There the similarity to hastiludes ended, however, for the battle continued until one of the parties admitted defeat or was killed. In the former case, the defeated combatant was taken outside the lists, disarmed and executed, since the outcome of the combat was a form of judgement just like the judicial duel.

Unlike the judicial duel, it could only be fought before the king, constable, marshal or their specially appointed deputies; it was fought in full armour and on horseback as well as on foot, and the judge could stop the fight at any moment and subject the matter to the king's arbitrary judgement.[105] This last happened frequently, especially in the fourteenth century, as the king could not afford to allow two men of high rank to put their lives at stake in such a cause. The combats between Otto of Brunswick and Henry, duke of Lancaster in 1352, and the Dukes of Norfolk and Hereford in 1398, for example, were both taken into the king's hands before the combat began.[106] Some combats involving men of lesser rank were fought out to the bitter end, however, like that between John Annesley and Thomas Katrington in 1380, and John Walsh and a Navarese knight in 1384.[107] In all cases the duellists were men of chivalric rank, being either knights or esquires. Although personal honour played an important part in the conduct of such affairs, men did not deliberately seek to participate in chivalric combats as they did for hastiludes. In the former they were seeking to vindicate their reputation and honour, which had been impugned, and failure meant not only death but also dishonour, whereas in the latter the mere participation, regardless of victory or defeat, increased their standing and enhanced their dignity. Moreover, even in hastiludes fought *à outrance* killing an opponent was a matter for regret and even reproof, since this was not the specific object of the game; using sharp weapons was simply a method of proving one's personal courage in the face of a danger which had been voluntarily sought, hence conferring honour on those who used them. There was not

[105] G. Neilson, *Trial by Combat* (Glasgow, 1890), pp. 188-9; Honoré Bonet, *Tree of Battles*, ed. Coopland, pp. 199-203, 206-7.

[106] *Chronicon a Monacho Sancti Albani*, p. 32; *Historia Vitae et Regni Ricardi Secundi*, ed. G. B. Stow (Pennsylvania, 1977), p. 149.

[107] *Chronicon a Monacho Sancti Albani*, pp. 261-5, 361.

only a difference in purpose between the chivalric combat and the hastilude, but also a difference in intention. For these reasons, and because its history belongs to that of the judicial duel rather than the hastilude, the chivalric combat has not been dealt with at length in this study.

The many different forms of hastilude which were available to the medieval knight offered him a wide choice. He could fight informally, on the spur of the moment, in a *behourd*, or he could meticulously plan elaborate challenges and settings which would encourage pageantry in a Round Table or joust. He could practise his lance skills on his own at the quintain, or as part of a large company in the tournament. He could fight his neighbour *à plaisance* or his enemy *à outrance*. By the end of the fourteenth century he could also choose whether to fight on horseback or on foot, with lances only, or with weapons more usually associated with war. The tourneyer's options were wide, and the flexibility of the sport no doubt encouraged *ad hoc* forms of hastilude which did not fit into any of the categories here defined. What does emerge, however, is that there were two mainstreams of tourneying development. Firstly, there was the hastilude *à outrance* which descended from the great *mêlée* tournament, through seeking adventures and jousts of war to feats of arms. Secondly, though no less important, there was the hastilude *à plaisance* which developed through Round Tables and jousts of peace. The two were coeval, so that there was always a choice of fighting for fun or for a more serious purpose, depending on the mood of the occasion.

CHAPTER EIGHT

Tournament Armour

The emergence of different forms of hastilude presented a new problem to the tourneyer. Each specialized form of the game had its own particular risks and dangers, and it was no longer practical simply to wear the normal armour of war for hastiludes, as had happened in the early days of tourneying. In the great *mêlée* tournament it had been appropriate to wear war armour because the same sort of hazards were to be faced; the lance thrust and the sword buffet, in particular, were features of both forms of combat. The joust, however, was a different matter. Here the knight had to be able to receive a single blow with the full weight of horse and rider behind it. Clearly a different sort of armour was necessary to withstand this type of assault. The development of tourneying armour was, therefore, in part a response to the specialized needs of hastiludes.

It was also an attempt to reduce the risks of personal injury which were inherent in tourneying. The list of English mortalities in tournaments is very long and includes some of the most notable names among the English nobility: Geoffrey de Mandeville, earl of Essex in 1216, Gilbert Marshal, earl of Pembroke in 1241, William, son and heir of John Warenne, earl of Surrey and Sussex in 1286, and John Hastings, earl of Pembroke in 1390.[1] At least four members of the Mortimer family were killed in hastiludes over the years, and even the royal family did not escape unscathed for Geoffrey of Brittany, fourth son of Henry II, was killed tourneying near Paris in 1186.[2] These are just a few of the socially important men who were killed tourneying. There must have been many hundreds more casualties from the ranks of 'simple' knights.

---

[1] Ralph de Coggeshalle, p. 179; Matt.Paris, iv, 135-6; *Chronicle of Bury St Edmunds*, p. 87; *The Brut*, ii, 344-5.
[2] *Monasticon Anglicanum*, vi, pt. i, 349, 350, 351, 352; Roger of Hoveden, ii, 309.

On top of the fatalities, there was a serious problem of those who were afflicted with severe mental or physical disabilities as a result of tourneying. Roger Bigod, for example, never recovered from the injuries he received at the Blyth tournament of 1256 and Robert FitzNeal's lands had to be put into the hands of guardians when he was struck on the head while jousting which rendered him permanently mentally incapable.[3] The risk of death or serious injury in hastiludes was one of the main objections which secular and ecclesiastical authorities had to tourneying, as we have seen. The development of higher standards of armour was, therefore, of two fold interest to tourneyers: their personal safety was increased but also, if the sport became less dangerous, then there would be less justification for prohibiting it.

Tourneying armour was specially developed to provide maximum protection in the variant forms of hastilude. It also became more highly decorated over the years, as increasing emphasis was laid on the spectacle presented by the tourneyers. The materials for hastiluding armour reflected those employed in war armour. The lightest defences, which were used throughout the period, were made from quilted fabric and *cuir bouilli*, leather which had been boiled and then dried to an extremely hard consistency. Metal armour was eschewed at first simply because, to be effective, it had to be so thick that the weight was unbearable. Mail armour, formed from linked metal chains or rings, was a partial answer to this problem which was not satisfactorily solved until the end of the fourteenth century. At this period, great advances in metalworking skills, pioneered on the continent, enabled plate metal armour to be so well tempered that it was both effective against blows and yet comparatively light. The history of tourneying armour is, therefore, a history of the trials and errors involved in combining the different defensive materials available: new pieces of armour were, in fact, fairly rare.

To give a clear idea of what developments were made it is necessary to study each piece of armour individually. This chapter will examine the tourneyer's wardrobe item by item throughout the period 1100 to 1400; the first section will deal with functional armour, the second with decorative armour. The chapter will end by drawing these different threads together to give a brief comparative description of the well-dressed tourneyer at the beginning and end of the period.

---

[3] Matt.Paris, v, 557, 609; *CPR 1348-50*, p. 413.

Part One: Functional Armour

The Helm

The huge helm, which was such a distinctive feature of tournament armour, remained remarkably unchanged throughout the period. From the twelfth century to the mid-fourteenth century it was cylindrical in shape with a flat top. Vision was restricted to one or two eye-slits which had to be narrow enough to prevent a lance passing through, but which could not prevent slivers from broken lances occasionally blinding or even fatally wounding the tourneyer. Ventilation was provided by means of a number of holes which also had to be small enough to prevent weapons entering or catching in them, and which were not very efficient. The helm was often airless and unbearably hot,[4] especially after hard exertion, and yet it was the main head protection for war as well as tournaments. The helm rested on the shoulders, protecting the knight's neck, and was fastened by means of buckled straps and laces to the body armour. This means of fastening caused innumerable problems. On one occasion William Marshal's helm turned round completely on his head so that his sight and breathing were impaired. It was only by means of hearty wrenching, which eventually broke the laces, that he was able to pull it off.[5] After another tournament he was found kneeling with his head on an anvil while the blacksmith tried to beat his helm back into shape so that it could be removed.[6] Incidentally, this was taken to be outstanding proof of his great valour because it clearly showed that he had been in the thickest part of the *mêlée* and had withstood tremendous blows. Lace fastenings could be used to advantage by the unscrupulous. When Sir Reginald de Roye jousted *à outrance* against Sir John Holland in 1387 he deliberately fastened his helm with only one thong. As a result, whenever Holland hit him on the head, the Frenchman's thong broke and his helm flew off, enabling him to keep his seat. This caused an uproar among the spectators who claimed it was unfair, but when they appealed to John of Gaunt as an arbiter, he declared that the stratagem was not illegal, merely unchivalrous.[7]

The helm was often highly decorated. At the turn of the fourteenth century John Bromyard complained that the elaborate gilded helms of tourneyers cost forty pounds each.[8] This was a huge

[4] *Parzival*, p. 139.
[5] *HGM*, ll. 1451-61.
[6] *Ibid.*, ll. 3102ff.
[7] Froissart, xii, 120-1.
[8] *Summa Predicantium*, fo. ccxlii(v).

exaggeration, but in 1391-2 Henry, earl of Derby paid 53/4d each for two helms for jousts *à plaisance*. Simon Burley, at about the same time, possessed seven helms of this type, which were painted white and bore his green device upon them.[9] Removable crests and *contoises*[10] completed the helm decoration.

An inventory of the goods of Roger Mortimer dating from 1322 divided his helms into three distinct groups: three helms for jousts, one for war and six for tournaments.[11] At this period there are no indications what, if any, were the differences between these helms, and it is not until the end of the fourteenth century that the differences become clearer. A steel skull cap called the *cervellière* or bascinet, worn over the mailed coif but under the helm, had given protection to the knight's head if he was unhelmed in the fight. In the latter part of the fourteenth century, the cumbersome helm was discarded for the purposes of war and the bascinet, which became more conical in shape, replaced it completely. This type of bascinet was probably also worn for jousts *à outrance* instead of the helm. In 1397 Richard, earl of Arundel owned eleven helms and three 'bacynets pour courses de guerre' and Thomas, earl of Gloucester, even more specifically, owned 'iii healmes p[ou]r joustes de pees' and 'ii basnets p[ou]r joustes de guerre'.[12] These bascinets for war and jousts *à outrance* had additional pieces to increase protection since they did not rest on the shoulders like the helm. Instead, the neck was more satisfactorily protected by a collar of steel, which was less vulnerable to lances slipping off the body armour under the helm, which could sever the jugular vein.

At the very end of the fourteenth century the great helm was also abandoned for hastiludes *à plaisance* in favour of the frog-mouthed helm. There had been a tendency for the eye-slits to become longer and join together to form a single slit. To combat the danger to the eyes caused by the increasing size of this *veue*, the helm below the eyes was given a more exaggerated curve and the top of the helm also became more rounded. These developments deflected and reduced the weight of blows received to the head. The frog-

---

[9] PRO DL28/1/3 fo. 14r; Bodleian MS Eng.Hist.B229 fo. 4.

[10] See *infra*: pp. xxxx.

[11] A. Way, 'Inventory of the Effects of Roger Mortimer', *Archaeological Journal*, xv (1858), p. 359. Hereinafter referred to as 'Mortimer Inventory'.

[12] L. F. Salzman, *The Property of the Earl of Arundel, 1397*, (Sussex Archaeological Collections, 91, 1953), p. 46. Hereinafter referred to as 'Arundel Inventory'. Viscount Dillon & W. H. St John Hope, 'Inventory of the Goods and Chattels belonging to Thomas, Duke of Gloucester (1397)', *Archaeological Journal*, liv (1897), p. 305. Hereinafter referred to as 'Gloucester Inventory'.

mouthed helm developed these traits to their logical conclusion, creating a much more spherical helm which fastened securely to the cuirass by means of hasps instead of laces. It had an exaggeratedly curved front with the lower piece jutting out beyond the upper to such an extent that the wearer only had a clear view when he was leaning forward in the correct position for couching the lance and taking aim. At the moment of impact, the jouster would straighten up to receive the blow of his opponent and in doing so, his eyes were protected, though the same action also rendered him virtually blind.[13] The old great helm made of heavy steel or even *cuir bouilli*, which had served the knight for so long in war and hastiludes was in this way replaced by the finely tempered steel bascinet for all combats *à outrance* and the frog-mouthed helm for jousts *à plaisance*.

Linen Body Armour

To prevent metal or *cuir bouilli* armour chafing or cutting the skin, the knight wore quilted fabric defences beneath his other armour for war and tournament. These defences also served to deaden the weight of blows received and this helped to minimize bruising, though it has to be said that they do not appear to have been particularly effective in either case. The *aketon* and the *gambeson* were both quilted coats worn for this purpose, though the latter was often made of rich silk and was also intended to be worn over other armour and in addition to the *aketon*.[14]

The first references to a specialized form of armour being adopted for hastiludes involved quilted defences. In 1216 the rebel barons held a tournament against their erstwhile allies, the French invaders, in which the participants fought 'cum hastis tantum et lineis armaturis'.[15] This restriction on armour and arms was presumably declared beforehand to reduce the chances of injury. Unfortunately, it proved ineffectual as Geoffrey de Mandeville was killed tourneying there. Similarly, the Blyth tournament of 1256 at which the participants fought 'in lineis et levibus', presumably because the lord Edward was tourneying there for the first time, was marked by heavy casualties.[16] At about the same time, Thomas du Cantupré recorded that the knights of Brabant used to meet regularly near

[13] Blair, *European Armour*, pp. 157-8.
[14] *Ibid.*, pp. 33-4.
[15] Matt.Paris, ii, 650.
[16] *Ibid.*, v, 557.

Brussels to hold tournaments 'sine ullo armorum praesidio exceptis lanceis, scuto et galea, induti tantum plicata linea tunica'.[17]

Perhaps because it proved ineffectual in limiting the consequences of combat, linen armour seems to have dropped out of fashion as the sole defence of the tourneyer, though it continued to be used in conjunction with other forms of armour. In 1307 Prince Edward gave over twenty pounds worth of armour 'tam lineorum quam ferri' to five of his knights and esquires in anticipation of a tournament at Wark and the Scots war.[18] The knight in the *Modus Armandi* armorial treatise of the early fourteenth century wore a *camisia de Chartres* over the top of his *aketon*, but beneath his hauberk and cuirass, and Roger Mortimer had an 'aketon cum una camisia de chartres' stored at Wigmore Abbey in 1322.[19] The exact nature of this elusive garment remains a mystery. Du Cange quotes an undated treatise which states that knights fighting duels should wear the *chemise de Chartres* between their armours. This, combined with the evidence of Guillaume de Tudèle that Chartres was renowned as a centre for producing helms and *gambesons*, suggests that the *camisia de Chartres* was also a quilted fabric defence for the body.[20]

A later form of linen armour which was current in the fourteenth century was studded armour. The fabric was covered with metal studs which could deflect a sword blow and it served as a light-weight addition to tourneying armour. A mid-fourteenth century manuscript of the romance, *Meliadus*, in the British Library has a particularly fine illustration of tourneyers wearing studded sleeves and in 1388 Simon Burley had a pair of white velvet sleeves worked with gilded nails ('clowes').[21] By the mid-fifteenth century at least one armorial treatise recommended that a whole *brigandine*, a corselet, studded in the same way, was the best piece of body armour available for the tourneyer.[22]

Linen armour, worn as a sole defence, was only suitable for hastiludes in which the main part of the fighting was done with the broadsword, as it clearly would not withstand the stabbing blow of the lance. It was not suitable for jousts nor for war despite its cheapness, lightness and flexibility: for these purposes, therefore, it

---

[17] Thomas du Cantupré, pp. 446-7.
[18] BL MS Additional 22923 fo. 10v.
[19] BL MS Additional 46919 fo. 87r; Mortimer Inventory, p. 361.
[20] Du Cange, *Glossarium*, ii, 'Chemise de Chartres'.
[21] BL MS Additional 12228 fos 150v-151r; Bodleian MS Hist.B.229 fo. 4.
[22] R. de Belleval, *Du Costume Militaire*, pp. 8-9.

formed only a subsidiary defence in conjunction with metal or *cuir bouilli* armour, to muffle the shock of blows received.

The Hauberk

The hauberk was an essential piece of armour for war and hastiludes throughout the period. It was a shirt of mail made of interwoven steel rings which was light and flexible compared to plate armour. It was worn over the quilted defences but beneath any rigid metal or *cuir bouilli* armour, giving particular protection to joints which needed flexibility but were vulnerable, such as the armpits. An extension to the hauberk, and often forming one piece with it, was the mail coif, a hood which defended the neck and head, leaving only the face uncovered. An evocative description of the effects of wearing mail armour is given in the *High Book of the Grail* where Perceval and Lancelot jousted together so hard that the mail of their hauberks stamped rings on their foreheads and faces.[23]

In the twelfth and thirteenth centuries the hauberk was the main metal defence of the tourneyer. Waleran de Luxembourg, for instance, appeared at the tournament at Chauvency in 1285 wearing a 'Haubert saffre menu maille'.[24] By this time, however, it is possible that a hauberk had been specially developed for hastiludes. When the crusader, Joinville, was lying ill on the deck of his ship near Damietta in 1250, his men clad him in 'un haubert a tournoier' to protect him from Saracen darts. Raoul de Nesle also possessed a 'haubers a tournoier' according to an inventory of his goods made in 1302.[25] How such hauberks differed from ordinary ones worn for war cannot be determined.

By the end of the fourteenth century mail had almost completely been superseded by plate armour which had many advantages over mail. Problems had been caused by mail armour in at least two eventualities. Firstly, because of its matted surface it did not encourage weapons to glance off the armour, thereby causing heavy bruising. Secondly, if the mail gave way under the impact of a blow, it was liable to become embedded in the wound, causing healing problems. By the end of the fourteenth century, therefore, mail was only used as a secondary defence, beneath plate armour to protect the joints where flexibility was essential.

---

[23] *The High Book of the Grail*, p. 93.
[24] *Le Tournoi de Chauvency*, l. 3439.
[25] Jean, Sire de Joinville, *Histoire et Chronique du très-Chrétien Roi Saint Louis*, ed. M. F. Michel (Paris, 1859) p. 96; Blair, p. 157.

Plate Body Defences

From the 1330s onwards, the pair of plates begins to be depicted in armorial brasses, though it was probably introduced well before this date. This was a cloth or leather garment lined with overlapping metal plates, which was worn over the hauberk, and it features regularly in the financial accounts of tourneyers because the fabric had to be repaired or changed to match the colour theme of the tourneyer's outfit. Edward III paid 50s. each for three new pairs of plates covered with white leather for the Windsor jousts of 1340, but in 1386 Richard II had to pay fully twice that amount for each of the pairs of plates he bought for the March Smithfield jousts, as did Henry, earl of Derby in 1395-6.[26] Fashion and the quality of the fabric used could considerably increase the cost of a pair of plates. The Black Prince had to pay £6.13.4d for two pairs of plates covered with black velvet which he gave to two of his knights in 1355, plus a further 20s. just for having his own old pair of plates recovered with red velvet.[27] Henry, earl of Derby even had a new pair of plates dagged (given a scalloped edge) to match the rest of his outfit for a hastilude *à plaisance* in 1391-2. The extensive jousting wardrobe of Simon Burley included one pair of gilded and silvered plates, six pairs of plates covered with velvet or leather, four uncovered ones and three coats in to which the plates could be inserted, made of tartaryn and decorated with his personal badge.[28]

The breastplate was introduced towards the middle of the fourteenth century. This was a single plate of steel, covered with cloth, which protected the chest: it had developed from the cuirass and the pair of plates. Breastplates emerge suddenly and in large numbers in the royal accounts in the 1340s, when Edward III was charged 16s. each for several 'poitrines pur joustes'.[29] Though the breastplate effectively replaced the cuirass for hastiludes, it was worn in addition to, and over the top of, the pair of plates. Henry, duke of Lancaster was given both 'a pair of plates for the jousts and a brestplate' by the Black Prince in 1358, and Froissart has many descriptions of knights jousting *à outrance* being pierced through steel breastplate, pair of plates and all the other layers of armour right through to the flesh.[30] As late as 1397 Richard, earl of Arundel

---

[26] H. Dillon, 'An Armourer's Bill, Temp. Edward III', *The Antiquary*, xx (1890), p. 150; PRO E101/401/15 m2; PRO DL 28/1/5 fo. 21v.
[27] *Register of the Black Prince*, iv, 123-4.
[28] PRO DL28/1/3 fo. 2v; Bodleian MS Eng.Hist.B.229 fo. 4.
[29] 'Armourer's Bill', p. 150.
[30] *Register of the Black Prince*, iv, 247; Froissart, x, 196-8.

possessed four 'brestplates pur turnement' as well as many other breastplates for war made in London and Flanders.[31]

In the 1380s a new device was introduced specifically for the jousts. The *arrêt de la cuirasse* was a metal bracket soldered on to the right side of the breastplate on which the jouster could take the full weight of his lance, thereby achieving a steadier aim. By locking into the lance it also prevented the backward movement of the lance on impact, thus increasing the likelihood of the lance breaking or the opponent being unhorsed.[32]

The tendency in body armour was, therefore, to move away from mail and *cuir bouilli* towards more rigid defences made of steel which covered a larger area of the body.

Arm Defences

The same developments are also true of limb armour. Rigid defences were introduced over the mail sleeves of the hauberk in a piece-meal fashion and in varying materials. Raoul de Nesle, for example, possessed a shoulder piece for the tournament made from whale-bone[33] which was presumably intended to give additional protection to the right shoulder which was not covered by the shield. Roger Mortimer, some twenty years later, already possessed *bracers* which were plate defences for the whole arm[34] though it was not until about 1340 that the *vambrace* and the *rerebrace* were introduced. The *vambrace* was a plate defence for the forearm to the elbow, and the *rerebrace* from the elbow to the shoulder.[35] This new development is marked in one of the royal household accounts for the year 1341 when Edward III paid 30s. for a pair of *vambraces* and *rerebraces* 'foubiz ... de la novelle maner' for the Norwich jousts.[36]

About the same time another piece of armour was introduced, this time specifically for the jousts. This was the *maindefer*, a rigid plate defence for the left hand and lower arm, which replaced the old leather or whalebone gauntlets which were now only worn on the other hand. The hand holding the rein was thus given added protection whilst the right hand remained unrestricted so as to give

---

[31] Arundel Inventory, p. 47.

[32] F. Buttin, 'La Lance et l'Arrêt de la Cuirasse', *Archaeologia*, xcix (1965), pp. 77-178, esp. pp. 102-4.

[33] Blair, p. 157.

[34] Mortimer Inventory, pp. 359, 361.

[35] Blair, pp. 44-5; James Mann, 'Arms and Armour', *Medieval England*, ed. A. L. Poole (Oxford, 1958), i, 324.

[36] 'Armourer's Bill', pp. 149-50.

better manoeuvrability of the lance. The earliest references to *maindefers* occur in 1338 when Edward III was purchasing arms and armour for jousts in Ghent. A single *maindefer* cost him 6s.8d whereas in the 1380s and 1390s Richard II and Henry, earl of Derby were paying at least twice that sum for the same item.[37] By this later period the *maindefer* and its fellow, the plate gauntlet (*cirothec' de plate*), appear to have been confined solely to hastiludes *à plaisance*. Thomas, duke of Gloucester, for example, only possessed *maindefers* as part of his harness for jousts of peace.[38] This points to the conclusion that the *maindefer* was one of those pieces of armour which were considered to give an unfair advantage to the wearer, and were prohibited in jousts *à outrance* and chivalric combats.

Leg Defences

Armour for the lower limbs did not develop as rapidly as for the arms, simply because the legs were not as vulnerable, since customary rules obliged jousters and tourneyers only to aim above the waist. As late as the tournament at Chauvency, knights were still using mail leggings to protect their legs,[39] though it was more usual to wear metal or *cuir bouilli* plates over the top. Even in 1388 Simon Burley was still wearing defences for the legs (*legh[ar]nois*), feet (*sabatons*) and arms (*j paire de vambras et rerebras*) made from *cuir bouilli* covered with velvet, and displaying his badges even though most of his armour was made from steel.[40] By the end of the century, most jousters were wearing complete plate defences for the leg, jointed at the knee, together with plate defences for the feet.

Since the greatest danger to the legs was that of being crushed when horses collided or fell in the joust, a saddle was developed to improve the jouster's safety. Until the fourteenth century there is no indication to suggest that knights used any saddle other than their war saddle for hastiludes. In the 1390s, however, jousting challenges began to make a distinction between high saddles and low saddles for jousts.

The high saddle was usually associated with jousts of peace, though there is an important exception in that Henry, earl of Derby purchased several items for his high saddle when preparing for his

---

[37] *Ibid.*, p. 150; PRO E101/401/15 m2; PRO DL28/1/1 fo. 6r; PRO DL28/1/5 fo. 21v; PRO DL28/1/4 fo. 13v.
[38] Gloucester Inventory, pp. 305-6.
[39] *Le Tournoi de Chauvency*, l. 3437.
[40] Bodleian MS Eng.Hist.B.229 fo. 4.

duel against the Duke of Norfolk.[41] It is possible that it simply had a higher front and back than normal war saddles, thus giving the knight a more secure seat, but at the turn of the fifteenth century de Gamez described how Pero Niño, a Castilian nobleman, observed that the French jousted in *cuir bouilli* saddles which covered their legs nearly to their feet.[42] As the English tended to follow the French in chivalric fashions, it is not unlikely that this type of jousting saddle had been introduced into England too. De Gamez' description tallies well with the form of wishbone shaped saddle used in the fifteenth century for the German *Hohenzeuggestech*. The special object of this type of joust was to splinter lances, rather than unhorse the opponent and so, to further this purpose without endangering the jouster's personal safety, the seat of the saddle was raised some ten inches above the horse's back. The jouster was held in a standing position by two wooden bars curving round his thighs which considerably reduced his freedom of movement and the front saddle bow was raised and extended in a fork shape to form a shield which protected the knight from his waist to his feet.[43] Though there is no indication in chronicles to suggest that this type of joust was practised in England, the emergence and proliferation of references to high saddles in the last decade of the century suggest that this was possible.

The alternative to the high saddle was the low saddle, which probably had a very low front and rear. Again there is a fifteenth century German parallel in the *Scharfrennen* saddle which had neither front nor rear supports, because the object of the joust was complete unhorsing and nothing impeded the knight's fall. Just as the high saddle seems to be associated with jousts *à plaisance*, low saddles seem to be especially, though not exclusively, associated with jousts *à outrance*.[44]

Although household accounts distinguish between saddles for tournaments and saddles for jousts,[45] there is no indication what, if any, the differences were. It may even be that the clerks were varying their terminology, rather than attempting to draw a hard and fast distinction between different saddles. The only obvious difference between saddles for hastiludes and for other purposes was that the former required much stronger means of attachment.

[41] PRO DL28/1/6 fo. 43r.
[42] *The Unconquered Knight*, p. 142.
[43] Blair, p. 160. An example of this type of saddle cen be seen in the Tower of London Armouries.
[44] Clephan, *Defensive Armour*, pp. 86-7.
[45] e.g. PRO E361/2 m12.

Double girths were usually issued for all such saddles[46] to ensure that they did not slip off backwards in the shock of the encounter. Gilbert Marshal had been killed in 1241 because his saddle girths broke when he reined in too sharply during a tournament: he was thrown off his horse and because he could not disentangle his spurs from his stirrups, he was dragged until dead.[47] The disadvantage of double girths, which was the reason why they were not employed outside the lists, was that they restricted the horse's breathing and so could not be used over a long period of time.[48]

The other feature common to all hastiluding saddles was that they were much more highly decorated than those used for war or pacific horses. In 1383, for example, John of Gaunt paid ten marks for a saddle covered with cloth of gold, and three years later Richard II paid 100s. for a saddle worked 'ad modum Boem' for the Smithfield jousts.[49] Thomas, duke of Gloucester had a saddle for jousts of war gilded with his arms, and Richard, earl of Arundel owned four tourneying saddles, three of which were painted and the fourth embroidered.[50]

Horses

The quality of a tourneyer's horse was almost as important as the quality of his armour. A weak horse could be overthrown by even a fairly feeble blow and if a knight fell and tangled his spurs he might be dragged to his death, like Gilbert Marshal and Geoffrey of Brittany.[51] Just as knights trained themselves for war by participating in hastiludes, so they trained their horses by the same means so that they were unafraid of the noise and crush of combat and were taught to ride head on for the encounter, which went against their natural inclinations. In the early days of the tournament, therefore, horse and rider trained together in hastiludes so that they were ready for combat in the event of war.

The horse was the most valuable booty to be won in hastiludes so that killing or wounding one was greatly frowned upon. Inevitably, however, accidents happened to them with even greater frequency

[46] Nicolas, 'Observations', p. 99; PRO E101/390/2 m6; PRO E361/3 m49.
[47] Matt.Paris, iv, 135-6.
[48] C. Lefebvre des Noëttes, *L'Attelage: le cheval de selle à travers les ages* (Paris, 1931), pp. 242-3.
[49] *John of Gaunt's Register 1379-83*, Hodge & Somerville, p. 259; PRO E101/401/15 m2.
[50] Gloucester Inventory, p. 307; Arundel Inventory, p. 47.
[51] Roger of Hoveden, ii, 309; Matt.Paris, iv, 135-6.

than to their riders, for they were less well protected. In 1293, for instance, John of Brabant had to put aside 15s. for the care of two of his horses wounded at the Northampton tournament.[52]

The value of horses could vary tremendously. John of Brabant bought a *runcin* to give to one of his knights on the tournament field at Dunstable and it cost him only 40s. In the same year, Thomas Corbet was trying to recover £20 in a lawsuit as the value of a horse which had been mortally wounded in jousts at Salisbury.[53] Because the expense of losing horses in hastiludes was so prohibitively high, it was common practice to look to the lord to pay for replacements. The lord Edward, for instance, ran up debts of nearly seventy pounds in this manner while on his tourneying tour of France in 1260-2: they were still unpaid over twenty years later.[54] On a smaller scale, Gilbert, earl of Gloucester had to pay £6.13s.3d and 100s. for two of his retainers' horses lost at the Dunstable tournament of 1309, plus a further twenty pounds for another retainer's horse which was captured there and presumably had to be ransomed or replaced.[55]

From the middle of the fourteenth century, references begin to horses used specifically for hastiludes only. Four horses for war and four for peace, each ridden by a man in the appropriate armour, were presented as an offertory at Sir Ralph Nevill's funeral in Durham Cathedral in 1355, though his heir bought back the four 'better' horses for a hundred marks. In 1369, Thomas, earl of Warwick willed his best and next best jousting horses to Sir John and Sir Roger Beauchamp respectively.[56] Some knights obviously kept large stables of horses: Pero Niño bred and trained horses to his liking, 'some for war, some for parade and others for jousting', and Renaut de Trie, admiral of France, still possessed twenty horses, including some for war and some for jousting, even when in retirement due to old age and ill health.[57]

It is significant that these references to horses specifically intended for jousts appear at a time when the joust was replacing the old *mêlée* style tournament. The jouster not only wore more and heavier armour than the tourneyer or warrior, but also required his

---

[52] *Account of the Expenses of John of Brabant*, ed. J. Burtt, p. 5.

[53] *Ibid.*, p. 10; *Year Books of the Reign of Edward I: Years XX & XXI*, ed. A. J. Horwood (R.S., 1866), p. 223 & Appx. ii.

[54] *Records of the Wardrobe and Household*, ed. Byerly, pp. 63, 244.

[55] PRO SC6/1109/12.

[56] *Wills and Inventories*, ed. J. Raine, p. 27; *Testamenta Vetusta*, ed. N. H. Nicolas (London, 1826), i, 80.

[57] *The Unconquered Knight*, pp. 41, 135.

horse to perform a specialized function quite distinct from war or tournament. The jousting horse had to run head on against a single opponent and bear the full shock of the encounter. It was also required to perform this function repeatedly, for there was no switch to sword play at close quarters as in the tournament and war. The training of horses solely for jousts had two effects: it decreased the risk of accident or injury caused by frightened or inexperienced horses and it increased the chances of jousters making contact, since the horse was more likely to perform the course in a reliable manner. Even so, the number of horses at the St Ingelvert jousts of 1390 who crashed, crossed over in their paths, swerved or refused altogether to complete their courses[58] is striking testimony to the difficulty in persuading even trained horses to act contrary to their natures. The introduction of the barrier in the fifteenth century must have greatly contributed to the smooth running of the joust.

Horse Armour

Trained horses were obviously more valuable than untrained ones, and this was reflected in the increasing care taken to ensure their safety in hastiludes. In 1278, for example, Edward I provided thirty-eight leather horses' heads (*copita cor' de similitud' capit' equ[orum]*) and thirty-eight leather cruppers for his Windsor Park tournament.[59] The former were probably *cuir bouilli* headpieces, otherwise known as 'testers' or *chanfreins*, which protected the whole head apart from the eyes. The cruppers were leather straps buckled to the back of the saddle and passing round under the horse's tail to prevent the saddle slipping forward. The tester and crupper, together with the piser, which probably protected the chest, formed the basis of most horse armour from the thirteenth century. Usually they were covered with velvet or taffeta so that the horse was as gaily decorated as its rider. Edward III, for example, spent £9.19s.3d on blue velvet, gold plate and silk for covering a crupper, tester and piser for the Lichfield hastiludes of 1348. All were embroidered with branches and flowers of columbine, lions and other fanciful devices.[60]

In the late fourteenth century another piece of armour designed to protect the jousting horse was introduced. This was a crescent-shaped buffer, padded with straw or cotton and covered with

[58] Froissart, xiv, 105-51.
[59] 'Copy of a Roll of Purchases for a Tournament at Windsor Park', pp. 302, 305.
[60] PRO E372/207 m50.

leather, which hung across the horse's chest to prevent injury if it collided with the opponent's horse. Edmund Mortimer owned a buffer of this type in 1393: one of his wardrobe accounts records 'j pilwe stuffato et la stuff' coopert' cu[m] cor[eo] rub[eo]'.[61]

Much of the rest of the horse's equipment seems to have been designed for hastiludes; there being abundant references to tournament bits, fanstirrups, stirrups, spurs, girths and reins. How these articles differed from the usual articles for war it is impossible to tell.

Over all the tournament armour worn by horses there was usually a trapper, which served the same purpose as a knight's surcoat. It was a long flowing cloth covering the horse's back and reaching almost to the ground, decorated with the coat of arms, badge or temporary tournament device of the tourneyer. In 1227, for example, Ulrich von Liechtenstein persuaded a large number of knights to fight on his side in a tournament and as a mark of their allegiance they wore Ulrich's coat of arms on their trappers.[62] Sir Hugh Hastings, father of the defendant in the Court of Chivalry case at the end of the fourteenth century, had also been seen displaying the disputed arms on his shield and on his trappers in 'divers joustes'. At about the same time, Simon Burley's wardrobe included two trappers for war, one decorated with his coat of arms, the other with his badges, and two trappers for peace, both decorated with his badges.[63] The practice was evidently a continuing one.

Shields

As was the case with almost all forms of armour, it was common practice to use the same shield for war and hastiludes until the fourteenth century. Shields were made from wood and reinforced with various hard materials such as sheets of metal or horn. Because of their prominence, shields provided an ideal place to display their owner's coat of arms. William Marshal, for instance, was recognized by the Count of St Pol across a tournament field because of the arms displayed on his shield.[64]

In the fourteenth century, the *écranché* shield was invented. Instead of being triangular, as in the past, this new type of shield

---

[61] BL MS Egerton Roll 8738 m1.
[62] Ulrich von Liechtenstein, p. 164.
[63] College of Arms, *Processus in Curia Marescalli*, i, 545; Bodleian MS Eng. Hist.B.229 fo. 4.
[64] *HGM*, ll. 5997-8.

was oval with a rounded indentation on the right hand side on which the lance rested. As it did not impede the lance, this shield could be held more centrally so that it gave better protection to the body. Its use was limited to hastiludes *à plaisance* and most challenges relating to such hastiludes state that the shield should not be covered with metal.[65] Shields of this type were usually covered with cloth of the same colour and design as the rest of the tourneyer's outfit, like the red velvet 'cov[er]ture p[ou]r lescu' restored to Edmund Mortimer in 1331, or Henry, earl of Derby's shield covered with dagged black and white cloth in 1391-2.[66] Simon Burley owned eight shields 'p[u]r les ioustes de pees' in 1386 which are all included in his inventory of jousting armour. His shield for jousting *à outrance*, (*target p[u]r iouster en guerre*), on the other hand, is not to be found in this category but rather in the separate list of war armour.[67]

Reinforced shields continued to be used for jousts of war and were a vital part of a tourneyer's defences. A French knight jousting *à outrance* against Sir John Colville in the mid-fourteenth century refused to complete his three courses of war when his shield split after the second course. He refused to fight with the broken shield or without it, declaring that both alternatives were too dangerous to himself and Colville.[68] Knights who were especially anxious to win renown for prowess, however, sometimes stipulated in their jousting challenges that their shields for jousts of war should have no metal coverings,[69] just like shields for jousts of peace.

The shield only gave full protection to the left side of the body and the left arm. This left the lance arm vulnerable and so the *vamplate* was developed in the fourteenth century. The *vamplate* was a convex, circular metal guard on the lance immediately in front of the hand grip. It gave protection to the hand and, as it increased in size throughout the fourteenth and fifteenth centuries, to the lower arm. As early as 1322 it appears in an inventory of the goods of Roger Mortimer, and thereafter it features regularly in purchases for war and hastiludes.[70]

---

[65] e.g. Bodleian MS Ashmole 764 fo. 35r; BL MS Lansdowne 285 fo. 46v.
[66] *Ancient Calendars of the Exchequer*, ed. F. Palgrave (Record Commission, 1836), iii, 165; PRO DL28/1/3 fos 3r, 6v.
[67] Bodleian MS Eng.Hist.B.229 fo. 4.
[68] *The Anonimalle Chronicle*, p. 18.
[69] e.g. BL MS Additional 21357 fo. 4r.
[70] Mortimer Inventory, p. 359; PRO E361/2 m12; PRO E101/388/11; PRO E101/401/15 m2.

Lances

In the twelfth and thirteenth centuries tourneyers used the same lances for tournament as for war, though when fighting *à plaisance* the sharp warhead was removed and replaced by the coronal, also known as the *socket*, *roche* and *rochet*. The first mention of a coronal in English tourneying history occurs at the Waltham Round Table of 1252, where Matthew Paris describes it as 'brevem formam habens vomeris, unde vulgariter vomerulus appellatur, Gallice vero soket'.[71] By the fourteenth century this had given way to a crown shape which gave the coronal its name. The three or more blunt projections prevented the lance piercing the armour and helped to spread the effect of the blow. The coronal was inter-changeable with a sharp blade used in war and hastiludes *à outrance*, so that the same lance shafts could be used for either purpose.

By the late fourteenth century, however, there was a difference between the war lance and the jousting lance. In place of the *arrêt de la lance*, a leather grip behind the hand grip which prevented the hand slipping down the shaft in the encounter, the jousting lance was fitted with a grate (*agrappe*). This device had a series of cog-like projections which interlocked with the lance rest on the breastplate (*arrêt de la cuirasse*). The grate and the lance rest ensured that the jouster took the full weight of his own lance on his chest and increased his chances of breaking his lance by preventing it rebounding backwards on encounter.[72]

Jousting challenges for all hastiludes and chivalric combats commonly specified that the lances should be *de mesure*, that is, of equal length as measured against a standard provided by the organizer. This prevented any knight having an unfair advantage in length, though it would seem that a knight could voluntarily put himself at a disadvantage by having a lance shorter than the measured standard.[73]

Whether intended for hastiludes or more deadly combats, lances were usually painted in bright colours and decorated with pennons of the bearer's arms. The lances which Osbert of Arden arranged to be carried for him in war and tournament in the twelfth century were all painted and in the mid-thirteenth century poem, *Le Tornoiement de l'Antéchrist*, the Lord of the Firmament's lance was painted azure with golden angels and jewels. As late as 1386,

---

[71] Matt.Paris, v, 318-9.
[72] Buttin, 'La Lance et l'Arrêt de la Cuirasse', pp. 96-104, 148, 177-8.
[73] See: Gloucester's *Ordinances for Combat Within Listes* in Bodleian MS Ashmole 764 fo. 87v.

Richard II was still having his lances painted red to match the rest of his harness for jousts.[74] The pennon was fixed below the lance head and usually bore the tourneyer's coat of arms, though in the late fourteenth century it tended to match the colour schemes of the hastilude and bore the temporary tourneying devices of the day. Similar ones were often made for the trumpets of heralds and minstrels who attended the tournament and gave the signals for combat to begin and end.[75]

Weapons

In contrast with the rest of tourneying equipment which grew progressively more complex, hastiluding weapons grew more simple over the years because they were more restricted. In the old *mêlée* style tournament of the twelfth and thirteenth centuries almost any weapons of war were permissable. Bows and crossbows are mentioned in this period,[76] usually, it is true, with disapprobation, but nevertheless these were the weapons of foot soldiers who were allowed to participate in hastiludes at that time. By the fourteenth century ballistic weapons had been banned from the sport, a development encouraged by the exclusion of foot soldiers from hastiludes.

The primary weapon of the fighting at close quarters in the *mêlée* was the broadsword. It was mainly used for buffeting and therefore had to be long enough to wield on horseback and have no sharp edges or point which might wound an opponent. Most tourneying swords were valuable enough to warrant bequeathing from father to son, as Sir Fulk Penbridge did in 1326:[77] they could also be made from more expendable materials, for Edward I provided swords made from whalebone and parchment for his Windsor Park tournament of 1278, perhaps because the tourneyers wore only *cuir bouilli* armour.[78]

The secondary weapon of the *mêlée* was the mace. Many of the tournaments attended by William Marshal were fought with lance, sword and mace,[79] so it is not surprising that the noise of resounding blows on helms is so prominent in romance accounts of tourna-

---

[74] *Facsimiles of Royal and Other Charters in the British Museum*, ed. Warner & Ellis, no. 12; Huon de Mery, p. 39; PRO E101/401/14 m1; PRO E101/401/15 m2.
[75] PRO E361/2 m12, 13; PRO E361/3 m10, 13; PRO 28/1/4 fos 8r, 13v.
[76] See *supra*: pp. xx, xx.
[77] BL MS Stowe Charter 622.
[78] 'Copy of a Roll of Purchases for a Tournament at Windsor Park', pp. 302, 304.
[79] *HGM*, ll. 2510, 2966, 3797, 5003.

ments, nor that William Marshal required a blacksmith to extricate him from his own mis-shapen helm. At the tournament of Chauvency in 1285 the tourneyers were also equipped with lance, sword and mace as suited each man's preference, but then the mace disappears from accounts of hastiludes until the mid-fifteenth century tournament treatises arm their tourneyers with *bastons* and *masses de mesure*.[80] The intervening silence may reflect the more stringent restrictions on weaponry in hastiludes introduced at the end of the thirteenth century or, more simply, the gradual falling into abeyance of the *mêlée* tournament which was the only hastilude in which the mace was appropriate.

The development of the feat of arms *à outrance* at the end of the fourteenth century introduced the dagger to hastiludes. Previously it had been excluded because, as a weapon for fighting at close quarters, it was unsuitable for most hastiludes. It was only in unusual cases, such as the Combat of the Thirty at Ploërmel in Brittany in 1351, that daggers had been allowed and in this instance the combatants also used axes and war hammers, as well as more conventional weapons.[81]

Apart from the feat of arms, which stands apart from other hastiludes in other ways as well, the general trend in tourneying weaponry was towards a more restricted choice and a more closely regulated quality of equipment. Less was left to chance than in the early days and skill in the handling of weapons was placed at a premium.

Part Two: Decorative Armour

Crests

The crest, which fastened to a staple on top of the tourneying helm, assumed varying shapes and sizes over the years. At first it seems to have been purely decorative. Ulrich von Liechtenstein and his opponents, for instance, often wore crests of feathers tipped with gold and silver leaflets.[82] Towards the end of the thirteenth century, however, crests became more individual and more personal. Gerard de Canle, for example, appeared at the Le Hem jousts wearing a

---

[80] *Le Tournoi de Chauvency*, ll. 3350-1; Bodleian MS Ashmole 764 fo. 40r; Prost, *Traités du Duel Judiciaire*, pp. 213, 215; René d'Anjou, 'Traité de la Forme et Devis d'un Tournoi', pp. 28, 33.
[81] Jean le Bel, ii, 194-7.
[82] Ulrich von Liechtenstein, pp. 106, 165.

crest in the form of a 'Oisiaus vis en une gaiole' – a fantastic choice more typical of the fifteenth century.[83] The commonest type of crest was the one dictated by the personal badge of the tourneyer. The Black Prince wore a *cuir bouilli* lion derived from the royal coat of arms for his crest, Richard II had a great golden sun made for his helm at a period when the sun appears to have been his personal emblem and Henry, earl of Derby had the forgetmenot, the flower which he had adopted as his personal device, depicted on his jousting crests.[84] The increasingly personal and heraldic associations of the crest made it an important part of the tourneyer's wardrobe. By the fifteenth century some heraldic treatises even claimed that no-one could participate in hastiludes unless they possessed a crest[85] and elaborate ceremonies were evolved for heralds to view tourneyers' crests and arms before the sport began.

By the fourteenth century it was also common to wear a form of cloth mantling over the helm, known as a *contoise*. Though it was not actually part of the crest, it was usually portrayed on the full coat of arms drawn up by heralds from the fifteenth century onwards. As early as 1285 John of Brittany included the cost of making 'queyntises' among his expenses for attending the Croydon tournament, and in 1344 an indenture of the goods preserved in the king's wardrobe in the Tower revealed two ancient and worthless tournament helms and an entire 'quoyntise' made of Aillesham cloth and displaying the arms of a 'Sir Robert de ... [lacuna]'.[86]

Aillettes

Aillettes, like the crest and the *contoise*, seem to have had no practical defensive function and were probably purely decorative. They were rectangular or square pieces of cloth or leather fastened to the shoulders for both war and tournament. Although some armorial brasses have the *aillettes* turned so that they faced forward and displayed their design to the front, in fact they were worn, not at right angles, but parallel to the profile. Often they were highly decorated and made of expensive material, like the ones owned by Gaveston which were garnished and fretted with pearls.[87] On the

[83] Sarrazin, p. 309.
[84] PRO E101/401/15 m2; PRO DL28/1/3 fo. 15r; PRO DL28/1/4 fos 15r-v.
[85] Bodleian MS Ashmole 764 fo. 36v. See also A. C. Fox-Davies, *Heraldic Badges* (London, 1907), p. 64.
[86] *Records of the Wardrobe and Household*, ed. Byerly, p. 47; PRO E101/390/7 m6.
[87] *Foedera*, iii, 38.

other hand, Edward I supplied leather *aillettes* for the tourneyers at Windsor Park in 1278 which cost only eight pence per pair. The four hundred pairs of *aillettes* made in 1329,of which half bore the arms of Sir Maurice de Berkeley and Sir John Neville quarterly, and the other half bore the arms of St George, were made of fine linen (*sindon*) and stiffened linen (*bokeram afforc*').[88] Usually the *aillettes* displayed the coat of arms, and most manuscript illuminations and armorial brasses show the knight wearing his own arms upon them. They could, therefore, serve as an additional means of identifying tourneyers, especially from the side, which was useful because the rest of his personal arms were displayed on his front and back. The four hundred pairs of *aillettes* made in 1329 further suggest that they might also be used to identify which team of tourneyers each knight belonged to, since he could wear his personal arms on his shield and surcoat and those of his team leader on his *aillettes*.

The Surcoat

The surcoat was vital as a means of identifying knights in war and tournament for the shield, though important, was frequently dropped or lost during combat. The four knights who had declared the tournament in Marie de France's *Lay of the Dolorous Knight* were more hard pressed than any of the other tourneyers because they were recognized by the arms embroidered on their surcoats. After the battle of Crécy, it was their surcoats which allowed the dead to be identified by a committee of knights and heralds.[89] Even when the long flowing surcoat was replaced by increasingly shorter and tighter fitting garments such as the *jupon* and *paltock*, the coat of arms or the personal badge of the tourneyer continued to be displayed there. In 1331 Edward III restored to Edmund Mortimer 'une cote p[ou]r les joustes de rouge velvet ove une frette dargent ove papillons des arms de Mortem[er]' which had been seized from his father.[90] Edward himself spent £7.7s.6½d. on embroidering an extremely elaborate *tunica ad arma* for the Dunstable tournament of 1342. It was patterned with small gold and silver saracens, each holding a jewel with the king's motto engraved upon it, and two large saracens holding a shield of the king's arms between them.[91] Similarly, though he also had a large number of gowns and *paltocks*

---

[88] 'Copy of a Roll of Purchases', p. 302; Bodleian MS Ashmole 1111 fo. 206v.
[89] Froissart, v, 73.
[90] *Ancient Calendars of the Exchequer*, ed. Palgrave, iii, 165.
[91] PRO E101/389/14 m3.

(sleeveless doublets) which had no personal identification on them, Henry, earl of Derby had several embroidered with his badge, the forgetmenot, and his motto 'Soveinez vous de moy'.[92] Sometimes the armorial devices and badges were repeated from the surcoat on other items in the suit of arms. Prince Edward, for example, gave Gaveston a whole harness of arms for man and horse in green velvet worked with piping and pearls and fretted with golden eagles taken from Gaveston's coat of arms. This highly decorated suit of arms, which was intended for wearing in tournaments abroad, since Gaveston was under threat of exile again, cost the prince a massive £24.4s.4½d – as much as a good war horse would have cost.[93]

Badges

The fourteenth century saw a gradual eclipse in the popularity of the coat of arms in favour of the personal device or badge on tournament clothing. In fact, the badge was particularly associated with hastiludes and was deliberately contrasted with the coat of arms which should be worn for war. It was a frequent provision in fourteenth century wills that armed men should appear before the corpse in the funeral procession, some wearing arms of war and displaying the coat of arms and others wearing arms of peace and displaying the badge of the deceased,[94] presumably to indicate that the knight had excelled in both fields.

Some badges made claims on behalf of their wearers, such as the swan device which was adopted by both the Tony family and the Bohuns[95] in token of the descent which they claimed from the legendary Swan Knight. Others were intended as puns or rebuses on the names of their owners, such as the white hart chained and gorged with a golden crown of Richard II (*Rich-hart*), or on places particularly associated with them, such as the so-called sunburst badge of Edward III which was probably a pictorial representation of golden winds (*winds-or*), as Windsor Castle was a favourite residence of Edward III.[96] Although the badge was primarily a

---

[92] PRO DL28/1/4 fos 6r, 14v.
[93] BL MS Additional 22923 fo. 10v.
[94] A. Nichols, *A Collection of all the Wills ... of the Kings and Queens of England* (London, 1780), pp. 67-8; Raine, *Wills and Inventories*, pt. i, 27, 41; *Testamenta Eboracensia* (Surtees Soc., ii, 1836), p. 42. On this subject see: M. G. A. Vale, *War and Chivalry*, pp. 88-93.
[95] N. H. Nicolas, *The Siege of Carlaverock* (London, 1828), p. 42; Fox-Davies, p. 50.
[96] Fox-Davies, pp. 50, 53.

personal and not a hereditary device, unlike the coat of arms, variants of a device were often used by different members of a family. The Black Prince, his illegitimate son Roger of Clarendon, his brothers Thomas of Woodstock and John of Gaunt and the legitimate and illegitimate offspring of John of Gaunt all bore variant forms of the ostrich feather badge. The golden rose of Eleanor of Provence similarly descended through the three Edwards, the Black Prince and Richard II, while her second son Edmund, earl of Lancaster varied her badge to a red rose which was adopted by all the house of Lancaster, including the descendants of John of Gaunt who had married the last of the direct line from Edmund.[97] It has been suggested that the badge was the feminine equivalent of the coat of arms, which correctly only belonged to men, and therefore the adoption of badges for hastiludes suggests that knights were carrying the wearing of ladies' favours and tokens one step further: unfortunately, the evidence for badges being 'inherited' from the female side of the family is very sketchy and indeed in some cases can be rebutted, though it is undoubtedly true that sons often did adopt their mothers' badges.[98]

The habitual wearing or displaying of such badges appears to have given rise to the *sobriquets* applied to certain knights. The Black Prince, for instance, had a black background to his ostrich feather badge and therefore his armour may have been painted black to match; his retainers may also have worn livery of the same colour.[99] The same explanation may lie behind the nickname applied to Ralph Holmes, an English esquire killed defending Don Pedro of Castile, who was known as the 'Green Esquire' and to Amadeus VI, known as the 'Green Count of Savoy'.[100]

Sometimes, however, a device or badge was adopted only for the duration of a single hastilude by a team of knights, who were thus identifiable as a simple tourneying society. In 1398, for example, forty knights and forty esquires dressed in green and bearing a device of a white falcon jousted against all comers at Smithfield.

[97] *Ibid.*, pp. 44-8; C. W. Scott-Giles, *The Romance of Heraldry* (London, 1965), pp. 89-91, 127-8.

[98] Scott-Giles, p. 89, following N. H. Nicolas. Fox-Davies rejects this theory, pp. 44-8.

[99] Fox-Davies, pp. 26-7. Although Fox-Davies rejects the painting of armour as an explanation, Richard II certainly had all his armour painted red as a background to his sun device for hastiludes in 1386: see PRO E101/401/15 m2; PRO E101/401/16 m15.

[100] Froissart, vii, 272; E. L. Cox, *The Green Count of Savoy* (Princeton, 1967), pp. 97-8, 362-4, esp. p. 364.

Eight years earlier, sixteen knights bearing a silver griffin on a green field had also jousted against all comers at Smithfield.[101] Both these badges were transitory, like so many others, but in the 1390 jousts the knightly *tenants* wore a white hart chained and gorged with a golden crown: according to at least one source,[102] this was the first public appearance of Richard II's favourite badge. Prior to this, Richard seems to have been trying to associate himself with his more glamorous grandfather, Edward III, by deliberately adopting his famous sun badge. In 1378-9 he had a whole harness and gown coloured red and decorated with golden suns and in 1386, for the March hastiludes at Smithfield, he had a whole suit of arms including six lances, six vamplates, one breastplate, two *vambraces*, two *rerebraces*, one *maindefer*, one plate gauntlet, six grates and six coronals painted red to match his red gown, harness, stockings and horse trappers embroidered with golden suns and gold and silver clouds which he had also ordered for the occasion.[103]

Although the suggestion that the Garter began life as a tournament badge has been effectively quashed,[104] the fact remains that after the order's foundation, the Garter was used as a hastiluding device. In 1348 twelve garters bearing the motto were made for a harness for the king to wear at the Eltham hastiludes and the Black Prince gave twenty-four garters to the knights of the order for the Windsor tournament.[105] The Garter knights were also the *tenants* of the Smithfield jousts of 1390, they received a challenge from the senechal of Hainault in 1408 and in the same year Richard Beauchamp was challenged by a Veronese knight to defend the honour of the Garter, of which he was a member.[106] It would therefore seem that membership of the Garter, and wearing its badge, sometimes acted in much the same way as the adoption of a specific tourneying device in provoking tourneying challenges, if only because membership of a chivalric order indicated some claim to belong to a military elite.

The badge was, therefore, an important feature of tournament armour and clothing: later it became a vital part of heraldry too, the knight's badge frequently becoming the supporters of his coat of

---

[101] Froissart, xvi, 151; BL MS Lansdowne 285 fo. 47r.
[102] *The Brut*, ii, 343.
[103] PRO E101/401/4 m3, 4; PRO E101/401/15 m15.
[104] J. Vale, *Edward III and Chivalry*, pp. 76-91.
[105] PRO E372/207 m50; *Register of the Black Prince*, iv, 72.
[106] *The Brut*, ii, 343; BL MS Additional 21370 fos 1r ff; *Pageant of Richard Beauchamp*, p. 25.

arms.[107] Why knights wore badges for hastiludes and coats of arms for war is a matter of some doubt. It has been suggested that the badge was more easily recognizable in combat than the elaborately quartered coat of arms of the fifteenth century,[108] but this argument applies even more strongly to warfare where identification was vitally important. Moreover, as we have seen, the badge was already familiar in fourteenth century hastiludes when coats of arms were not yet so elaborate as to cause difficulty in identifying the wearer. What seems most likely is that the wearing or displaying of a badge was a symbol of the limited and peaceful intention of the combat, for the badge was especially associated with hastiludes *à plaisance*.

Part Three: Summary

The jouster at the end of the fourteenth century cut a very different figure from the tourneyer of the twelfth century. His ancestor would have appeared on the tournament field in his usual armour for war and riding his usual war horse. His trunk and limbs would have been covered with mail, perhaps reinforced with *cuir bouilli* or steel greaves. On his head he would have worn the huge pot helm and he would have carried a shield decorated with a simple coat of arms. As a concession to the sporting nature of the occasion his weapons might have been rebated, but this was by no means the rule.

A hundred years later, the tourneyer was still using much the same equipment, with the addition of more elaborate decoration and more rigid armour pieces, such as the pair of plates, which gave him a greater number of protective layers.

A hundred years further on again and his appearance was revolutionized. The jouster came into the lists clad from head to foot in steel plate armour, moulded closely to the shape of his body and presenting a much smoother surface to his opponent's lance than his ancestor had done. He had the advantages of specialized equipment, such as the *maindefer*, grate and *arrêt de la cuirasse*, which were designed to give him a steady aim for the specific purpose of the joust. On his head he wore the frog-mouthed helm which gave him better protection than the old pot helm but which was useless outside the lists. His horse was specially trained for the

---

107 Fox-Davies, p. 67.
108 M. G. A. Vale, *War and Chivalry*, p. 96.

joust and his saddle and tackle were expressly designed for the particular form of hastilude in which he participated. Both horse and rider were richly and elaborately decorated with expensive cloth, gold and jewellery: heraldic coats of arms, badges and mottoes were prominently displayed.

The jouster of the late fourteenth century was better protected by his specialized armour than his twelfth century counterpart. He was also more highly ornamented. The combined effect of improved standards of safety and increased ornateness was to make tourneying a more expensive sport. The tourneyer could no longer use the same armour for war and hastiludes but required more sophisticated and increasingly disparate armour for each form of combat. Even in the twelfth century knights such as William Marshal, and even the Young King himself, had sought patronage in order to equip themselves to a reasonable standard. By the end of the fourteenth century patronage had become essential, since few knights could hope to afford all the different pieces of armour now necessary for the sport. The sheer cost of jousting at this period must have put hastiludes, particularly those fought *à plaisance* before cultured audiences expecting a spectacle, beyond the pocket of all but the very rich. Of necessity, therefore, the tourneying society became smaller and more select than it had been in the early days.

Conclusion

The period 1100 to 1400 was one of great change and development in the history of the English tournament. For almost the first century of its existence, tourneying was a prohibited sport which could only be freely indulged in on the continental circuits or during moments of political weakness. But Richard I's momentous decree of 1194 changed things in this aspect completely. From then on, English knights, if they obtained due licence, were able to tourney legitimately with royal approval and often, as time went by, with royal patronage and participation. Whenever a policy of repression was tried the result was only to lead enthusiasts to flout prohibitions. In these circumstances tourneying could easily become a useful political and military tool for the disaffected. On the other hand, English kings especially from Edward I onwards, were quick to realize that judicious patronage reaped great rewards, particularly in the field of propaganda at home and abroad.

The sport itself changed considerably over the period. Different forms of hastilude emerged offering opportunities to practise with different types of weapons under different conditions. The general trend, however, was away from the tournament, the hastilude for the masses, towards the more individual emphasis of the joust. This was, perhaps, a natural development in view of the obsessional desire of most tourneyers to have their personal valour publicly recognized and rewarded. The joust lent itself more readily to personal gratification since the acts of each individual were more easily observed than in the sprawling confusion of the *mêlée*, and were acclaimed with more effect by the attendant heralds. The popularity of the joust gave a new prestige to the participants who were, of necessity, fewer in number and therefore more easily identifiable. It also gave added impetus to the adoption of imaginative settings and costumes which turned the joust *à plaisance* into a pageant designed to gratify and impress spectators as well as the participants. The consequent rising level of costs, combined with the opportunity for propaganda, made the joust *à plaisance* a much more court centred cult than the tournament had ever been. Alongside these developments, there was a powerful parallel development of hastiludes *à outrance* designed for the dedicated knight who wished to prove his courage and strength in more dangerous forms of combat and at greater personal risk to himself.

Throughout the period, there was a great interaction between English and continental tourneyers, and the pattern of English tourneying history very much follows that of northern France. English knights continually sought out French opponents with varying degrees of good humour or serious intent. In the same way, knights from France, the Low Countries and the Iberian Peninsula were also to be found in English tourneying circles, particularly when English prestige abroad was high. It is not surprising, therefore, that England should follow the model of France in most things relating to hastiludes, just as she did in most things chivalrous.

Where England did differ from France, the differences were considerable. The most important and significant distinction was the deep involvement of English kings in tourneying from a remarkably early date. Until the mid-fourteenth century, French kings did not personally participate in hastiludes and therefore English kings had a head start on them. This is most apparent in two fields: the regulation and control of hastiludes and their use for propaganda purposes. A chivalrous king like Edward I or Edward III not only won the personal respect of his subjects and fellow tourneyers by his successes in the lists, but also won a European reputation by fostering the chivalric cults which meant so much to knights of all nationalities. In England the king, and not his wealthy and powerful nobility, was the greatest patron of chivalry.

If there were far-reaching changes in the organization, conduct and setting of hastiludes which made the twelfth century tournament very different from the fourteenth century joust, certain important features remained exactly the same. The inspiration to tourney, for instance, was unchanged. Knights at the end of the fourteenth century still sought to win renown and approval, particularly in the eyes of the ladies, just as their forbears had always done. Periods of war and political or military tension were still as conducive to tourneying as they had been in the past. Essentially, too, it was the same sort of people who tourneyed – men who moved in knightly circles and shared the same sort of education and upbringing. The hold which tourneying had on the knightly imagination is perhaps best illustrated by the very fact that tourneying not only survived but flourished and eventually became respectable, despite the initial prolonged (and often combined) opposition of church and state. Its survival must, to a large extent, be attributable to the powerful ideology of the romances as typified in romances. Without it, the tournament must have been suppressed, despite its value as military training. With it, the tournament became not simply a military exercise but rather a celebration of all the values that chivalrous society held dear. The principles of courtly love, gentlemanly behaviour and courage in adversity were carried over into a wider sphere of influence, but nowhere were they so strongly defined as in hastiludes.

The Statuta Armorum

The only detailed study of the *Statuta Armorum* was made by Denholm-Young in 'The Tournament in the Thirteenth Century'. Unfortunately, the corruption of the texts led him to perpetuate some misconceptions about the *Statuta* and to introduce another important one about the dating of the provision which preceded the statute. The printed texts variously offer an Edward *fiz le Roy* with an Edmund *frere le Roy*, or an Edward *fitz le Roy* with an Edmund *son frere* among the supervising committee. Denholm-Young accepted the latter version and argued from the extreme youth of Prince Edward and the advanced age of Edmund of Lancaster, Gilbert de Clare and William de Valence in 1292 that the provision dated from 1267, when the king's sons and nephew were taking such an interest in tourneying:

> Instead of three men well advanced in years and one child fresh from the nursery, we have four young men in the prime of life.

Conveniently, he ignored the fifth member of the committee, Henry de Lacy, for in 1267 he was a ward in the king's custody and even when he received livery of his lands in the following year he was still under age.[1] In fact, both the provision and the statute date from 1292: Edward I drew up letters[2] patent dated from Westminster on 5 February 1292 which gave power to administer the provision to

> Edward noster fiz Edmon noster frere Willame de Valence noster uncle Gilbert de Clare cunte de Gloucestre e a Henry de Lacy counte de Nicole

The royal family and the senior earls of England, all of whom, except the eight year old Prince Edward, had had a lifetime's personal experience in tourneying, were appointed to the committee to give it respect and authority. The youth of the prince, though it precluded him from taking an

---

[1] *CCR 1264-8*, pp. 412-3; V. Gibbs, *Complete Peerage* (London, 1926), viii, 680.
[2] PRO DL10/186. I am indebted to Dr M. H. Keen for this reference.

active part in administration, did not prevent his being the nominal head of the committee.

Many of the errors which have been caused by the corruption of the texts can be corrected by using an unpublished version of the *Statuta* which can be found in BL MS Harleian 69 fo. 17r. It is more internally consistent than the printed versions and often provides a better reading. For example, when the printed texts say that 'nul **fiz** de graunt Seignur' should be armed except with knee, thigh and shoulder pieces and bascinet, the Harleian text says 'nul **fors** de grans seigneurs'. Instead of the sons of nobles being limited in their armour we find that it is the rest of the men in the lists, excluding these noble tourneyers, whose armour is limited. Similarly, instead of the nonsensical 'E qe[si: Lib Horn) nul sake Chivaler a terre, fors ceus qe serrunt armez pur lur Seign[ou]r servir . . .' the Harleian version offers 'Et si aucun tire chevalier a terre fors ceux que seront armes pour leur seigneur servir . . .' Denholm-Young construed the printed text as meaning that only the three esquires could aid their own fallen master, whereas the Harleian version proposes that these same esquires could actually legitimately pull a knight from his horse.

The consistency of the Harleian manuscript's readings makes it quite clear that the tourneyers, which it differentiates from the rest of the field by calling them *grans seigneurs*, are excluded from all restrictions on arms and armour. The fact that the lance is omitted from the list of permitted weapons, which Denholm-Young appeared to think meant that the lance was not used in the tournament, is thus irrelevant to the tourneyers, for the restrictions applied only to their followers: so the *grans seigneurs* could fight with lance, broadsword and mace if they so wished.

Because the Harleian readings are so superior to the printed texts I have followed the manuscript in preference to the latter throughout my discussion of the *Statuta Armorum*.

Tourneying Retinues

Table I: tourneying retainers of the Earl of Pembroke.

The earl's retainers have been ascertained from the lists in Phillips, *Aymer de Valence*, Appx.2, supplemented by references from the Patent and Close Rolls and the Protection Rolls which show that a knight served regularly in the earl's company on campaign or had close personal links with him. The table shows for each retainer the year he is known to have tourneyed and the source of this information.

NAME	YEAR	REFERENCE
Walter Gacelyn	1309	DTR no.185
John Gacelyn	1309	DTR no.186
John de Ryvere	1309	DTR no.184
William Munchesny	1265	CPR 1258-66, p. 406
Walter Beauchamp	1309	DTR no.25
Aymer de la Zouche	1309	DTR no.183
William de la Zouche	1309	DTR no.40
Warin Bassingbourne	1305	CCR 1302-7, p. 299
William Mareschal	1309	DTR no.71
John Darcy 'le neveu'	1309	Bain, v, A11547
John Darcy the uncle	1309	DTR no.104
Robert Darcy	1309	DTR no.2
William Hastings	1309	DTR no.180
William Melksop	1318	CPR 1317-21, p. 124
Philip Hastings	1309	DTR no.116
Robert Hastings	1309	DTR no.69
Constantine de Mortimer	1309	DTR no.129
William Rydell	1309	DTR no.52
John de Argentine	1309	DTR no.123
Thomas Latimer 'Burchard'	1309	DTR no.60
Roger Wateville	1309	DTR no.100
Henry de Dene	1309	DTR no.166
William de Bayous	1309	DTR no.51

Anselm le Mareschal	1309	DTR no.73
John Exning	1305	CCR 1302-7, p. 299
William Lovel	1309	DTR no.128
John Moubray	1309	DTR no.130
Roger Damory	1309	DTR no.11
Robert FitzPayn	1303	Bain, ii, A1407

Berkeley sub-retinue

Thomas Berkeley, snr.	1309	DTR no.178
Maurice Berkeley, snr.	1309	DTR no.80
William Wauton	1309	DTR no.176
Thomas Gournay	1309	DTR no.175

Hastings sub-retinue

John Hastings, jnr.	1309	DTR no.181
Nicholas de Clare	1309	DTR no.16
Robert Clifford	1309	DTR no.47
William Latimer	1309	DTR no.55

Table II: tourneying retainers of the earl of Gloucester

NAME	YEAR	REFERENCE
Roger Tyrell	1309	DTR no.4
Gilbert de Elsefield	1309	DTR no.8
John de Elsefield	1309	DTR no.17
Thomas Lovell	1309	DTR no.12
Nicholas Wokingdon	1309	DTR no.3
Nicholas Poinz	1309	DTR no.9
John Belhus	1309	DTR no.10
Robert Boutevilain	1309	DTR no.20
Geoffrey de Say	1309	DTR no.22
Richard de Clare	1309	DTR no.13
Nicholas de Clare	1309	DTR no.16
John de St Oweyn	1309	DTR no.19
Henry de Penbrigge	1309	DTR no.5
William Fleming	1309	DTR no.18
Hamo Sutton	1309	DTR no.220
Roger Bilney	1309	DTR no.75

Giles de Argentine	1309	DTR no.7
John Bluet	1309	DTR no.145
Edmund Bacon	1309	DTR no.45
Robert Etchingham	1309	DTR no.64
Bartholomew de Baddlesmere	1309	DTR no.74
Gilbert de Clare	1306	Cal.Fine Rolls, i, 543
Oliver de St Amand	1309	DTR no.15
Roger Damory	1309	DTR no.11
John Giffard	1313	CPR 1307-13, p. 520
Philip Coleville	1305	CCR 1302-7, p. 299.
	&	
	1306	Cal.Fine Rolls, i, 543

Table III: tourneying retainers of Nicholas Segrave

NAME	YEAR	REFERENCE
Nicholas Segrave	1309	DTR no.117
Henry Segrave	1309	DTR no.126
Stephen Segrave	1309	DTR no.125
John Filliol	1309	DTR no.121
Gerard de Lisle	1309	DTR no.122
Robert de Lacy	1309	DTR no.124
Richard Caple	1309	DTR no.170
Geoffrey de Wateville	1309	DTR no.120

Bibliography

This bibliography represents only those sources to which continual reference has been made. Tournament references are scattered throughout such a wide variety of sources that it is impractical, if not impossible, to list all the works that have proved useful. The following bibliography therefore is not comprehensive, and where a source has only been used once or twice, a full citation will be found in the notes to the text, rather than in this bibliography.

I. Manuscript Sources

Berkeley Castle, Gloucestershire

Select Charter 490 — Letters patent of Nicholas de Cryel testifying to his being retained by Stephen de Segrave (undated).

Select Roll 60 — Account of Thomas de Schypton, keeper of the Wardrobe to Sir Thomas Berkeley, 24 April 1328–September 1328.

British Library

Additional MS.21357 — Jousting challenges between English and French knights, 1398-1402.

Additional MS.21370 — Jousting challenges relating to the Senechal of Hainault.

Additional MS.22923 — Wardrobe account of Edward, Prince of Wales 20 November 1306–7 July 1307.

Additional MS.46919 ff. 86v-87r — *Modus Armandi Milites* treatise.

Cotton MS.Nero Dii ff. 260v-262r — Jousting challenges at the marriage of Lady Blanche, 1401.

Cotton MS.Otho Div ff. 187r-192v — Dunstable Tournament Roll of 1334.

Egerton Roll 8738 — Wardrobe account of the Earl of March, 24 April 1393–23 April 1394.

Lansdowne MS.285 ff. 46v-47r — *Le Crie des Joustes* for the Smithfield jousts 9-12 October 1390.

Stowe Charter 622 — Will of Sir Fulk Penbrigg (1325).

196

Bodleian Library

MS.Ashmole 764
ff. 30v-43 | La façon des criz de tournois et des joustes.

MS.Ashmole 856
ff. 83-93 | Of the Mannier and Order of Combating within Listes delivered by Thomas Duke of Gloucester unto King Richard the Second.

MS.Eng.Hist.B.229
ff. 1-10 | Inventory of the goods of Simon Burley (1388).

College of Arms

MS. Processus in
Curia Marescalli | Grey v. Hastings case in the Court of Chivalry. (1407).

Public Record Office

C47/6/1 | Lovell v. Morley case in the Court of Chivalry (1385).
DL10/186 | Letters Patent of Edward I, 5 February 1292.
DL25/92 | Retaining indenture: Earl of Hereford/Bartholomew D'Enfield (1309).
DL25/1981 | Retaining indenture: Earl of Hereford/Thomas de Maundeville (1309).
DL28/1/1 | Household expenses of Henry, earl of Derby M'mas 1381–M'mas 1382.
DL28/1/2 | Wardrobe expenses of Henry, earl of Derby 30 September 1387–30 September 1388.
DL28/1/3 | Wardrobe expenses of Henry, earl of Derby 13 May 1391–13 May 1392.
DL28/1/4 | Wardrobe expenses of Henry, earl of Derby 30 June 1393–15 February 1394.
DL28/1/5 | Wardrobe expenses of Henry, earl of Derby 1 February 1395–1 February 1396.
DL28/1/6 | Wardrobe expenses of Henry, duke of Hereford 1 February 1397–1 November 1398.
E40/A11547 | Retaining indenture Earl of Pembroke/John Darcy le neveu (1309).
E101/27/11 | Retaining indenture Earl of Pembroke/Robert FitzPayn (1303).
E101/382/17 | Compotus of Hugh Tyrel, undated. (c.1329).
E101/400/4 | Liberation Roll of the Wardrobe M'mas 1377–M'mas 1379.
E101/401/14 | Account of Alan de Stokes, keeper of the Great Wardrobe 9-11 Richard II.
E101/401/15 m2 | Expenses of Alan de Stokes, keeper of the Great Wardrobe 9-11 Richard II.
E101/401/16 | Roll of the Expenses of the Wardrobe 9-11 Richard II.

E372/207 m50   Account of John de Colonia, king's armourer 26 July 1333–18 October 1354.

Printed Sources.

I. Primary sources

Account of the Expenses of John of Brabant, 1292-3, ed. J. Burtt (Camden Misc., ii, 1853).

Ancrene Wisse: parts six and seven, ed. G. Shepherd (Thomas Nelson, 1959).

d'Anjou, René, 'Traité de la Forme et Devis d'un Tournoi', *Verve*, iv no. 16 (1946).

'Annales Londonienses de Tempore Henrici Tertii', *Chronicles of the Reigns of Edward I and Edward II*, ed. W. Stubbs (R.S., 1882), i, 1-251.

Annales Monastici, ed. H. R. Luard (R.S., 1864-9).

'Annales Paulini de Tempore Edwardi Secundi', *Chronicles of the Reigns of Edward I and Edward II*, ed. W. Stubbs (R.S., 1883), ii, 253-370.

'Annales Ricardi Secundi et Henrici Quarti', *Johannis de Trokelowe et Henrici de Blaneford, Chronica et Annales* ed. H. T. Riley (R.S., 1866), pp. 155-422.

Anonimalle Chronicle 1333-1381, ed. V. H. Galbraith (Manchester, 1927).

Ancient Calendars and Inventories of the Exchequer, ed. F. Palgrave (London, 1836), 3 vols.

Ardres, Lambert of, *Chronicon Ghisnense et Ardense*, ed. D. Godefroy (Paris, 1855).

'Armourer's Bill temp. Edward III', ed. H. Dillon, *The Antiquary*, xx (July-Dec, 1890), pp. 148-50.

Avesbury, Robert of, *De Gestis Edwardi Tertii*, ed. E. M. Thompson (R.S., 1889).

'Aye d'Avignon', ed. M-M. F. Guessard & P. Meyer, *Les Anciens Poètes de la France* (Paris, 1861), vol. 6.

Baker, Geoffrey le, *Chronicon*, ed. E. M. Thompson (Oxford, 1889).

Barbour, John, *The Bruce*, ed. W. W. Skeat (EETS, 1870).

Bel, Jean le, *Chronique*, ed. J. Viard & E. Déprez (Paris, 1904), 2 vols.

Brakelond, Jocelin de, *Cronica*, ed. H. E. Butler (London, 1949).

Bretel, Jacques, *Tournoi de Chauvency* ed. M. Delbouille (Liege, 1932).

Bromyard, John, *Summa Predicantium* (Nuremburg, 1518).

Brunne, Robert of, *Handlynge Synne*, ed. F. J. Furnivall (London, 1862).

The Brut or Chronicles of England, ed. F. W. D. Brie (EETS, 1906-8), 2 vols.

Calendar of Close Rolls, Henry III-Richard II.

Calendar of Documents relating to Scotland, ed. J. Bain (Edinburgh, 1881-1884), vols i & ii.

Calendar of Fine Rolls: Edward I 1272-1307 (London, 1911).

Calendar of Patent Rolls, Henry III to Richard II.

Cambrensis, Giraldus, *The Historical Works*, ed. T. Wright (London, 1863).

Cantupré, Thomas de, *Miraculorum, et Exemplorum Memorabilium sui Temporis Libri Duo* (Duaci, 1605).

Chansons de la Croisade, ed. J. Bédier (Paris, 1909).

Charny, Geoffroi de, 'Le Livre de la Chevalerie', *Oeuvres de Froissart*, ed. K. de Lettenhove (Brussels, 1873), i, pt. iii, 463-533.

Charny, Geoffroi de, 'Le Livre Messire Geoffroi de Charny' ed. A. Piaget, *Romania*, xxvi (1897).

Chronicle of Bury St Edmunds, ed. A. Gransden (Nelson, 1964).

Chronicon a Monacho Sancti Albani, ed. E. M. Thompson (R.S., 1874).

Chronique du Religieux de St Denys, ed. M. Bellaguet (Paris, 1839), 6 vols.

Coggeshalle, Ralph de, *Chronicon*, ed. J. Stevenson (R.S., 1875).

Condé, Baudouin de, *Dits et Contes de Baudouin de Condé et son fils Jean de Condé*, ed. A. Scheler (Brussels, 1866-1867), 3 vols.

'Copy of a Roll of Purchases for a Tournament at Windsor Park in the Sixth Year of Edward I', ed. S. Lysons, *Archaeologia*, 1st series, xvii (1814), pp. 297-310.

Corpus Juris Canonici, ed. A. Friedberg (Lipsiae, 1881), 2 vols.

Cuvelier, *Chronique de Bertrand du Guesclin*, ed. E. Charrière (SHF, 1839).

Eschenbach, Wolfram von, *Parzival: a romance of the middle ages*, ed. & trans. H. M. Mustard & C. E. Passage (New York, 1961).

Facsimiles of Royal and Other Charters in the British Museum, ed. G. F. Warner & H. J. Ellis (London, 1903), vol. i.

FitzStephen, William, 'Descriptio Civitatis Londoniae', translated by H. E. Butler in *Norman London: an essay* by F. M. Stenton (London, 1934), pp. 25-35.

Flores Historiarum, ed. H. R. Luard (R.S., 1890), 3 vols.

Florilège des Troubadours, ed. A. Berry (Paris, 1930).

Foedera, ed. T. Rymer (London, 1704-9), 7 vols.

French Chronicle of London, ed. G. J. Aungier (Camden Soc., xxviii, 1844).

Froissart, Jean, *Oeuvres*, ed. K. de Lettenhove (Brussels, 1867-1877), 25 vols.

Gamez, Guttiere Diaz de, *The Unconquered Knight: a chronicle of the deeds of Don Pero Niño*, ed. & trans. J. Evans (London, 1928).

Guisborough, Walter of, *Cronica*, ed. H. Rothwell (Camden Soc., lxxxix, 1957).

Higden, Ranulph, *Polychronicon*, ed. J. R. Lumby (R.S., 1882-86), vols viii & ix.

High Book of the Grail, ed. & trans. N. Bryant (Cambridge 1978).

Histoire des Conciles, ed. C. J. Hefele & H. Leclercq (Paris, 1912-3), v, pts i & ii.

L'Histoire de Guillaume le Maréchal, ed. P. Meyer (SHF, 1901), 3 vols.

Hoveden, Roger of, *Chronica*, ed. W. Stubbs (R.S., 1868-1871), 4 vols.

'Inventory of the Effects of Roger Mortimer', ed. A. Way, *Archaeological Journal*, xv (1858), pp. 354-62.

'Inventory of the Goods and Chattels belonging to Thomas, duke of Gloucester', ed. Viscount Dillon & W. H. St John Hope, *Archaeological Journal*, liv (1897), pp. 275-308.

Issues of the Exchequer: Henry III to Henry VI, ed. F. Devon (London, 1837).

Jakemes, *Le Roman du Castelain de Couci*, ed. M. Delbouille (SATF, 1936).

Knighton, Henry, *Chronicon*, ed. J. R. Lumby (R.S., 1895), 2 vols.

Lancaster, Henry of, *Le Livre de Seyntz Medecines*, ed. E. J. Arnould (Anglo-Norman Text Soc., ii, 1940).

Legend of Fulk FitzWarin, ed. J. Stevenson in Ralph de Coggeshalle, *Chronicon Anglicanum* (R.S., 1875).

Liechtenstein, Ulrich von, *Service of Ladies*, ed. & trans. J. W. Thomas (University of North Carolina Studies in the Germanic Languages and Literature, 63, 1969).

Malmesbury, William of, *Historia Novella*, ed. K. R. Potter (Oxford, 1955).

Mery, Huon de, *Le Tornoiement de l'Antéchrist* (Rheims, 1851).

Monasticon Anglicanum, ed. W. Dugdale (London, 1830), vi, pt. i.

Mons, Gislebert of, *Chronique*, ed. L. Vanderkindere (Brussels, 1904).

Murimuth, Adam, *Continuatio Chronicarum*, ed. E. M. Thompson (R.S., 1889).

Newburgh, William of, 'Historia Rerum Anglicanum', *Chronicles of the Reigns of Stephen, Henry II and Richard I*, ed. R. Howlett (R.S., 1885), i, 1-408; ii, 409-500.

Novare, Philippe de, *Mémoires: 1218-43*, ed. C. Kohler (Paris, 1903).

Ordonnances des Roys de France, ed. M. de Laurière (Paris, 1723), 21 vols.

Pageant of the Birth, Life and Death of Richard Beauchamp ed. Viscount Dillon & W. H. St John Hope (London, 1914).

Paris, Matthew, *Chronica Majora*, ed. H. R. Luard (R.S., 1872-82), 7 vols.

'Property of the Earl of Arundel, 1397', ed. L. F. Salzman *Sussex Archaeological Collections*, 91, (1953), pp. 32-52.

Reading, John of, *Chronica*, ed. J. Tait (Manchester, 1914).

Records of the Wardrobe and Household 1285-6, ed. B. F. & C. R. Byerly (London, 1977).

Register of Edward the Black Prince (London, 1932-3), iii & iv.

Roman de Perceforest (Paris, 1528), 6 vols.

Rotuli Scottiae, ed. Macpherson (London, 1814-9), 2 vols.

Sarrazin, 'Le Roman de Ham', ed. F. Michel, *Histoire des Ducs de Normandie et des Rois d'Angleterre* (SHF, 1840).

Scalacronica, ed. J. Stevenson (Edinburgh, 1836).

Scrope and Grosvenor Roll, ed. N. H. Nicolas (Chester, 1879 & London, 1832).

Statutes of the Realm (London, 1810), i, pp. 230-1.

Traités du Duel Judiciaire, ed. B. Prost (Paris, 1872).
Trivet, Nicolas, *Annales*, ed. T. Hogg (London, 1845).
Vita Edwardi Secundi, ed. N. Denholm-Young (Nelson, 1957).
Vitry, Jacques de, *Exempla*, ed. T. Crane (London, 1890).
Wyntoun, Andrew of, *Original Chronicle*, ed. F. J. Amours (Scottish Text Soc., 1903-14), 6 vols.
Zatzikhoven, Ulrich von, *Lanzelet*, trans. K. G. T. Webster (Columbia University Press, 1951).

II. Secondary Sources

Anglo, S., 'Financial and Heraldic Records of the English Tournament', *Journal of the Society of Archivists*, ii (1960-4), pp. 183-95.
Ashdown, C. H., *British and Foreign Arms and Armour* (London, 1909).
Barber, R., *Edward, Prince of Wales and Aquitaine* (London,1978).
Barber, R., *The Knight and Chivalry* (London, 1970).
Barnard, B., *Illustrations of Ancient State and Chivalry* (London, 1840).
Barnie, J., *War in Medieval Society* (London, 1974).
Beeler, J., *Warfare in England 1066-1189* (Cornell University Press, 1966).
de Behault de Doron, A., 'La Noblesse Hennuyère au Tournoi de Compiègne de 1238', *Annales du Cercle Archéologique de Mons*, xxii (1890), pp. 61-114.
de Behault de Doron, A., 'Le Tournoi de Mons de 1310', *Annales du Cercle Archéologique de Mons*, xxxviii (1909), pp. 103-250.
de Belleval, R., *Du Costume Militaire des Français en 1446* (Paris, 1866).
Bernard, B., *Illustrations of Ancient State and Chivalry* (London, 1840).
Blair, C., *European Armour c.1066-c.1700* (London, 1958).
Brush, H.R., 'La Bataille de Trente Anglois et de Trente Bretons', *Modern Philology*, ix (1912), pp. 511-44 & x (1912), pp. 82-90.
Bullock-Davies, C., *Menestrellorum Multitudo: minstrels at a royal feast* (Cardiff, 1978).
Buttin, F., 'La Lance et l'Arrêt de la Cuirasse', *Archaeologia*, 99 (1965), pp. 77-178.
Chênerie, M-L., ' "Ces Curieux Chevaliers Tournoyeurs" ... des Fabliaux aux Romans', *Romania*, 97 (1976), pp. 327-68.
Clephan, R. C., *The Defensive Armour and the Weapons and Engines of War of Medieval Times and the Renaissance* (London, 1900).
Clephan, R. C., *The Tournament: its periods and phases* (London, 1919).
Cline, R., 'The Influence of the Romances on Tournaments in the Middle Ages', *Speculum*, xx (1945), pp. 204-11.
de la Colombière, Vulson, *Le Vray Théâtre d'Honneur et de Chevalerie* (Paris, 1648), 2 vols.

Cooke, A. S., 'Beginning the Board in Prussia', *The Journal of English and Germanic Philogy*, xiv (1915), pp. 375-88.

Cripps-Day, F. H., *The History of the Tournament in France and England* (London, 1918, reprinted New York, 1982).

Denholm-Young, N., 'The Tournament in the Thirteenth Century', *Studies Presented to F. Powicke*, ed. R. W. Hunt, W. A. Pantin & R. W. Southern (Oxford, 1948), pp. 204-68.

Du Boulay, F. R. H., 'Henry of Derby's Expeditions to Prussia 1390-1 and 1392', in *The Reign of Richard II*, ed. F. R. H. Du Boulay and C. M. Barron (London, 1971).

Duby, G., *The Chivalrous Society*, ed. & trans. C. Postan (London, 1977).

Duby, G., *Le Dimanche de Bouvines* (Gallimard, 1973).

Du Cange, C., 'Dissertations sur la Vie de St Louis par Joinville', *Glossarium*, x (Niort, 1887).

Ferguson, A. B., *The Indian Summer of English Chivalry* (Durham, N.Carolina, 1960).

Flori, J., 'Qu'est-ce qu'un Bacheler? Étude Historique de Vocabulaire dans les Chansons de Geste du XIIe Siècle', *Romania*, 96 (1975), pp. 289-314.

Flori, J., 'La Notion de Chevalerie dans les Chansons de Geste du XIIe Siècle', *Moyen Age*, 81 (1975), pp. 211-44, 407-45.

Fowler, K., *The King's Lieutenant : Henry of Grosmont, First Duke of Lancaster* (London, 1969).

Fowler, K., *The Hundred Years War* (London, 1971).

Fox-Davies, A. C., *Heraldic Badges* (London, 1907).

Giffin, M. E., 'Cadwalader, Arthur and Brutus in the Wigmore Manuscript', *Speculum*, xvi (1941), pp. 109-20.

Harvey, R., *Moriz von Craûn* (Oxford, 1961).

Haskins, C. H., 'The Norman *Consuetudines et Iusticie* of William the Conqueror', *Eng.Hist.Rev.*, (1908), pp. 502-508.

Jackson, W. H., *Knighthood in Medieval Literature* (Cambridge, 1981).

Jeayes, I. H., *Descriptive Catalogue of the Charters and Muniments ... at Berkey Castle* (Bristol, 1892).

Kilgour, R. L., *The Decline of Chivalry* (Cambridge, Mass., 1937).

Langlois, C. V., 'Un Mémoire Inédit de Pierre du Bois', *Revue Historique* (1889), pp. 84-91.

Lecoy de la Marche, A., *La Chaire Française au Moyen Age* (Paris, 1886).

Loomis, R. S., 'Chivalric and Dramatic Imitations of Arthurian Romance', *Medieval Studies in Memory of A. K. Porter* (Cambridge, Mass., 1939), i, 79-97.

Loomis, R. S., 'Edward I: Arthurian Enthusiast', *Speculum*, xxviii (1953), pp. 114-27.

Maddicott, J. R., *Thomas of Lancaster 1307-22* (Oxford, 1970).

Neilson, G., *Trial by Combat* (Glasgow, 1890).

Nicolas, N. H., 'Observations on the Institution of the Most Noble Order of the Garter', *Archaeologia*, xxxi (1846), pp. 1-163.

Owst, G. R., *Literature and Pulpit in Medieval England* (Oxford, 1961).

Phillips, J. R. S., *Aymer de Valence: Earl of Pembroke 1307-1324* (Oxford, 1972).

Poole, A. L., *Medieval England* (Oxford, 1958), 2 vols.

Prestage, E., *Chivalry* (London, 1928).

Prestwich, M., *War, Politics and Finance under Edward I* (London, 1972).

Prestwich, M., *The Three Edwards* (London, 1980).

Rosny, M. Lucien de, *L'Épervier d'Or* (Valenciennes, 1839).

Russell, P. E., *English Intervention in Spain and Portugal* (Oxford, 1955).

de Sainte Marie, H., *Dissertations Historiques et Critiques sur la Chevalerie* (Paris, 1718).

Sainte-Palaye, M. de la Curne de, *Mémoires sur l'Ancienne Chevalerie* (Paris, 1759), 2 vols.

Sandoz, E., 'Tourneys in the Arthurian Tradition', *Speculum*, xix (1944), pp. 389-420.

Strutt, J., *Sports and Pastimes of the People of England*, enlarged and corrected by T. C. Cox (London, 1801).

Tomkinson, A., 'Retinues at the Tournament at Dunstable 1309', *Eng. Hist.Rev.*, lxxiv (1959), pp. 70-87.

Toulmin-Smith, L., *Expeditions to Prussia and the Holy Land made by Henry, Earl of Derby: 1390-1 & 1392-3* (Camden Soc., New Series, lii, 1894).

Vale, J., *Edward III and Chivalry* (Woodbridge, 1983).

Vale, M. G. A., *War and Chivalry* (London, 1981).

Verbruggen, J., *The Art of Warfare in Western Europe during the Middle Ages*, trans. S. Willard & S. C. M. Southern (Amsterdam, 1977).

Webster, K. G. T., 'The Twelfth Century Tourney', *Anniversary Papers Presented to G. L. Kittredge* (Boston & London, 1913), pp. 227-234.

Withington, R., *English Pageantry* (Cambridge, Mass., 1918), 2 vols.

Index